Talking about Immersive Theatre

ALSO AVAILABLE IN THE THEATRE MAKERS SERIES

The Art of Making Theatre: An Arsenal of Dreams in 12 Scenes
Pamela Howard with Pavel Drábek
ISBN: 978-1-3502-7798-4

The Dramaturgy of Space
Ramón Griffero, translated by Adam Versényi
ISBN: 978-1-3502-3559-5

Toward a Future Theatre: Conversations during a Pandemic
Caridad Svich
ISBN: 978-1-3502-4105-3

The Art of Resonance
Anne Bogart
ISBN: 978-1-3501-5589-3

Adrian Lester and Lolita Chakrabarti: A Working Diary
Adrian Lester and Lolita Chakrabarti
ISBN: 978-1-3500-9277-8

The Uncapturable: The Fleeting Art of Theatre
Rubén Szuchmacher, translated by William Gregory
ISBN: 978-1-3501-3884-1

Julie Hesmondhalgh: A Working Diary
Julie Hesmondhalgh
ISBN: 978-1-3500-2569-1

Julius Caesar and Me: Exploring Shakespeare's African Play
Paterson Joseph
ISBN: 978-1-3500-1118-2

Simon Stephens: A Working Diary
Simon Stephens
ISBN: 978-1-4742-5141-9

Devising Theatre with Stan's Cafe
Mark Crossley and James Yarker
ISBN: 978-1-4742-6704-5

Meyerhold on Theatre
Edward Braun
ISBN: 978-1-4742-3020-9

Joan's Book: The Autobiography of Joan Littlewood
Joan Littlewood, introduced by Philip Hedley
ISBN: 978-1-4742-3322-4

Talking about Immersive Theatre

Conversations on Immersions and Interactivities in Performance

EDITED BY
JOANNA JAYNE BUCKNALL

methuen | drama
LONDON • NEW YORK • OXFORD • NEW DELHI • SYDNEY

METHUEN DRAMA
Bloomsbury Publishing Plc
50 Bedford Square, London, WC1B 3DP, UK
1385 Broadway, New York, NY 10018, USA
29 Earlsfort Terrace, Dublin 2, Ireland

BLOOMSBURY, METHUEN DRAMA and the Methuen Drama logo are trademarks of Bloomsbury Publishing Plc

First published in Great Britain 2023
This paperback edition published 2024

Copyright © Joanna Jayne Bucknall, and Contributors, 2023

Joanna Jayne Bucknall has asserted her right under the Copyright, Designs and Patents Act, 1988, to be identified as editor of this work.

For legal purposes the Acknowledgements on p. xiii constitute an extension of this copyright page.

Cover image: Persis Jade Maravala as Medea in ZU-UK's Hotel Medea, London 2010. (Photographer © Ludovic Des Cognets)

All rights reserved. No part of this publication may be reproduced or transmitted in any form or by any means, electronic or mechanical, including photocopying, recording, or any information storage or retrieval system, without prior permission in writing from the publishers.

Bloomsbury Publishing Plc does not have any control over, or responsibility for, any third-party websites referred to or in this book. All internet addresses given in this book were correct at the time of going to press. The author and publisher regret any inconvenience caused if addresses have changed or sites have ceased to exist, but can accept no responsibility for any such changes.

A catalogue record for this book is available from the British Library.

Library of Congress Cataloging-in-Publication Data

Names: Bucknall, Joanna Jayne, editor.
Title: Talking about immersive theatre: conversations on immersions and interactivities in performance / edited by Joanna Jayne Bucknall.
Description: London; New York: Methuen Drama 2023. | Series: Theatre makers | Includes bibliographical references and index.
Identifiers: LCCN 2022025616 (print) | LCCN 2022025617 (ebook) | ISBN 9781350269330 (hardback) | ISBN 9781350269347 (epub) | ISBN 9781350269354 (ebook)
Subjects: LCSH: Theatrical producers and directors–Great Britain–Interviews. | Participatory theater–Great Britain.
Classification: LCC PN2597 .T35 2023 (print) | LCC PN2597 (ebook) | DDC 792.0280922–dc23/eng/20220829
LC record available at https://lccn.loc.gov/2022025616
LC ebook record available at https://lccn.loc.gov/2022025617

ISBN: HB: 978-1-3502-6933-0
PB: 978-1-3502-6937-8
ePDF: 978-1-3502-6935-4
eBook: 978-1-3502-6934-7

Series: Theatre Makers

Typeset by Deanta Global Publishing Services, Chennai, India

To find out more about our authors and books visit www.bloomsbury.com and sign up for our newsletters.

For Mark Bucknall
Dad, I know you will never get to read this book but look,
I did it!!

CONTENTS

List of figures ix
List of contributors x
Acknowledgements xiii

    Introduction 1
    Joanna Jayne Bucknall

1. Underground adventures with Oliver Lansley and James Seager from Les Enfants Terribles 33
2. Playable worlds with Owen Kingston from Parabolic Theatre 57
3. Gamified experience with Bertie Watkins from COLAB Theatre 83
4. Socially engaged interactions with Natalie Scott, Joseph Thorpe, Antigoni Spanou and Joe Iredale from The Lab Collective 99
5. Intimate encounters with Ruth Cross from Cross Collaborations 127
6. Post-immersive interventions with Jorge Lopes Ramos and Persis Jadé Maravala from ZU-UK 151

7 Possible futures round-table discussion with Joanna Bucknall, Oliver Lansley, Persis Jadé Maravala, Jorge Lopes Ramos, Joseph Thorpe, Ruth Cross, Bertie Watkins, Owen Kingston and James Seager 177

Conclusion 205
Joanna Jayne Bucknall

References 221
Index 224

FIGURES

1. Immersive theatre spectrum diagram 18
2. Image from *Alice's Adventures Underground* (2015), at the Vaults, Waterloo 32
3. Image features Christopher styles and Zoe Flint performing in *For King & Country* at the COLAB Factory 56
4. Image details a live public performance of *CROOKS 1926* taken at the COLAB Tavern 82
5. Image details *Love: Inc* at Rose Bruford College of Theatre & Performance, featuring performers from the BA (Hons) European Theatre Arts programme with lighting design by Jeremy Jason 98
6. Image details performers Billie Beckly and Ruth Cross of *Meridian* by Cross Collaborations at Battersea Arts Centre 126
7. Image details live performance of *Goodnight, Sleep Tight* by ZU-UK 150
8. Image details Dr Joanna Bucknall in the process of recording a TAIT episode at her residence 176

CONTRIBUTORS

Oliver Lansley is an actor, writer, director and artistic director of Les Enfants Terribles, which he founded in 2002. As an actor, he is best known for playing Kenny Everett in the BAFTA-winning *The Best Possible Taste* (2012), which earned him a Best Actor nomination at the RTS Awards. Other credits include *The Wrong Mans* (2013), *Sherlock* (2010–17) and *Misfits* (2012).

James Seager is Les Enfant Terribles producer and Company Director. He has fifteen years of experience in theatre, television and film. Involved with Les Enfants Terribles initially as an actor, he moved to producing and directing shows in 2005. In 2015, he co-directed and produced Les Enfants Terribles' *Alice's Adventures Underground*, which was seen by over 95,000 people and was nominated for an Olivier award. James is an experienced TV presenter and actor.

Owen Kingston is the artistic director and founder of Parabolic Theatre, a prominent UK-based immersive and interactive theatre company pushing the boundaries of interactive experiences. Owen has a long history of working in the entertainment industry; he worked in conventional theatre, film and immersive theatre, as a director, producer and screenwriter. He has managed venues such as Matthews Yard and COLAB Factory. In 2022, Owen launched his own immersive theatre venue, The Crypt in Bethnal Green, London.

Bertie Watkins is the founder and artistic director of COLAB Theatre. It has grown from a one-person company to a company that now runs three productions a year and has four venues within London Bridge, most notably the COLAB Factory, which housed many theatre companies, including *The Immersive Great Gatsby*. Starting at a young age (and even performing in Punchdrunk's

Masque of The Red Death at age thirteen), he, instead of attending university, worked across fringe venues before he started to work for immersive companies such as Coney, Look Left Look Right, the Battersea Arts Centre and RIFT.

Natalie Scott is the co-founder and artistic director of The Lab Collective. As well as her work with The Lab Collective, Natalie has worked within the Outdoor Arts Sector and was previously the general manager for Outdoor Arts UK. Natalie has delivered performer and practitioner training with companies such as Specifiq (Zurich UOA MA programme), Rose Bruford (European Theatre Arts) and UEL (for ZU-UK), as well as directing for Dank Parish and producing for Emergency Exit Arts. Natalie was the company manager for Punchdrunk's live broadcast The *Third Day* (2020) and freelances as a producer alongside her work with The Lab Collective.

Joseph Thorpe is a founding member of The Lab Collective, and together with his directing credits for the Lab Collective, he has worked with immersive companies such as Specifiq and Hartshorn Hook (the *Great Gatsby*, South Korea). He is also a director of Dank Parish (Boomtown Fair and *Peaky Blinders*). Joe was the company coordinator for Punchdrunk's live broadcast *The Third Day* (2020).

Antigoni Spanou is a creative associate and core company member of The Lab Collective. Antigoni is a Greek theatre maker, dramaturg, director and solo artist. Her artistic practice is centred on the concepts of performative truth and vulnerability. She creates work that is intimate, emotive and interactive at its core, generating a shared experience for all. As well as her work with The Lab Collective, Antigoni has created work for Camden People's Theatre and regularly works with Rose Bruford College.

Joe Iredale is a multidisciplinary artist who has worked with The Lab Collective for over ten years and is now a core company member. Joe is intrigued by function and form, drawing inspiration from the everyday. His development from theatre making has led him to work with design and construction for companies such as Punchdrunk, The National Theatre, Darkfield, Dank Parish and

Interim Spaces. Joe's work has featured in *Beyond Immersive Theatre* by Adam Alston and *Total Theatre Magazine*, and he is a guest director at Rose Bruford.

Ruth Cross is a facilitator, director, project designer and changemaker with a background in choreography and theatre arts. She founded Cross Collaborations in 2009, a collective of makers dedicated to social and ecological activism, and spent a decade organizing arts festivals and making immersive and site-specific performance, including the letter project *Post Present Future*. Ruth is now using creative tools to support transition within diverse communities and running international arts for justice residencies. She is the co-founder of La Bolina, an intercultural association working with people with a migrant and refugee background to create dignified regenerative livelihoods in Granada, Spain.

Jorge Lopes Ramos is Co-founder and Executive Director of ZU-UK. He is also Associate Professor of Contemporary Performance at the University of Greenwich. Jorge has worked with Artistic Director Persis Jadé Maravala to create *#RioFoneHack* (2012–), *Binaural Dinner Date* (2016–) and *Pick Me Up & Hold Me Tight* (2018–), as well as in the creation and delivery of the DRIFT International Residency (2006–), Body Brain Bingo for UCL/Wellcome Trust (2017–18) and Garota Hacker for British Council's DICE Programme and Battersea Arts Centre's Co-Creating Change (2019). Jorge recently co-authored the *Post Immersive Manifesto* (2020).

Persis Jadé Maravala has been an artistic director of ZU-UK's projects (London) since 2006. Her artistic work has won awards and nominations in the fields of interactive theatre, hybrid art and innovation. Her most acclaimed project *Hotel Medea* was the highest-rated event by both public and press, becoming the standout hit of the Edinburgh Fringe, 2011. Her work has focused more recently on mediating relationships between strangers, particularly using sound design and instruction-based performance. Jadé is committed to reclaiming public spaces as sites for people to gather, as a way to reduce barriers to audience participation and actively push for fairer and more equal opportunities for working-class people.

ACKNOWLEDGEMENTS

The generosity of the theatre makers included in this book has been astounding; I am deeply grateful for their magnanimity in sharing their time and expertise. I feel truly humbled to be able to champion their fiercely generative creative spirit and practices with the wider world. Deep gratitude must be extended to Ella Wilson and Mark Dudgeon at Bloomsbury for their mighty expertise in wrestling the manuscript into shape but also in holding together all of the technical threads that such an endeavour demands! This book would never have been possible without the supportive temerity and insistent nudges that I received from my life partner Nigel Tuttle and closest friend Kirsty Mills to start the TAIT podcast series in 2016. I was sceptical, but they were utterly convinced that it needed to be done and that I was the best person to do it. They have been my biggest cheerleaders, not only giving me the confidence to launch TAIT in the first place but also in spurring me on through the many challenges of bringing this volume to fruition. Kirsty, I am so thankful for all of those long phone conversations where you empathized with my frustrations and beat down my anxieties. Nigel, you have supported me in so many ways from late-night transcribing to single handily wrangling our rambunctious toddler; 'thank you' does not even go towards covering it. I would also like to offer gratitude to my sister Emma Bucknall for her keen copyediting eye. Emma your tenacity in trawling through my erratic typescripts, hunting down typos and spelling gaffs cannot be thanked enough. I would also like to extend my heartfelt thanks to a dear colleague Dr Adam Ledger, who championed my initial proposal to Bloomsbury and throughout the process has offered incisive feedback that has transformed the shape and tone of this volume. I would also like to thank the University of Birmingham for providing the financial support that has enabled a serious chunk of the transcribing work to be undertaken. Finally, I would like to thank my wonderful mum, Lorraine Bucknall, for always believing in me and my vision, but more so for picking up the childcare slack and holding the fort with my son Tristan with uncompromising, unconditional love.

Introduction

Joanna Jayne Bucknall

Introduction

This volume provides a platform for current immersive and interactive makers to not only reflect on their own approach to making experiential work but also consider where their work might rest in relation to the broader experience economy and creative cultural industries. I expect that this book will become a valuable primary resource, one that gets underneath the desires, dreams and intentions of some of the key immersive makers currently working within the audience-centric landscape.

This volume has emerged out of the knowledge exchange work that I have been doing since 2016 on the podcast series Talking About Immersive Theatre (TAIT). I began producing the series to fill a gap in knowledge and resource. The gap in the immersive canon has had implications for not only my own research endeavours but also my work as a pedagogue. Since 2015, I have been developing practical and theoretical modules for undergraduate drama and theatre arts students that explore audience-centric performance practices, but, as I have already suggested, beyond the existing scholarship that addresses immersive theatre, there is little resource that offers insight into *how* this work is made or how audiences experience it. This has made it challenging to provide resources that support students' development of their own practice, as well as their access to professional practice in order that they might develop their conceptual understanding of the form. Students struggle to access the work as audience because of its London-centric position culturally, its price point (there is no infrastructure to subsidize or offer reduced ticket prices to students) and the lack of available documentation.

The TAIT podcast series is open access and designed to reach non-academic audiences so that it has value for emerging or aspiring practitioners, as well as audiences and fans of this type of experiential performance. It is a site in which the creatives working in the sector can reflect upon and share not only the nuts and bolts of their particular dramaturgies but also their location within the sector and their desires for its future. The TAIT podcast series began the work of building a new primary resource in 2016 – a resource that situates the voices of makers first and foremost in the public sphere – and that project continues to consolidate its worth and value in this volume.

The conversations in this book are an accessible way to encounter the discreet perspectives of a diverse range of makers. It presents the opportunity to gain an understanding of a variety of different approaches to making audience-centric theatre experiences. The immersive scene in the UK is notoriously secretive; as Alston has previously observed, 'secrecy has played an important role in the design of audience participation' (Alston in Harpin & Nicholson 2016: 184). However, the conversations shared here in this book work to dissolve some of that secrecy, offering fresh and exclusive access to the inner workings of the various creatives' ethos, intentions, design and rehearsal methods. The featured discussions offer a practical understanding of the ways in which a diverse range of immersive and interactive performance is made, articulated by the makers themselves. Each discussion is a space in which makers unfold the peculiar intimacies and intricacies of their creative practice, approaches that in most instances were pioneered by those practitioners.

Immersion and interactivity in performance is now a firmly established feature within the contemporary theatre landscape in the UK and, as Miilo Norros acknowledges, 'globally' (Norros 2015: 131). Despite the rich, vibrant variety of practices nestled beneath the banner of 'immersive theatre' and the increasing body of scholarship that attends to such practices (Gareth White 2012 & 2013, Josephine Machon 2013 & 2016, Adam Alston 2013 & 2016, James Frieze 2016, Rose Biggins 2017, Jason Warren 2017, Nandita Dinesh 2018 & 2019 and Liam Jarvis 2019), access to the practical processes of *how* such work is made but also by whom remains somewhat elusive. This volume begins the work of addressing both gaps in current scholarship. It is a novel knowledge exchange resource of praxical 'know how', articulated by previously unrevealed or marginalized creative voices. This volume offers exclusive insight into the ways in which some of Britain's leading immersive makers both think and work.

Despite the global trend towards experiential dramaturgies and entertainment, such as large-scale immersive events like *World of the Worlds* (2021), the emergence of escape rooms in cities across the UK and the numerous scare attractions hosted in theme parks and derelict proprieties, the canon is distinctly UK-centric with very few exceptions. Beyond the work of 'giants' of the field like Punchdrunk and Secret Cinema, understanding how immersive and interactive performance is made by practitioners working outside of these highly visible endeavours remains overshadowed by these dominant practices. Over the last decade, the immersive theatre canon has emerged as a somewhat narrow proposition populated by a few dominant voices (White 2012 & 2013, Machon 2013 & 2016 and Alston 2013 & 2016); the space occupied by makers' voices within that canon is even more select. The dissemination and knowledge exchange of embodied, practice-based knowledge and 'know how' are astonishingly limited, which I suspect is in many ways impacted by the (syn)aesthetic, kinaesthetic and experiential nature of the form.

Over the course of the Introduction, I will consider briefly the cultural and contextual scholarship that has led to this gap in knowledge, but first I will outline the ways in which this book seeks to address the yawning chasm of immersive makers' practical 'know how'. Crucially, this volume offers insight into immersive theatre makers' processes, practices, methods and strategies in a direct manner. It also provides a reflective space in which contributing creatives have been afforded the opportunity to articulate perspective on the nature of their dramaturges, sharing their intentions and desires but also the concrete ways in which they construct experiences for audiences. This volume thus provides a new platform for makers' voices to be added to the currently under-represented body of practice-based expertise. The discussions presented across these pages provide original access to new understandings of the ways in which the companies and artists featured make their work. Each chapter brings novel and exclusive access to the ways in which a more diverse range of artists make their work. The intimate conversations featured redirect and enrich the existing but narrow immersive canon with a more diverse range of insights and expertise. Together the discussions here provide a cross section of the current immersive performance landscape.

Many of the makers are UK based, though there are a couple of notable exceptions: Ruth Cross of Cross Collaborations is currently working out of Spain and ZU-UK's work has always been an international affair, working simultaneously out of the UK and Brazil. Common themes and threads run across each of the discussions, but each one unfolds a unique and localized perspective along with a set of approaches to immersive and interactive performance making. The volume is a welcome illumination of the current experiential turn that has over the last decade consolidated itself within the creative cultural industries in the UK and beyond. As Alston so astutely observes:

> this centralisation of experience in immersive theatre, a form of cultural production, chimes with a late-twentieth-century economic paradigm shift that led James Gilmore and Joseph Pine to introduce the term 'experience economy', that has signalled a broad cultural experiential turn.
>
> (ALSTON IN FRIEZE 2016: 248)

Positionality

I have already given some indication of my role as the producer and host of the TAIT podcast series and its significance in the relationships that I have forged with the immersive makers' community. I wanted to clarify the nature of my positionality as the instigator, facilitator and curator of the conversations in this book and to acknowledge the ways in which that positionality has informed and impacted upon the nature of the intimate conversations captured within these pages. I am a practitioner-scholar and since 2005 have been making audience-centric work, which might now be considered 'immersive' (I started making work with my company Vertical Exchange Performance Collective (VEX), which included the audience in fundamental ways before the culture of immersive work had become established as a mode of designating experiential practices).

As I have previously explicated (Bucknall 2017), my practice and scholarship exist in a holistic relationship, impacting upon one another in reflexive ways that generate a localized, subjective form of praxis. To be clear, my usage of praxis and praxical here is aligned with the mode of thinking about the relationship between theory and practice that has emerged out of the PARIP project and 'Palatine'. As Stephen Farrier suggests:

> Rather than seeing practice and theory at opposite ends of a shape that values one over the other, a cyclical relationship can be used to describe to what extent theory and practice can be seen as equally interrelated. Given certain circumstances, practice is part of post-structuralist theory and theory part of practice; they are not discrete or mutually exclusive features but inexorably wedded together.
>
> (FARRIER 2005: 131)

The central concerns of my praxis have been, and still are, researching, thinking, reflecting, analysing and conceptualizing around audience engagement, inclusion, interaction and activation, as well as concerns of embodied research methodologies, experiential documentation and dissemination.

Since 2005, I have found that practice and scholarship have, for me, become more and more imbricated into an entirely holistic and symbiotic relationship. Over the last fifteen years in the pursuit of understanding experiential dramaturgies, I have also wanted to forge a methodology through which the specialist practice of being an expert immersive audience member can be utilized as a distinctive practice-based research strategy – one that is again implicated into my own practice-based scholarship and creative mindset. The convergence of my scholarly, practice-based and audience behaviour generates a unique positionality from which I am able to cultivate a dialogical relationship with the immersive creative sector – a creative community that I am fundamentally a part of.

It is my academic position and perceptions of its standing that afford me the privileged position of 'validity' from which to make approaches to immersive makers. However, it is my shared stake, creative expertise and sometimes empathy that have enabled me to earn and maintain the trust of the immersive community. It is the trust that I have cultivated which has facilitated the reified level of access I have been afforded, which has in turn made possible the extension of that access through the insights shared in these pages. As I have previously unfolded (Bucknall 2017), my specialist expertise as an audience member further consolidates my knowledgeable position and ensures that my explicitly embodied perspective maintains a connection to the central feature of the form, which is experiential, kinaesthetic and (syn)aesthetic. Machon suggests that (syn)aesthetic dramaturgies are a 'fusing of sense (semantic "meaning making") with *sense* (feeling both sensation and emotion), [which] establishes a double-edged rendering of making-*sense*/sense-making and foregrounds its fused somatic/semantic nature' (Machon 2009: 14, emphasis in the original). This core trope of immersive dramaturgy means that what is being marketed and promoted is the opportunity to have an experience of one kind or another. It is the relational, holistic convergence of these positional conditions that informs and defines my relationship to the work that is being discussed with the makers in these conversations. This positions the conversations as highly localized, contingent and subjective. This does not diminish their value but instead increases the worth of the contribution because of its peculiar originality and because I do not operate as an external objective interviewer in these discussions but instead meet the makers on shared terms, as a maker and a collaborator. This ethnographic approach to the generation of primary resource material that is presented in this volume is a novel approach to the dissemination of immersive practical 'know how' and expertise. I am simultaneously revealing my own praxis while providing insider insights into the work of other makers' processes too.

In my own research endeavours, I am interested in seeking to understand the nature of the audience's role within experiential dramaturgies, but again the lack of a primary resource in this field which documents or disseminates the dramaturgies, or their reception, is stark and significantly prohibitive for undertaking that mode of research. It is this yawning chasm that was the driving impetus for developing the TAIT podcast series in the first instance. Since 2016, embarking upon developing TAIT as a novel primary resource, I have been working to cultivate relationships with immersive makers to begin the task of filling that gap in resource, knowledge and understanding. The relationships at first were, indeed, London-centric, but as the podcast's reach has become increasingly international in its listenership, there is an increasingly evident need to address this dearth in scholarship that stretches far beyond the shores of the UK and is evidently[1] a global concern.

The objective of TAIT is to have frank and intimate conversations with immersive performance makers in their own creative spaces to offer a praxical perspective on both how and why they make work in the ways that they do. The approach is ethnographic as it is taken up from a distinctly kinaesthetic and embodied methodological position. As the host, the instigator and facilitator of the discussions, I can take up a unique methodological position not just as a practice-based scholar but also from an informed position as a seasoned immersive 'reflective participant' (Bucknall 2017). In over ten years of seeking out audience-centric performance work as a participant, it is inevitable that my praxis and audience-based research activity have generated a unique ethnographical positionality from which, for this volume, I have been able to forge direct access to the work of the creatives included.

Until Covid-19 prohibited travel and social contact, I have always made a concerted effort to attend the work of the makers as an audience member before engaging in conversation with them. In this way I became part of the experience as an audience participant, giving me an embodied authority from which to work as an interlocutor with the creatives to generate the type of dialogical discourse presented in this book. I am firmly convinced that this uniquely embodied position has enabled me to build the trust, rapport and understanding that have facilitated the space for frank, intimate and reflexive knowledge transfer to occur: first, via the TAIT podcast series and now in the pages of this book.

The mode of knowledge transfer that the TAIT podcast offers is of course significant in meeting my own agenda for developing the resource for both my students and, of course, myself. My objective has been to build a resource that captures and disseminates the approaches, methods, strategies, attitudes and reflections of immersive and interactive performance makers in an *accessible* form. Podcasting is becoming increasingly recognized as a form for its accessibility, which is acknowledged by Jonathan Gill in *Forbes* magazine:

> [M]any of the products showcased at this year's Consumer Electronics Show (CES) also reflect an increased focus on

inclusive design and accessibility. Podcasting is no different, and the future of the medium will be largely defined by inclusive design and accessible listening experiences.

(GILL 2021)

A reflective methodology was employed in developing the structure of the conversations that nestle here; the original recording was reviewed, and the threads that arose in the round-table conversation were also considered along with current working practices, concerns and shifts in attitude since the originating discussion. The relationship between the TAIT podcast episodes and the discussions that are printed here is not an explicitly direct one. These discussions are not transcripts of the TAIT episode discussions; instead, new discussions were recorded that came about through a review process in collaboration with each contributor of the original TAIT episodes. I worked collaboratively with the creatives to identify discussion points that we wished to return to, as well as new areas for discussion that have arisen since the original recording (some of which were five years ago).

I have curated the discussions here to offer shifted perspectives, reflections and focus from the originating TAIT episode to ensure that they pick up current concerns, anxieties and challenges in the contemporary immersive landscape. It must be noted too that all of the new conversations were recorded in the 'zoom-sphere' and each well over two hours in length, which means a considerable collaborative editing process has been employed to craft each chapter into the documents that are found within this volume. In most cases, a considerable amount of time has elapsed between the TAIT episode broadcast and the new conversations that make up each chapter, thus requiring careful curation on my part to navigate the new conversations into the territory of vital and current concerns facing the maker and wider sector. This curatorial steer was necessary to capture the material shifts makers have encountered due to the context of the global pandemic. Covid-19 seriously disrupted the sector in fundamental ways.

The shift in context has in some cases significantly altered the tone and nature of the discussion with each of the makers. This volume extends beyond the ethos of TAIT, which is to give performance makers a platform for knowledge transfer and attempts the broader task of offering some cultural custodianship for the sector in the form of generating legacy.

This volume seeks to offer a snapshot of the variety of practices from the theatrical through to the pervasive and into more ethically charged, socially responsible approaches that make up the wide net of immersion and interactive performance dramaturgies. The voices included cannot claim to be an exhaustive coverage of the sector but might be recognized as indicative of some of the dominant approaches currently operating within the spectrum of the immersive landscape. Each contributor's work has achieved recognition, acclaim or success with audiences in one form or another, with Les Enfants Terribles' work nominated for an Olivier Award and ZU-UK's *Hotel Medea* (2006–12) recognized as an iconic cultural work. The work included here reveals some of the prominent dramaturgical strategies being employed within contemporary live immersive and interactive practices and the cultural concerns that frame them.

Immersions and interactivity landscape

Immersive theatre has become culturally synonymous with the work of Punchdrunk, Secret Cinema and large-scale intellectual property (IP) projects such as *Great Gatsby* (2019), *Wolf of Wall Street* (2019), *Dr Who (2022)* and *War of the Worlds* (2021). However, as noted earlier, access to the inner workings of how such work is made is problematically scarce. It must be acknowledged that Machon's seminal text *Immersive Theatres: Intimacy and Immediacy in Contemporary Performance* (2013) was presented in two parts, with the second section of the volume presenting conversations between some of the key first-wave audience-centric makers such as Felix Barrett, Christer Lundahl and Silvia Mercuriali. The conversations offer a substantive collection of discourse around the nature of the practices that collect each maker into the variously focused discussions, but they do not offer a direct access into the ways in which the various modes of work are made. The discussions are mostly conceptual rather than praxical and address broader themes taken from Machon's analysis. It is important to recognize the contribution made to the emergence of immersive theatre but also to build upon them. Machon's volume was published ten years ago this year (2013) and thus requires the insights it held to be extended to consider developments within the contemporary immersive landscape.

Warren (2017) offers a handbook for making immersive theatre, as does Dinesh's work (2018), which offers a fresh perspective from beyond the UK. Warren's *Creating Words: How to Make Immersive Theatre* is one of the few contributions to the field that is written by and for performance makers. It is an earnest sharing of Warren's own immersive making experience, crafted into an in-depth articulation of the practical ways in which one might address some of the central concerns that arise in making audience-centric work.

In his own words, he suggests that the book

> is written for theatre makers, artists and students who want to create this kind of work. It is also for those who are interested in the guts and ideas that fuel the performance they love.
>
> (WARREN 2017)

Warren shares what remains a comparatively rare praxical 'know how', developed out of his own localized experiences, and offers strategies for how to approach key dramaturgical tropes of the experiential form. His book also offers approaches to understanding and anticipating audience behaviour and designing space and journeys, as well as methods for running complex rehearsal processes. It is a refreshingly frank and open dissemination of a maker's own process which shares the pitfalls as well as the moments that led to discovery and insight. Warren's welcome contribution to the canon has begun to open the space in which makers can explicate their approaches to performance making, and this volume will not just occupy that same space but diversify and extend it.

Dinesh is a practitioner-scholar whose recent two volumes (2018 & 2019) have also contributed to broadening the offer of makers' voices and adding praxical insight of the field, particularly her latest scholarly edition *Immersive Theater and Activism: Scripts and Strategies for Directors and Playwrights*. Like Warren's book Dinesh's latest contribution brings more practical strategies and approaches to immersive theatre making into the public sphere. What is particularly striking about this volume is the non-Western practice context that informs the approaches that it explicates.

Dinesh's work firmly broadens out the euro-centricity of the current scholarship, offering a strong female, practice-led and experienced voice to the discourse of immersive theatre performance making. The conversations that can be found here in this volume have synergies with some of the dramaturgical concerns that Dinesh raises in her own two publications. Warren and Dinesh are much-needed praxical voices; however, this volume will significantly broaden and contemporize the space of 'know how' in the canon, adding further diversity and variety to the embodied knowledges that both Warren and Dinesh have begun to disseminate. Beyond the contributions of Warren and Dinesh, practical 'know how' is limited and hard to find. This book will serve, then, as a new primary source that both captures and transmits one of the most cutting-edge cultural trends of the early twenty-first century from a variety of contexts and perspectives.

The scarcity of resource for praxical 'know how' is likely partly to do with commercial pressures and legal constraints around IP; many large-scale immersive companies have understandable concerns surrounding the protection of creative strategies as an asset. Many of the current generation of immersive makers in the UK have adopted a different approach to financing work than more traditional theatre funding routes such as Arts Council England (ACE), grants and subsidies. As Alston asserts, what

> is different, though, is that an embrace of the private sector is no longer balanced against public funding and institutional support, which is threatening the prospect of a resilient creative economy over-exposed to the whims of commerce and competing interests in the market.
>
> (ALSTON 2019: 239)

In addition to the pressures of commercial funding models, the form is also perhaps a casualty of the 'elusivity' (Bucknall 2023) that is often central to those immersive and interactive dramaturgies. Immersive theatre, particularly of the large-scale variety, is a commercial venture with investors' and stakeholders' financial interests to protect. Those interests generate a need for the 'praxical know how' to be kept secret because they have commercial value as an asset. As such, the 'know how' does not entirely belong to the performance makers, thereby creating a barrier to the sharing of practical knowledge. This is an issue that will continue to pervade the immersive performance landscape because, as Alston recognizes, 'the pace of immersive theatre's commercialisation in London is moving at an alarming rate of knots' (Alston 2019: 240) and is a condition of the production of this mode of performance that will need to be reconciled if more access, visibility and knowledge transfer opportunities are to be developed.

In addition to the financial pressures, there is a more fundamental aspect to the nature of the 'elusivity' that shrouds this mode of performance making: secrecy. Building on Alston's work, I have previously suggested (Bucknall 2023) that this secrecy is driven by a fundamental anxiety of the form: keeping the experience 'virgin' for each individual participant. Secrecy is employed to ensure that each participant has the possibility of a unique, bespoke and personal experience. It is the practice of secrecy that keeps alive the radical potential of the liminal spaces of experiential dramaturgy regardless of the length of the run or the number of 'bodies' that pass through it. The withholding of details beyond the aesthetic or thematic produces mystery that ensures each participant can take full advantage of the uniqueness of the experience on offer (Bucknall 2023). Secrecy protects the audiences' experience and keeps the promise of something bespoke, personal and exclusive alive. It ensures the promise of an encounter, an experience, something that can be lived through.

Secrecy may be part of the allure of the work and an enticing proposition that requires some faith on the part of the spectator. But it also demands more than a little 'productivity' from its audiences. Alston has written extensively on the nature and role of productivity for immersive audiences, suggesting that

> [w]hile an audience's affective relationship to a work arises from engagement with something represented, as it does in all theatre, and while this may well carry great and personal significance, as it might in all theatre, the promotion of productive participation in immersive theatre and the introspection that comes with immersion in a contemporary experience machine means that affective experience itself tends to become utterly absorbing as a centrally significant and memorable feature of immersive theatre aesthetics.
>
> (ALSTON 2016: 10)

There is something seductive about the 'not knowing' of the form, a mix of anticipation and expectation that is generated by the lack of concrete information, insight and understanding as to the ways in which these encounters are made. However, albeit seductive, the secrecy inherent in the form is a barrier for emerging artists, students and scholars trying to gain insight into the praxical ways this work is funded, conceived and produced. The conversations shared here push through that barrier to illuminate the dark corners of practicalities such as finance, casting and the rehearsal process. This volume widens insight into the particular nuts and bolts of the way that the contributors make their work. In Chapter 1, Les Enfants Terribles expose the challenges they faced with the technical and structural innovations they developed for *Alice's Adventures Underground* (2015), whereas in Chapter 7 ZU-UK talk about the importance of starting with the 'human' in their process.

'Elusivity' is extended beyond just the form itself. Immersive work is hard for audiences to find; it utilizes non-theatrical spaces and venues, which means that it must be sought out, discovered or hunted down. Audiences of immersive theatre need to know how to find the work because of its negation of established venues of theatre and culture and the 'elusivity' of marketing practices. In this volume I have curated a selection of work that operates outside of the usual institutions where culture can be readily accessed. The practices showcased across the chapters of this book mainly operate out of non-theatrical, pop-up spaces; therefore, a crucial ambition for the volume is to generate more visibility for some of these groundbreaking approaches. All the theatre makers in this volume talk about their struggles to access space. In Chapter 3, Bertie Watkins opens up about the sheer serendipity that led to him acquiring the old carpet factory in 2016 that later became the COLAB Factory. Owen Kingston outlines his struggles in Chapter to acquire space in Croydon and the way in which he was able utilize Matthews Yard Café to establish Parabolic. Ruth Cross and ZU-UK outline the ways in which their work has evolved in and through the use of public spaces, such as phone boxes and seaside piers. The lack of cultural visibility is a condition that Alston has also signalled as a cultural condition of the immersive landscape:

> pressure on space and resource, particularly for more ambitious projects, means that artists keen to explore immersive practices are

less likely to be programmed within established, publicly-funded venues unless there is a proven track record of success, which can force the hand of artists to make use of temporary 'pop-up' theatre spaces without institutional support and the experience, expertise and security that such support brings with it.

(ALSTON 2016)

Instead, the work pops up in DIY or found spaces for limited periods of time with finite capacity.

For audiences, finding immersive performance means one must learn to be productive in order to penetrate the mystery that envelopes the form as a cloak of 'elusivity'. As I have already shown, there is a precarity at the heart of the immersive UK creative culture, from the financial models utilized in funding the work to the utilization of found and pop-up spaces. Financial and geographic precarity are driving factors for the 'elusivity' that surrounds the form, as well as the secrecy inherent in the making processes. There is scant primary resource available to offer a sense of what the work is like for audiences, or detailed explanation of how it is made. This volume will begin the work of demystifying the 'elusivity' that currently eclipses access to understanding the ways such work is made, by whom it is made and where it often can be found. Outside of large-scale events the immersive creative community is a tight-knit sub-culture of makers and audience. This volume provides access to some of the key companies at the heart of that sub-culture, generating access to a previously impenetrable sector of the cultural landscape.

It is 'professional commentators who have historically controlled the formation of cultural discourse' (Bucknall & Sedgman in Saint 2017: 120) in the theatre especially rather than the documentation of performance per se. This poses two barriers to cultural visibility for immersive practice; first, they are often pop-up and do not run long enough to attract those professional commentators. Second, documentation is a task that must be undertaken purposefully, which is a time-consuming and costly business many of the creatives cannot afford to undertake. There are two main barriers that 'elusivity' poses to the development of a more accessible, inclusive and lively body of knowledge and practice that this volume seeks to overcome. First, these experiential practices resist capture and elude meaningful documentation, which troubles their cultural currency and potential cultural legacy. Second, they remain impenetrable to the next generation of audiences and performance makers alike. Therefore, in this book, it is imperative that makers are given the opportunity to contribute their voices, perspectives and 'know how' to the knowledge community of the immersive canon, to grow it, broaden it and of course challenge it. Beyond the academy, the contribution of this volume is far more vital; it opens the impenetrable 'elusivity' of the form, ensuring a more diverse and rich cultural future through the sharing of practical expertise and 'know how'. While the discussions captured between the following pages enrich and extend the canon, they also help promote the future practice and cultural legacy of the form.

Curation and cultivation

In this section, I will outline the rationale for how and why I have chosen the makers, artists and companies for inclusion. The work included has been selected for both epistemological and very practical reasons. I have included contributions from practitioners whose work I am experientially familiar with, whose work has been featured in the TAIT podcast series and those that have been open to my approach for inclusion in the volume. I have had the privilege of attending at least one piece of work produced by each of the contributors, and in some cases I have encountered their work multiple times.

This of course has practical implications; it means that in some ways the selection for inclusion has been reliant at least in a small way upon my own financial and geographical access to the work, which has its limitations and I recognize is to some extent limiting on the breadth and variety of approach that is represented here. This volume is by no means exhaustive or even suggestive of any best practice or gold standard, but it does begin to broaden out the resource and discourse to include some new and previously marginalized creative voices. Covid-19 disrupted the methodology of the TAIT podcast series, as I was not able to attend work or chat with makers in their 'natural habitats' for a long time. Although this disturbed the experiential impetus of the epistemological logic for selection and inclusion for the TAIT podcast series, it did generate the conditions under which international practitioners began to reach out to me to share their newly developed digital practices and express a desire to be a part of the growing resource of conversations of TAIT.

The contributors in this volume are either UK based or have a very concrete relationship with the UK creative cultural industries. I have the ambition to continue the growth of the resource beyond these initiating conversations and intend to open up more internationally informed resources in the not-so-distant future. However, the UK has been the 'ground zero' for the emergence of immersive theatre as a cultural phenomenon and is still at the forefront of the experiential turn in performance. I want to suggest that despite the UK-centric nature of the volume in terms of the practices being represented, international interest will be captured because of the ways in which UK practices lead innovation within the global landscape. Indeed, the statistics of TAIT's reach suggest that there is significant global interest in the activity of the UK immersive sector, with over 6,400 listens in the UK but over 9,700 listens from outside of the UK (almost 6,000 of those listens are from within the United States and Canada but the rest of the almost 4,000 listens have been from locations across the globe, such as Korea, India, South Africa, China, The Netherlands, continental Europe, Australia, Russia and Japan).

I have reached out to many practitioners over the five years since TAIT was launched to keep up with emerging practices. As TAIT has grown in reach, many have reached out to me. I have been embraced by the immersive community, and the conversations captured here testify to the ways in which I have been able to use TAIT as a vehicle to begin to build a knowledge community. TAIT as a series was born out of my own desires, needs and hopes as a practitioner-scholar, reflective participant and pedagogue. It has grown through the generosity of makers and listeners, along with institutional support and a little sprinkle of serendipity. This volume, I hope, will offer a more robustly and rigorously curated document than the TAIT podcast series is able to attain and will shore up the foundations for the beginnings of a vital and urgent new primary resource for makers, scholars and students alike.

Immersive theatre is widely accepted as an umbrella term beneath which a multitude of approaches and practices nestle; as Machon first drew attention to in 2013, 'immersive' is now attached to diverse events that assimilate a variety of forms and seek to exploit all that is experiential in performance, placing the audience at the heart of the work' (Machon 2013: 22). Since that time, the term has persisted as 'an ambiguous and generic referent, not least because there is no consensus over what it is that draws companies and artists together as makers of immersive theatre' (Alston 2016: 5). Since there are practices that 'precede the currency of the immersive moniker' (Alston 2016: 6) and practices that are distancing themselves from it, it is important for me to keenly articulate my own approach to the selection and inclusion of voices and practices that make a contemporary and critical intervention into the too broad classification of immersive theatre making.

As the book demonstrates, there is a spectrum of practice that sits beneath the umbrella of immersive theatre. 'Fictive worlds' appear at one end, pervasive and gamified approaches in the middle and dramaturgies that operate to reframe the real at the opposite end of a continuum. The focus of this volume excludes work from within the broader immersive entertainment sector, and so I have not considered contributions from artists making work that does not have some fundamental relationship with practices that retain an explicit relationship with theatre. As I have already suggested, immersive entertainments such as scare attractions, escape rooms and large-scale IP events like Layered Reality's *The Gunpowder Plot* (2022) have complex investment models which are accompanied by equally complex issues of creative ownership. These IP complexities are one of the reasons why this sector has been difficult to penetrate and has some bearing on their absence in the podcast series and inevitably this volume.

In addition to the conditions surrounding access to the inner workings of immersive entertainments, there is also a more epistemological curatorial decision which excludes them from the discussions in this book. Immersive entertainments have emerged as a result of the growth of the experience economy and have a different genealogy to many of the practices which consider themselves theatre. The relationship between these cultural forms needs a more robust inspection than I am able to provide here; thus, the focus of this volume is on practices which fall beneath the immersive theatre umbrella rather than the broader moniker of immersive experience. In order to explicate the immersive theatre spectrum that provides a framework for understanding the logic of inclusion, it is necessary to briefly draw out some of the distinctions and definitions that are captured across the breadth of the spectrum because they inform the method that was employed for selecting the contributors and inform the order in which they appear.

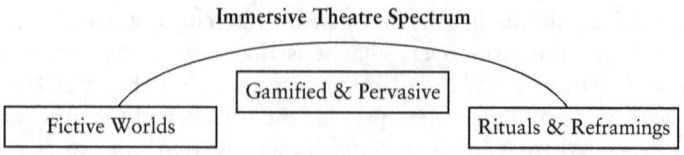

FIGURE 1 *Immersive theatre spectrum diagram.*

The distinctions I have drawn out in the immersive theatre spectrum are not founded on the aesthetic quality of the work but instead are made through a consideration of the *nature* of the experience that is on offer to the audience. There is little to connect immersive theatre in the way of aesthetic or thematic qualities; however, I have observed certain dramaturgical features that more tangibly cluster these approaches into similar 'types' of immersive theatre experience. This observation is made by reflecting upon over a decade of my own audience experience but, more significantly, has emerged out of the access TAIT podcast has afforded me to the inner workings of those dramaturgies. In this volume, I am able to extend that access as a new primary resource that will be the catalyst for further novel insights.

It is widely acknowledged that all immersive theatre relies upon liminal space, whether that be the construction of a liminal site for an audience to enter into, such as Les Enfant Terribles' highly aestheticized set of *Alice's Adventures Underground* (2015), which transformed the Waterloo Vaults to the Second World War bunker that Parabolic Theatre constructed in the COLAB Factory basement; the activation of 'real-world' spaces as liminal sites through gamification, such as the way COLAB Theatre's *Hostage* (2015), unfolded in the streets of Waterloo and ZU-UK's inhabitation of a café in Stratford for *Binaural Dinner Date* (2017); or the generation of liminal space in and through the committing of acts or rituals, such as Cross Collaborations' different iterations of *Post Present Future* (2009) and Lab Collective's provocative *Incoming/Exodus* (2017). Liminal space is a dramaturgical foundation of immersive theatre; '[t]he specific location of and/or the "transformation" of that space according to the aesthetic of the event is vital' (Machon 2013: 93).

Although the continuum of approaches I have identified in Figure 1 relies on liminal space as a foundational mode for engaging, activating or transporting audiences, I want to suggest that each mode of performance making employs a distinct way of constructing or generating the liminal space. Further, the character of that mode of liminality impacts upon the nature of the experience that it elicits for the audience. There are, of course, within those distinctions a variety of approaches, methods and strategies for creating audience experience, engagements or activations that have discrete genealogies snaking back through different traditions of performance making. However, in starting to recognize the spectrum of work in the immersive performance landscape, I have, in this volume, endeavoured to represent makers who might be understood to epitomize its three major modes of experience making.

Practices at the fictive end of the spectrum have been recognized by critics and audiences alike as the 'gold standard' of immersive theatre and are concerned with lifting the red curtains and letting the audience slide inside aesthetically complete theatrical worlds. Punchdrunk's much-anticipated return to London with their new work, *The Burnt City* (2022), will likely further consolidate their dominant position within the immersive landscape. As Lyn Gardener acknowledges, 'since Punchdrunk premiered *Sleep No More* (2011), in a disused school in Vauxhall in 2003, immersive theatre has become ubiquitous, but the company's return to London is likely to remind why they are still the leaders of the pack with work whose complexity, scale and attention to detail remains unparalleled' (Gardner 2021). These apparently dominant fictive worlds offer the tantalizing proposition to encounter the *inside* of the theatrical, to enter the world of a dramatized story.

This mode of immersion is most closely related to a recognizable mode of theatrical or dramatized storytelling. The theatrical world that the companies construct pre-exists the audience's encounter; they arrive at it and enter *into* it. Immersive theatrical worlds are realized through a cohesive and complete construction of aesthetic space in which the dramatized aspects of narrative and mimetic representation unfold around the audience. They are often fixed dramaturgies, and although the audience encounter them from within, they are rarely able to impact upon the theatricalized space or narrative in a concrete way. Les Enfants Terribles', Olivier-nominated show, *Alice's Adventures Underground* (2015) is an exemplary example of this mode of immersive theatre. In the chapter, Les Enfants Terribles explain the ways in which their process has certain dramaturgical resonance with more recognizable modes of theatre making. They talk about the role of the script within their process and its central role in the development of the realization of the project.

The first contributor in Chapter 2 is Les Enfants Terribles, whom I want to suggest represent approaches at the 'fictive world' end of the spectrum (see Figure 1, in this volume). Les Enfants Terribles' work to build an aesthetically complete experience that the audience encounter as in the liminal site of *Alice's Adventures Underground* (2015) has already been constituted. Spectators are required to pass into the fictive world that has been meticulously crafted for them; the whimsical proposition is to fall down the rabbit hole and take up the perspective of Alice as they pass through Les Enfants Terribles' striking aesthetic realization of Wonderland. The sites of Les Enfants Terribles' work thus exist as an 'alternative reality' that lays dormant, waiting to be inhabited by the audience. It is a hermetically sealed aesthetic construct with its own rules, social conventions and contracts that are drawn from the familiar existing IP of Lewis Carroll's beloved novels. Les Enfants Terribles' work offers the audience little agency or efficacy within that fictive world; the audience are not able to *affect* the narratives or structure of the work but instead are merely invited into it and to live through it.

Pervasive, action and gamified dramaturgies such as those pioneered by COLAB and Parabolic Theatre rely upon the audience taking up a designated role within the scenario's narrative; they are invited to become the protagonist within a scenario-based narrative that is activated through game and play. COLAB Theatre and Parabolic Theatre discuss their use of gamified approaches in their respective chapters; in Chapter 3, Bertie Watkins explains the ways in which he utilizes different strategies to locate the audience as the protagonist of the work: 'We always start with a protagonist and antagonist which I think is always our narrative basis' (see p.89). In Chapter 2, Owen Kingston gives insight into the role that gamified mechanics has in the process of devising the audience pathways through their work:

> Yeah, that character and story stuff needs to be front and centre. For King & Country (2018), burying the game mechanics was critically important because the core game that everything else must support is that you are an MP in 1940, and you are trying to save the country from being invaded by Nazis. So, everything must build that core game. (See p.94)

Watkins and Kingston offer an understanding of the ways gamified approaches rely on unfolding in 'real-world' spaces and others build aesthetic sites that hold the 'game'. However, regardless of the manner in which the liminal site is established, it is activated by and through the audience's capacity to engage in play. Unlike the fictive worlds of Les Enfants Terribles, gamified dramaturgies require activation to be brought into being. Both *Hostage* (2015) and *For King & Country* (2018) could not take place without the audience activating the gamified propositions of the scenario; as Watkins explains, 'we try and balance the narrative versus the game' (see p.86). In *For King & Country* (2018), the audience are asked quite early in the performance to formulate an emergency cabinet and elect each other to certain roles. The entire performance is structured with numerous choices to be made and played out. They must be inhabited *in* and *through* play, which affects the very nature of the ways in which the experience unfolds for the audience in any given performance. COLAB Theatre and Parabolic Theatre represent this mode of audience engagement in the volume. Their work requires the audience to activate the experience, and the outcome is often contingent on the nature of the audience's engagement. Gamified dramaturgies have a direct relationship and shared family tree with computer gaming, live action role play (LARP) and forms from within the immersive entertainment sector too, such as escape rooms.

Both Parabolic Theatre and COLAB Theatre have made work that has constructed gamified spaces which operate as 'alternate realities', such as *For King & Country* (2018) and *CROOKS* (2016), but they have also utilized strategies that rely on the 'game' unfolding against a 'real-world' backdrop, such as *Hostage* (2015) and *Morning Star* (2017). To bring the performance into being for themselves and the other audience members, gamified action and pervasive dramaturgies rely upon audiences taking up the play opportunities offered and inhabiting them. These dramaturgies thus offer the audience agency and efficacy through the gamified or action-based structures. They are structures that must be *activated* by participation; in short, they must be played.

What might be considered 'rituals and reframings' suggests approaches to building audience experience that rely upon collaboration between participant and audience to bring the liminal space and thus the experience into being. As I have previously asserted (2016), this mode of experiential dramaturgy functions to reframe the everyday or a set of particular social rituals to make the offer of a liminoid invitation, which is ultimately the offer of co-creation. It is an invitation to collaborate generating something unique, localized and personal in the moment between the participant and the performer's. It is usually structured as a set of provocations, rules, tasks or the offer to commit a series of acts in collaboration with the performer or, in instances such as ZU-UK's *Binaural Dinner Date* (2017), with other audience members.

As I have previously suggested (2016), these 'reframing' dramaturgies are built utilizing a hybrid of social practice and social space often ethically motivated to expose the underlying structure process and power dynamics of the social rituals being utilized. These dramaturgies rely upon the 'stuff' of everyday lived experience but extend an invitation to bring them into being in such a way as to trouble, challenge and transform them through a process of rendering them uncanny. In this volume, Cross Collaborations, ZU-UK and The Lab Collective discuss openly the various ways that their work operates in this ethically charged, radicalized space. It is the use of radicalized liminal space and the DIY approach or the use of the 'everyday' as an artistic medium that makes ethically charged modes of experiential performance making distinct along the spectrum of work. In this volume, the work of Cross Collaborations, The Lab Collective and ZU-UK reframes aspects of the 'real', the 'everyday' and social rituals to create socially engaged approaches to audience experience.

In Chapter 4, The Lab Collective explain the centrality of the relationship that they generate between all of the participants. They discuss the ways in which the performers are facilitating the collaboration between the audience, particularly in *Incoming/Exodus* (2017); as Natalie Scott explains, 'The performer needs to be OK relinquishing their material and sort of giving in to lead and facilitate the audience so that they actually get something meaningful from their experience' (see p.107). In Chapter 5, Ruth Cross shares her process of facilitation and the ways in which she is able to activate audiences through the instigation of acts rather than live performance. Ruth Cross explains the relationship that her work establishes between audience and performer, 'always with the sense of the audience going on a journey with the performers and they share their experience of going on this journey, so it's enabling the audience members again to step into the shoes of the performers' (see p.196). Cross' hugely influential project *Post Present Future* (2009) couches a performative proposition to audiences in her absence. She reframes the seemingly mundane task of letter writing as a performative act, one that continues to perform across five years. Cross explains the extended impact of the letter-writing act when she says:

> Obviously, there's this very intimate experience; when the letter arrives five years later, people are very sort of taken aback: 'This is my handwriting on an envelope.' That's another one-on-one performance, that happens with you and you. You receive this and then start to realize, 'Oh, it's a letter that I wrote to myself!' I just imagine people; they're making a cup of tea and sitting in their favourite chair or going for a walk maybe and finding a bench that they like to sit on or somewhere that they feel it's special for them and opening this letter that they've written to themselves. (See p.130)

Like Lab Collective and Cross Collaborations, ZU-UK's work is often generated *with* the audience; it is a collaboration, and without that process of collaboration, there would be no experience to encounter at all. Rather than offering a fictive world to explore or a game to play and win, socially engaged, audience-centric dramaturgies employ radicalized liminality or more precisely liminoid invitations to engage audiences in structures that utilize the everyday to explore the possibility of change, whether that be in perspective or behaviour. In Chapter 7, ZU-UK give in-depth insight into the ways they utilize and radicalize the 'stuff' of everyday experience to build meaningful encounters; as Jadé articulates:

> One of the biggest things that we learned, and I think that immersive needs to know more about, is allowing audience members to feel safe, comfortable, not, and I don't mean safe in that kind of 'this is a safe space' kind of way. I mean like literally, 'You are perfect, and we have been waiting for you and here's your space, it's been held for you'. I've always worked on that principle. (See p.158)

More recent works such as *Project Perfect Stranger* (2020) serve to facilitate meaningful exchange between audience participants rather than between audience and performer. ZU-UK advocate in their chapter and in the round-table discussion for the possibilities of radicalizing the real to generate meaningful human connection, 'what we're working with is the human being. We work with who they are, and we work very much in the here and now' (see p.167).

It is important (for reasons we explicate during our conversations in Chapters 5, 6 and 7) to recognize, though, that Cross Collaborations, The Lab Collective and ZU-UK do not consider their work to be immersive per se. ZU-UK and Cross Collaborations have been making audience-centric work before the immersive moniker became a cultural phenomenon, a positionality that they discuss in their respective chapters.

The Lab Collective have never comfortably allowed that label to adhere to their mode of making, preferring the term 'interactive'. ZU-UK have also recently published a manifesto (2020), in which they articulate their position as offering the experiential and propose instead that their work is post-immersive. The manifesto signals their connection with the umbrella term of immersive theatre but perhaps locates them in some ways as operating beyond it too. In the manifesto, ZU-UK suggest:

> Post-immersive performance, unlike immersive experience design, requires a deeper level of commitment and care from participants than the dominant scene currently offers. At the core is human social interaction and the constitution of a kind of performance collective, a temporary community. The use of technology, clever design and stage tricks cannot accomplish this.
>
> (RAMOS ET AL. 2020)

It is provocative for the group to have asserted this positionality because in many ways their work was one of the driving forces that seem to crystallize the context that the moniker of immersive emerged out of, particularly their iconic work *Hotel Medea* (2006–12). However, I suggest that although the inclusion of their work might not comfortably sit beneath the banner of immersive theatre that stretches the spectrum to recognize, include and account for work was instrumental in fuelling the turn towards immersion in performance and the work, which continues to test its elasticity as a category or genre of cultural production. In Chapter 6, the inherent friction of their positionality is felt through the various threads of the round-table discussion but particularly in the discourse around accessibility.

The chapters presented in this volume are not interviews with theatre makers but instead are carefully crafted and curated discussions. I did not approach the makers from an objective scholarly position, seeking to excavate their wisdom and 'know how', but instead I meet them eye to eye as a fellow immersive theatre maker. The conversations here are a series of discourses between two creative perspectives and positions. As I have already unfolded earlier in the chapter, I am a practitioner-scholar and I have been making audience-centric work since 2005. I have a stake in these discussions beyond just the scholarly curiosity or concerns of cultural custodianship one would expect of my role as a theatre scholar; I meet the makers from a position of my own practical expertise and experience of crafting audience-centric performance.

I have a pre-existing relationship with all of the contributors; thus, the focus, tone and texture of the discussions that are captured here are the accumulative result of the many conversations had and broadcast for TAIT since 2016, as well as those more informal exchanges in the COLAB Factory bar, many other damp basements and pop-up spaces around London over the last five years. The discussions here are intimate and deeply personal but constructed to draw out aspects of each contributing artist and companies' work that are usually hidden to those on the outside of their various processes. For the first time in immersive scholarship, each conversation explores and opens up topics that expose the creatives' ethos, desires, viewpoints and the practical 'know how' they have developed around aspects from casting, design mechanics, rehearsal, audience engagement tactics to the financial strategies.

The concluding round-table discussion seeds knowledge exchange through the sharing of approaches and concerns from across the spectrum of immersive theatre. The discussion between all of the contributors in the round table was thus curated to start the work of sharing attitudes, concerns and desires as well as practical expertise. Such knowledge exchange can not only enrich and enhance practice but also begin to address some of the urgent and pressing challenges that makers feel face the sector more broadly, such as accessibility, diversity, inclusion, support, infrastructure and stability, as well as safeguarding concerns for audiences and performers alike. There have been growing concerns about inclusivity in immersive theatre but also reservations about the safeguarding practices in operation for performers working in often intimate and close proximity to the audience.

The structure of the book

The order that the conversations appear in the volume has been curated to unfold from a place of familiarity with work that is more explicitly theatrical through to work that firmly moves away from comfortable, recognizable forms of experience building. The chapters build across a spectrum of immersion and interactivity, from immersive theatre through to pervasive and gamified approaches on to socially engaged work, ending with post-immersive dramaturgies. The first discussion in Chapter 1 is with James Seager and Oliver Lansley from Les Enfants Terribles; Chapter 2 is a discussion with Owen Kingston from Parabolic Theatre; Chapter 3 engages Bertie Watkins from COLAB Theatre; Chapter 4 is a discussion with The Lab Collective, led by Natalie Scott, Joseph Thorpe, Joe Iredale and Antigoni Spanou; for Chapter 5 I chat with Ruth Cross from Cross Collaborations; and in Chapter 6 I talk with Jorge Lopes Ramos and Persis Jadé Maravala from ZU-UK. Chapter 7 brings all of the contributors together for a round-table discussion in response to thinking about the future of immersive and interactive theatre.

The discussions conclude with the round-table conversation between all of the contributors that brings together the full spectrum of voices to reflect upon the future of their field of practice and marks the start of building a more diverse and inclusive practice-based knowledge community. The logic of the volume is constructed so that it opens with discussions that are most closely related to the familiar form of theatre with Les Enfants Terribles and then with each discussion that follows adding an under-represented and previously undisclosed approach culminating in a provocative discussion, with ZU-UK locating them firmly within the realm of post-immersive theatre.

Each discussion was recorded between April and July 2021 and has been collaboratively edited to meet the broader requirements of the book both epistemologically and stylistically. The conversations playfully take up some of the conventions of contemporary playscripts, an attempt to keep alive the conversational tone and energy of the original conversations. I have utilized the tropes of a contemporary play text to capture and preserve the texture of the different voices involved, so sentences have not been corrected or completed to satisfy the rules of grammar. The interruptions, cross-talking, pauses and laughter have been kept alive through the use of dramatic dialogue conventions and through the vitalization of emotive or sound expressions. My hope is that the unique qualities of each of the voices represented here are presented and communicated through a form of the contemporary dramatic text. I will now go on to offer some background information and context for each of the contributing artists and companies which will help to further frame the intimate and refreshingly frank conversations.

About the contributors

Les Enfants Terribles

Les Enfants Terribles is run by Artistic Director Oliver Lansley and Creative Director James Seager, who steer the Les Enfants Terribles creative team. Since their inception in 2002, they have been dedicated to creating original, innovative theatre to entertain and inspire a wide breadth of audiences. Since their humble origins, the company has received consistent critical acclaim, won top industry awards and established a large and loyal following for their unique work. They were nominated for an Olivier Award in 2015 and made the Stage Power 100 List in 2017 with a further nomination for the Stage Innovation Award in 2016. Over the course of their twenty-year history, the company has produced award-winning shows, including *The Trench* (2012) and *The Terrible Infants* (2007), as well as groundbreaking immersive productions such as *United Queendom* (2020), *Inside Pussy Riot* (2017), the dining experience, *Dinner at the Twits* (2016), and the smash-hit *Alice's Adventures Underground* (2015), which transferred to China in 2018 for a two-year run. Les Enfants Terribles are known for their striking visual aesthetic and innovative use of props, puppetry and live music. Their work explores new ways of telling stories and immersing audiences in the weird and wonderful worlds they create in our shows. Les Enfants Terribles have created shows about everything, from 'bad-ass feminist revolutionaries to a melancholy Mock Turtle. From immersive to stage, online to virtual reality, we love to push the boundaries of what it means to put on a show, and we do it all in our distinctive Les Enfants Terribles's style' (Les Enfants Terribles 2022).

Parabolic Theatre

Parabolic Theatre was founded by Artistic Director Owen Kingston and has been at the forefront of fringe interactive experiences since their emergence in Croydon in 2016. Parabolic shows are highly interactive and responsive to their audiences, utilizing Owen's concept of 'adaptive narrative' to fully engage the audience by giving them the power to meaningfully affect their worlds and the outcomes of their shows. Parabolic work hard to ensure that audiences never encounter the 'edges' of the worlds they create, and they believe that for a show to be immersive in the truest sense, an audience should not merely occupy the same space as the actors but also inhabit the same world with a concrete meaning to be present there and have the freedom to fully explore and interact with that world, which should extend beyond the physical confines of the performance space. The work they make operates beyond the 'trendy' immersive spectacle commonly found within the immersive landscape and instead aims to tackle the sociopolitical concerns of our time 'in creative and historically connected ways' (Parabolic Theatre 2021). Parabolic Theatre's novel approach to audience-centric performance was supported by the ACE/DCMS Culture Recovery Fund with previous commissions from Croydon Council, *Croydonites Festival* and Aimhigher London. Parabolic Theatre have received success with critics and audiences alike with their interactive live shows *Land of Nod* (2015 & 2018), *Morningstar* (2017), *For King and Country* (2018 & 2019) and *Crisis? What Crisis?* (2019 & 2021). They have more recently developed some exciting digital interactive works such as *We Have a Situation* (2020) and *The House of Cenci* (2021), which won an Immie award. This year (2022), Parabolic Theatre are taking the exciting step of launching a new immersive venue called *CRYPT*, in the Crypt of a church in Bethnal Green.

COLAB Theatre Productions

COLAB Theatre Productions was founded in 2012 by Bertie Watkins, the artistic director. It has grown from a one-person company to one of the lynchpins of the London immersive landscape. COLAB Theatre now runs three productions a year and has four venues in and around the London Bridge area. Their venues include the extraordinary catalyst COLAB Factory, which has supported influential companies such as Coney, Parabolic Theatre and Hartshorn Hook. Combining authentic immersive theatre with original interactivity and classic storytelling techniques, COLAB's work facilitates its audiences to navigate space, story and characters as the protagonist. Their work is designed to be accessible, providing 'rewarding experience that offers excitement, thrill and intrigue to the seasoned immersive theatre goer or newcomer alike' (COLAB Theatre Productions 2022). They take advantage of the London cityscape working in buildings and locations around London. COLAB have a distinctive mission, which is 'to put audiences centre stage in fantastical worlds that allow them to tell the story for themselves' (COLAB Theatre Productions 2022). They have made innovative interactive shows such as *Hostage* (2015), *CROOKS* (2016), *Hunted* (2017), *Montagues & Capulets* (2017), *CROOKS 1926* (2020) and, more recently, the horror experience *Flicker* (2021). COLAB has been at the heart of the growth of the immersive sub-culture in the UK, with the COLAB Factory serving as a nurturing environment for new and emerging talent.

The Lab Collective

The Lab Collective was founded by Artistic Directors Joe Thorpe and Natalie Scott in 2007 but began making audience-centric work in 2010. The Lab Collective's work is socially engaged and often provocative. They create interactive, visceral live experiences in forms that exist between theatre, game and installation in both physical spaces and virtual worlds. The Lab Collective utilize dramaturgies that explicitly empower their audiences. They have developed novel democratized approaches to facilitating audience participation that is both collective and collaborative and provide training in interactive and immersive practice for professional performers and HE students. In their commitment to activating ethically charged participation, they have 'worked in a variety of traditional and non-traditional performance spaces, exploring and playing across disciplines to generate an innovative theatrical experience' (The Lab Collective 2017). Working alongside a dedicated group of associate artists and creative collaborators, Scott and Thorpe suggest that they develop work which 'asks questions about issues which impact us all, giving a voice to unheard stories – told not only by our performers – but by the audience themselves' (The Lab Collective 2017). Some of their most successful socially and politically engaged work includes *Bullpen & Matador* (2010), *The Pinstripe Trilogy* (2013), *Between Us* (2014), *A Dedication* (2016), *Incoming/Exodus* (2017), *Burden of Proof* (2018) and *Vector* (2018–22). The Lab Collective have also been central to supporting new and emergent interactive creatives offering space and development opportunities out of their old home, The FlyPit, Stanley Halls.

Cross Collaborations

Since 2009, Cross Collaborations has been Ruth Cross' vehicle for creating collaborative interdisciplinary work, which moves between social arts, activism and immersive theatre.

Cross Collaborations create participative spaces where audiences imagine and shape possible futures. Their work poses questions such as 'If our reality depends on our collective actions, how do we want to act?' They take inspiration from the principles of gifting, cultures of care, decolonial embodiment, radical friendship, reflexivity, imagination, emergent strategy and delicate activism. Project-specific collaborators include intercultural regeneration project La Bolina (Spain), Dartington College of Arts alumni, filmmakers, researchers and ecologists. Cross Collaborations are best known for *Post Present Future* (2009–present). Touring festivals across Europe, it invites participants to write a letter to their future, posted back after five years. Ruth and her mum, Jane, have sent more than 5,000 handwritten letters for their owners to open in an intimate 'performance for one'. The letters inspired the production of immersive and site-specific theatre, a film, public letter readings and a research project on life transitions. Cross Collaborations are currently working on an art activism project about industrial food systems and migrant workers' rights, specifically focusing on 'The Plastic Sea', Almeria, Spain.

ZU-UK

Founded in 2009, ZU-UK are a multi-award-winning theatre and digital arts company based in East London. Renowned for their distinctive personal, political and sometimes humorous approach to creating interactive performance, and known for their attention to detail, care and complete respect for audience members, the company are leaders in participatory theatre and performance art. Led by immigrant working-class artists Persis Jadé Maravala and Jorge Lopes Ramos, ZU-UK is an independent not-for-profit company. Persis Jadé is ethnically Persian, coming from Yemen but raised in East London. Jorge was born and raised within Borel, one of Rio de Janeiro's largest favelas to a Polish and Romanian family. In a world where mainstream narratives normalize hate and fear, and where contemporary loneliness is a new epidemic, Persis Jadé and Jorge believe in the need for shared rituals, new narratives and experiences that empower those most vulnerable to have a voice and participate in a live culture. Renowned for their distinctive personal, political and sometimes humorous approach to creating interactive performance, and known for their attention to detail, care and complete respect for audience members, the company are leaders in participatory theatre and performance art. From the outset, work such as *Hotel Medea* (2009–12) and *The Humble Market* (2012) has been provocative and dramaturgically groundbreaking. ZU-UK's more recent interventions, *Missing* (2017–19) and *Project Perfect Stranger* (2020), are pushing at the boundaries between the everyday, performance and gaming

Note

1 The TAIT podcast has over 18,000 listeners with more than 7,000 from outside of the UK.

FIGURE 2 *Image from* Alice's Adventures Underground *(2015), at the Vaults, Waterloo. Photographed by Rah Petherbridge. ©Rah Petherbridge Photography.*

CHAPTER 1

Underground adventures with Oliver Lansley and James Seager from Les Enfants Terribles

Speaker key:

JB: *Joanna Bucknall*
JS: *James Seager*
OL: *Oliver Lansley*

[This conversation was recorded over Zoom on 21 June 2021.]

JB: Can we begin by discussing *Alice's Adventures Underground* (2015, 2017 & 2022)? This was your first immersive show and seems to have been the start of a big shift for the company. *Alice's Adventures Underground* (2015, 2017 & 2022) was nominated for an Olivier Award in 2015. Could you talk a little about the impact of the success that that show has had for you as a company?

JS: I suppose one of the biggest effects that it's had is that people have started to call us an immersive theatre company, which is not true. We're a theatre company.

OL: We're not *exclusively* in immersive theatre.

JS: Yeah. Absolutely – that show was the biggest thing we've ever done in terms of capacity and reach. So, I don't fight it. I don't mind it. It's understandable and since then, we've done quite a few immersive shows.

OL: I would say also, it was our first official immersive show, but I think we started doing immersive stuff before it was like a thing, really, I suppose, when we did *Vaudevillains* (2010, 2011 & 2016). The first time we did that was at *Latitude*,[1] and our idea was that it was a way to create the Cabaret Club. And when we first did it in *Latitude*, oh, and in Edinburgh, actually, we did one-night affairs in *Edinburgh Fringe Festival*[2] and in *Latitude*, which were absolutely insane. But we basically – we did the show and then they turned into these, you know, cabaret parties afterwards. And off the back of that, there's a band called *Edward Sharpe and the Magnetic Zeros*,[3] and it was their first UK performance. And we did this big, immersive gig. So, it's all been building up and learning stuff. But then, yeah, with 'Alice', it just kind of the scale of it, I think, just exploded.[4]

JS: It was the first time that we sat down, you know, probably a year, a year and a half ahead of when we did it, saying, 'Okay, let's do an immersive show'. And, usually, when we decide to do a show, it's because we've either seen something that sparks our interest or creative flows, like, Ollie and I see something and go, that's great, but wouldn't it be great if it did this, this, and this? Or let's do a musical, but let's put our spin on it. At the time, we'd started to see a few immersive shows and I think, storytelling was something that was missing for us and that's what we thought, wouldn't be great if we did one, but with storytelling? That's when the seeds were sown of doing a big-scale immersive show with storytelling at the forefront.

JB: Well, it has all the hallmarks of your work, as I said when we spoke many years ago. I saw your work back in, probably, 2006, 2007, in Brighton at the Nightingale Theatre. And, actually, a lot of those kind of aesthetics and dramaturgies I can see in 'Alice' and in the work that you've done since then. I think they're a really strong kind of element that run through that. And you're right, I the usage of immersive emerged after a lot of people that I'm talking to developed their work, and so it is a funny relationship. I wanted to pick up on something that you said, this idea of large-scale and getting lots of bodies through. For 'Alice', you developed a really innovative way of doing that which hadn't been seen before. And I wondered if you could talk just a little bit about that design and how you worked to get so many audience members through the experience every night.

JS: Yeah. You know, thinking back, it's tricky to say, chicken and egg, what came first? But I think the idea of always wanting it to be intimate was always there quite early on, we had been going to quite a few immersive shows where there were a lot of people and we thought, well, actually, it's much better to get intimacy and smaller numbers. So that was a driving force.

OL: Like with all of these things, it comes through, you know, its limitations. It's your restrictions that force you; you have to create new ways of doing things. Because, you know, like James said, we knew that our focus was to tell these stories and create these different experiences, but until you try and make it, you know . . . you go, okay, we want to tell a story, so what do we need? We need a beginning, a middle and an end. And, you know, most of the immersive theatre at that time was completely free-roaming. So, if you happen to be at the place where there was the beginning, and the middle and an end, you get your story. But if not, you couldn't guarantee that. So, it kind of started from there. And then it was also about the intimacy, and just bit by bit. We just sort of had to find ways of kind of controlling the experiences as much as curating the experience.

JS: And I suppose, we partnered with quite a commercial producer. We wanted as many people to see this as possible, so it wasn't really a surprise that the idea of entries. . .

OL: We had to balance the books. We were like, this is what we want to do. And it was basically, well, this is how much it's going to cost; therefore, this is how many tickets you need to sell; therefore this is how many people need to go through the doors.

JS: Yeah, absolutely. Saying that, at the same time, I guess we always have that thought in the back of our mind being creators as well as producers, in that, there's no way we could create 'Alice' the size that it was for only fifty-six people, which is, one entry.

OL: There's so much about the thing that we have to create. There's so many different – like, even when I think about it now, we've got the timed entries, but then you've also got a system where the actors play multiple parts, and they go on a rotation. All of it came through necessity, but it was like . . . if you've got a small number of actors, they can just kind of wander wherever they want. But if you've got, for example, you know, you've got entries every fifteen minutes, but you want your White Rabbit to spend more than fifteen minutes with one of your audiences, it means you're going to need another White Rabbit or a third White Rabbit to make that up to an hour. So suddenly you're then into these kinds of incredibly mathematical equations, where you're going. Right, we need three Rabbits because they need to cover this amount of time, and then five minutes of that is at the beginning of the show. The other five minutes is at the end of the show. So, you've got these kinds of rotations that your audience is on one show, your actors are on another show, and it's just, you know, when I even try and think about it now, it makes my brain hurt.

JS: Yeah. Talking about the 'Rabbits', that was a change because, initially, we did this route for the 'Rabbits'. I think we had maybe two at the time, well, there was a team of six, but in one evening, there were two 'Rabbits', two separate 'Rabbits'. And we gave this one actor, a guy called John, who is an incredibly fit actor, very energetic, and it was like the first test. It was like, well, can you do this? And he did it. And at the end of the night, it was like, Yeah, I don't think we can sustain it. Straightaway, we're like, okay, we need three 'Rabbits' in one evening. But there's a lot with immersive theatre of trying things out; going, actually, this isn't going to work, we need to try this. We need to change.

OL: In the first previews, all of the audience saw everything. And we were like trying to get how many people up these stairs, and then back down the same stairs, and that's the thing about a show like that, it very quickly tells you very loudly that it doesn't work. But also, what we realized is that the world feels bigger if people don't see everything. Weirdly. So, actually, what people didn't see became as important as what people did see. And so, you would have people coming out the show afterward, and some of them would go, 'Oh my goodness, did you see this bit, when it rained', and others would go, 'Oh, no, I didn't see that, but I saw the caterpillar'. So, you know, that idea of people meeting up and sharing their different experiences became a crucial part of what we wanted to bring. And as a result, the different routes sprung out of that, and then they became different stories, and they became different experiences. And so, yeah, it was all sort of organic in many ways, and it all came from trying to solve problems in a very basic way, we wanted our audience to *be* 'Alice', so we wanted to give them as rich an experience as possible.

JB: And so did it begin, then, with knowing the numbers that you needed to get through the door, then working out the mechanics and then testing them in the previews and adjusting, as you went through – is that the kind of process?

JS: A little bit. But also, you know, I think when we're doing a lot of immersive theatre, we ask ourselves and ask others and I think we ask ourselves probably even subconsciously. Why? Quite a lot. And even if it's just a little question, it has to be. So why fifty-six people? And, actually, it didn't start with fifty-six. It started with fifty-two because that's how many cards are in a deck. And so that means something. And we thought, okay, fifty-two people will go through and everyone will be given a card. And then you start thinking, well, why are they getting a card? Well, actually, if you're getting a card, you are the three of diamonds, what does it mean? And so, it led from there. And I think we probably looked at the economics. And I remember this meeting, going, this isn't financially going to work. And then I think Em (Emma Brünjes) and Ollie were like, What about fifty-six? We can't do fifty-six because it's not in a pack. And then someone went, Jokers? Fifty-six. There's four Jokers in a pack. So, you know, that's kind of how it got to fifty-six, really.

JB: What were the challenges of working in this rigid form? I know you've spoken in the past, you know, that literally, lights go out on a set timer. Things are fixed once the show begins. So, what are the challenges managing that on a nightly basis?

JS: So many.

OL: Firstly, like with 'Alice' (2015, 2017 & 2022), the challenge was, like you said, it had never really been done before on that scale. So, the challenge was convincing your huge cast that it was possible, was one of the main challenges – or that it was sustainable as well.

JS: And doing something completely new.

OL: You know, it's so interesting, you look at it six weeks in, and you've got actors sliding into a room, the light comes on, and they've got time. But the first couple of weeks of those shows, people are like, this is impossible. It's inhuman. It can't be done.

And at the time, we didn't know it could be done either. So, you know, now, when we do it, we have the confidence there. We go, guys, it will be fine, give it ten days and it will be second nature. But at the time, we didn't know if it was possible, so leaping into the unknown and trying to convince everyone to come with you was a challenge.

JB: So not just audience then, the performers, too.

JS: Absolutely. Yeah, in some ways, bringing it back in 2017, we knew a lot more then, so we knew it could work, as Ollie said. The difference between 2015 and 2017 is like climbing Everest. In 2015, you couldn't see the top. There are loads of clouds. So, when we're through one cloud, we're like, okay, I'm sure the tops are through that cloud, and then you get through that cloud, and then there's another cloud. But in 2017, when we did it, it was clear. There were no clouds, so we could see the top. I don't know which one is worse really, because, oh my god, we're going to get there?! But at least we knew. But I guess in 2015, it was like trying something entirely new. But that's exciting, and I think it was exciting doing something different and new. And there were times, looking back in 2015, or maybe '14, we were like, technically, I don't understand this. And we work with some very amazing people, but, obviously, we were learning, and we've learned a lot since then.

OL: And some people really thrive in that environment, and some people don't.

JS: Yeah. Then I guess on a nightly basis, you know, when it comes to the audience, you can never anticipate how an audience is going to react. And, initially, I think when Ollie and Anthony Spargo were writing the script, they were acting it out. But then Ollie and Anthony just had to guess how long a scene would be before the next scene, like one minute. So, we all had to put one minute in, and guess how long it would take fourteen people because, obviously, it gets divided fifty-six into four groups of fourteen, how long it would take them to walk from here to there, and we just didn't know. There was a lot of change in the initial period of, going, okay, well how long is it going to take? Also, how long is it going to take an actor to deliver a scene within a room? Must be seven minutes. But, you know, all plays, on the stage, they all last relatively, give, or take, a minute or two, the same every night.

OL: That's the thing. Because you tell an actor, 'This scene has to take three and a half minutes', and they panic. But, you know, as James says, if you're doing *A Midsummer Night's Dream* and you're doing a long run of it, the show times will usually come in between one and two minutes difference. And no one feels like they're consciously trying to do that. Things find their natural rhythm.

JS: So, you have to have a slight adaptability with that. The actors do. If an audience arrives ten seconds later, then they are going to pick the pace up within that scene to deliver that scene within four minutes and thirty-two seconds. Or they have to fill, either way. And sometimes audiences were a bit slow walking from there to there, or a bit fast, but over a course of six months, it finds its natural rhythm. Sometimes, Ollie and I would go and see the show and not watch the show, but go backstage, and you watch an entirely different show which is incredibly amazing watching people run from there to there and it all works. And that's really quite fulfilling, especially in 2017, when we made it even more complicated for ourselves and improved the show and made actors appear in more scenes, so they were popping in and running out. And so that was amazing to see when that worked, but quite hard to achieve.

JB: I wanted to talk just a little bit about the venue that you were working in because, of course, it was an incredible space underneath Waterloo in *The Vaults*,[5] but what was that like, and what were some of things you had to take into account working in those unusual spaces?

JS: What's really important to say is that sometimes, it's a bit of a chicken and egg when you get a new show of what comes first, the show or the venue? We were quite lucky that we knew we had that venue, and so we started planning the show around it. We were like, okay, well the tea party has to be in the – they call it 'The Long Wet One'. And, the 'Mock Turtle' has to be in that area. And it was complicated, but we knew because we had the venue first. But sometimes when you don't it's quite hard to know what does come first. But it was challenging working in the space of course.

OL: Yeah, and *The Vaults* was amazing, that it gave you the sense of being underground – you know, *Alice's Adventures Underground* (2015, 2017 & 2022), which was amazing. But at the same time, it was underground tunnels, and they hadn't been completely refurbished so there's one day that it flooded, the electrics. There was damp. Air conditioning was something that we never thought about, when it was hot, it was incredibly hot. But also, it could get cold. One of the biggest challenges, I think, the first time around was airflow and air conditioning, which was something that we'd never considered. On the first show, we didn't use LED lights. We used theatrical lights. So, you know, chucking a load of those lights in, an underground bunker heats the place up pretty quickly. About 40 actors and 700 audience members, it gets warm. And then you've got actors with makeup and rabbit heads on – it presents a big challenge. That's one of the first things we always think about now is temperature, air and soundproofing.

JS: Sound *play* that was another thing. Because, obviously, if you're splitting up groups and they're walking around, and then you've got other entries coming in in different groups, we didn't want them to hear each other because that's really distracting.

OL: Your whole show is happening at exactly the same time. Every scene is happening at the same point. So, you know, your big, loud finales are happening at the same time as your small intimate moments. So, finding a way of creating a space that allows for that to happen was another challenge.

JB: Would you say then that 'Alice', in some ways, was a little bit site-responsive, as well as being immersive?

OL: I mean, it had to be site-responsive.

JS: I think that tunnel, 'The Long Wet One', where the tea party was, that's a perfect example because Sam Wyer, the designer, his idea very early on was that tunnel is older than all the other tunnels and it's got exposed brickwork and it looks like a tunnel, so let's embrace that. His design early on was the tea party table was a train carriage and then it was slightly off the rails of a train track down the middle. It was very much where that design for that particular room was inspired and influenced and replicated and of the environment. And we didn't dress. I think we put green creepers at the side of the walls, but that was exposed brickwork, and it added to the atmosphere. So, in an environment like that and then immersive, site-responsive you have to respond to the environment you're in. And it was a great idea. But also, it can save a bit of money from not having to dress that particular space.

JB: You're very fortunate to have worked in quite unusual spaces. And I know you've done lots of work with cultural institutions, so I want to get into that a little bit as well, to chat about some of the challenges of working within existing sites and spaces. Could you talk a little bit about your collaboration with Madame Tussauds to make *The Game's Afoot* (2016), and how that sort of came about in the first place?

JS: I think it came about because 'Alice' was a big game changer for us in many ways because I think it came about because people had seen 'Alice' and thought, That's great. I think that would work in our environment or in our situation. And that happened with Madame Tussauds, but it also happened with a lot of corporate clients as well. You know, Toyota or agencies saw the show and thought this immersive theatre is not a fad. So, with Madame Tussauds, Emma [Brünjes], our co-producer on the show, knew someone there. They'd seen 'Alice'. And for a long time, Madame Tussauds were like, we really do need to do something about Sherlock Holmes because our building is on Baker Street, or at least, you know, the side of it is on Baker Street. And then they came to us, and that was that little seed in our mind of, okay, well, how could we do an immersive show but do it slightly, well, do it very differently, actually, to 'Alice'? And that got us excited. I remember exactly where we were and what tube we were on when I said, 'Hey, do you remember this game that I used to play? I think it was called 221B Baker Street'. I said, 'It wouldn't be as a board game, to do something that's similar to that?' And then me, Ollie, and Anthony, the co-writer and Sam the designer, I think we went away for about three days where we just talked about it and played that game, and the show ran from there. Then Ollie and Anthony went away and wrote it.

OL: Yeah, I think it was the mix of going, you know, they wanted the sort of smaller experience, but we kind of thought, well, if we do that and we create this set and everything, then what is it that would excite us about that? And for me, one starting point was wanting to create an immersive world where everything you touched, everything you looked at was relevant, you know. Like, I think people have been to these big, immersive experiences and seen these incredible designs and gone, what is this? How does this affect the experience? And we wanted every drawer you open, every piece of paper, every poster on the wall, if you picked up a phone, you could make a phone call. You know, basically trying to go, right, well, you know, there was a crime. And rather than it being a story as such, it was like, there's a crime and all the clues you need to solve it are here somewhere. But there's also a load of other stuff. There was over a hundred clues per case, as well as verbal clues, visual clues. But basically, every different version you could think of, we had to then think about the different order that people might see those clues in. And you had to train your performers. We'd kind of give them like a bible of information, but they didn't have a script. They were trained to kind of improvise based on this set of information. It was a really fascinating way of telling a story, I suppose, because it's not linear. Everybody's story will be different depending on the order that they decide to look at stuff. But, yeah, unlike the more conventional free-roaming, immersive stuff, they're free-roaming on a very, very clear objective.

JS: And I suppose we drip-feed the narrative for the experience. It was an hour and a half, maybe an hour and 20. And then the actors all had timings of when scenes would happen or information, so you would get that progression, but in a different type of free-roaming.

OL: All our characters were basically living within the space in that time. So, like, two characters would go and have an argument outside the chemists at a certain point. So, if your audience happened to be following one or two of those characters that moment, they would witness this argument. And so, they were on a kind of real-time storyline building up to the end of the show. And, again, it depended on who you were following or where you were if you saw these moments.

JS: And I suppose from Madame Tussauds' side It was 2016, it was large companies waking up to the possibilities of immersive and wanting to diversify, seeing the potential for it and the popularity of it. So that was starting to happen. We were starting to get very busy with the corporate world. And although it wasn't corporate, it was a collaboration with them, it was an insight that year of, like, wow, this is something that a lot of people are doing, wanting to do, and actually wanting to expand on.

JB: How did you have to negotiate some of the things that are fixed within that institution?

JS: Well, it was in the basement of Madame Tussauds, they did have this horror thing there for years. And they just totally got rid of all of it, knocked it all down in the basement, and they said, Right, it's yours, you build what you want. They demolished everything there and we built a Baker Street, and docks and a train carriage, which was really cool! We did a moving train and the moors. It's quite a small space, so we managed to compact it pretty well then started thinking about: well, actually, how do we get audiences through the whole thing? And then we thought, you can't have more than forty people, down there. So, we started to do three entries of forty people, so it was relatively small, audience-wise. We wanted more, but the museum – Madame Tussauds closes at half-five, and our show is on when it closed, in the basement, so we weren't allowed to start before half-six. And then we could only get three shows through. But, again, it was like, okay, after an hour, then the audience, we have to place them somewhere else, so the next audience, when they come in, don't see them, which is what we did. And we'd learned a lot through 'Alice' of doing that, and relatively speaking, it was a lot easier than 'Alice' to move audiences around that space.

JB: I experienced that at Madame Tussauds, and I liked having an objective and being able to hunt something down. I love rifling through drawers and just looking at stuff, but the objective puts you in the driving seat of the narrative in a way that roaming doesn't as much.

JS: Absolutely. We hundred per cent agree. You've got to have role and a reason, in immersive theatre, and an objective really pushes the audience and gets them immersed in the situation that they're in or the environment; the narrative, I suppose.

JB: Well, it gives you the stakes. Because that's why I always ask, 'What's at stake here? Why would I jump in? Why would I get involved? What's at stake for me? What's the win? What do I get out of doing this? Why do I get out of my seat?' What you're talking about is exactly that.

Do you want to talk a little bit about *Queendom* and the project that you did at the Historic Palaces?

JS: We went in and thought, we don't have to do any design work here because the palace is beautiful and, actually, we're recreating a story that actually happened in these rooms, which is pretty exciting. They approached us, similar to Madame Tussauds, and they said, 'We want to diversify our audience'. We want to get a younger audience in, a different type of audience. Like Madame Tussauds, when the museum or palace is closed at five o'clock, it's empty at night, so we think it'd be great to do some kind of show in the evening. And they actually said to us, we either want to do it about Anne. . .

JS: The *Favourite* (2018) film had just come out. We looked at the history of the other two women that they wanted to talk about; we knew nothing about these two women who are incredible, so far ahead of their time. So, it'd be great to do an immersive show and shine a bit of light on these two women. It was challenging because you do get frustrated with Historic Royal Palaces; on the one hand, it's fair play to them because they've never done something like this before. And good on them for trying something. And why would they know anything about our world? They're coming from here. We're coming from there. In working with them, we have to learn a lot. And Emilie Wiseman, who worked there, she was brilliant, and a kind of conduit between the museum world and our world, and she drove the project really well for us and was a great supporter for us because it must have been challenging from her side.

JB: Was there a different approach then in terms of starting to write, when you have that weight of real people and real histories and real stories behind what you're doing? Did you approach it any differently in terms of the writing and in terms of putting it together because of that?

JS: From the off we thought, well, two men telling this story – it shouldn't really be us telling this story. So, there was a female director (Christa Harris) and a female co-writer (Yassmin Abdel-Magied).

OL: You're working with an institution. They're obviously doing it because they have an intention. So, what story do they want to tell?

JB: I just wanted to start to draw out some of the work that you did with the Roald Dahl Estate because, of course, that must have been unusual and it's an interesting sort of project to take on. So how did that come about?

JS: Someone who worked at the Estate, a lady called Bernie, who's great, she had seen 'Alice' and loved it. So, 'Alice' was a big calling card for us and had got us meetings with the Estate, and it kind of rolled from there. And we were looking at properties, and *Charlie* (1964) was always a big thing for us, of wanting to do *Charlie and the Chocolate Factory* (1964), but the rights are so complicated, they actually wanted to do a show for adults, which was great. We were the first show ever specifically designed for adults. They were like, what about *The Twits* (1981)? What appealed to us about *The Twits* (1981) is that it's quite graphic in its descriptions and the descriptions of Mr Twit, the food, the world, the house, is very tactile. Quite early on we met *Bombas and Parr*, who worked a lot in food, drink and jelly. And what they could bring to the table in terms of food was actually, this could be quite exciting.

OL: The idea of creating a dining experience where the food was disgusting but tasted delicious, it was bird pie and it was worm spaghetti and all of that sort of stuff, I think appealed to our more macabre tastes.

JB: Absolutely! And I love *The Twits*. I think it's the grotesqueness of it. In terms of working with food and that existing, much beloved IP, how did you bring all of those things together to design that experience?

JS: I guess it was a different challenge for us because we knew at some point the audience had to be sat down because it was a dining experience, which is not what we'd done before. But then we started thinking, well, we want them to walk around. But why are they having food? And then suddenly, well, why? Maybe Mr and Mrs Twit are renewing their wedding vows. We thought because they hate each other but they love each other, it'd be quite fun to do a renewal of wedding vows. Why are they doing this? They want to lock everyone up. And the narrative kind of came from there, really.

JB: And was the food then designed in conjunction as you wrote? Or did the food come after that process?

OL: We knew what the bulk of the food would be because it was taken from the book, so we knew that our main course would be bird pie. And then we have these amazing pies that had chicken feet sticking out of the top of them. And I suppose, in a way, you look at your three courses as three acts, you know, for your story, so that's what we kind of did. We treated the meal as a three-act play.

JB: So back to that narrative drive that's at the heart of everything that you do, it's that telling a story, isn't – that beginning, middle and end, that really drives. . .

OL: Yeah, that's very much at the heart of everything we do. It kind of starts and ends with that. And then we spend a lot of time thinking about what is the coolest and most exciting and fun way to tell it? But ultimately, everything is about telling that story. Because, ultimately, that's what people are engaged with, you know. I think we've all had experiences where you can see the most exciting, cool stuff in the world, but it gets boring very quickly. Like 3D, or VR, or whatever, you know. For the first ten minutes, it's like, this is the most amazing thing that I've ever seen. But if there's nothing beyond that, if there's no story. Once you've got used to it, it's not interesting anymore. But at the same time, you could sit around a campfire and listen to one person tell you a story for an hour and a half, if it's a good story. So, all the bells and whistles and effects and lights and this, that and the other, like, they'll be cool for a bit, but, eventually, that will wear off and then you're left with. Either you've got your audience engaged or you haven't.

JB: You have huge casts especially in 'Alice', how do you start to populate that with actors? Do you have a specific casting process for hiring actors?

JS: Initially, in 2015, we had workshops when we were casting because 'Alice' *works* in teams, we had to cast five Alices, for example. We had an 'Alice' day, and people submit their CVs, headshots, and we selected probably sixty, seventy people to come to those workshops. During those workshops, you do group exercises. A lot more in 2017 because, you know, I think sometimes we don't want to undersell the script.

JS: 'Alice' was over 300 pages long, so you have to see what people are like with script and with improvisation as well. It was slightly easier in 2017, bringing it back, because you knew exactly what we're after. There are some actors who are amazing on stage but wouldn't be great in an immersive type of setting or situation, and vice versa.

JB: So, as well as doing that kind of script work that we all know well, are you testing their improv skills, their charisma that comes with working this way when you do the workshops?

JS: We do improv bits or give people situations and see. Sometimes those situations can be a bit difficult or misleading because, some people can really come to the forefront in front of another group/

OL: /is why we need people who can think on their feet and adapt, you know, yeah.

JB: Yes. Because it is a different proposition being in and amongst the audience, than to presenting yourself with that barrier that the audience/

JS: /if something goes wrong. Something went wrong on press night for 'Alice', which is one of the worst nights of our lives! There was a power cut in Waterloo. I mean who could predict that? And so suddenly, all the audiences couldn't move on, so they were stuck in rooms with actors for about ten minutes. So, all the actors had to improvise for ten minutes. Those poor actors having to improvise with critics.

OL: That was awful.

JS: You have to get people that are going to be okay with that. Hopefully, it'll never, ever happen again; luckily, we've worked with some amazing people.

JB: One of the really tricky aspects, I think, of this work is when it's so inhabited by the audience, so how do you rehearse that absence?

OL: A big part of it is training. You need to try and give people the tool kit that they will use. But, ultimately, you can't a hundred per cent rehearse the show until you've got an audience, you know. So, obviously, as a result, you need to try and do as many previews as you can. But a lot of the early parts of our rehearsal process, you know, is boot camp. It's understanding what you're going to be doing. It's understanding the routes, and where you're going to be running, and how long have you got, and how long it takes to say this scene or that, you know.

JS: We had to be quite military with our rehearsals. Ollie and I sat down for a week and wrote down the show. The rehearsal process, the three weeks rehearsal, like, right, from ten to twelve, we're looking at that scene. Because there's so many scenes and so many rooms, and you've got teams.

OL: You've got thirty-plus scenes and forty-plus actors. In our shows, your actors play up to six different characters. So, you know, when you think about the tea party, you're trying to rehearse a scene with six different Hatters, four different Alices, the combination of actors might meet once every six months, so you can't rehearse it like you normally would a scene because it is completely unique and that's one of the things about noting the shows as well. You go and note the show, but you realize that that exact combination of shows may never happen again. You've got to kind of build the structures for people to work within.

JS: There are probably seven or eight rooms going on at the same time, like me and Ollie doing a scene and then Joe, our associate, Roddy, our assistant, there's puppetry rehearsal as well. And you have to make sure that they're all running concurrently. The rehearsals were as military precision and timing as the show, and they had to be so that we could get through it all.

JB: Does it take a little longer? Because theatres usually have a two-week rehearsal period. So is your period that kind of length, where you have to fill it all in? Or do you have a little bit longer to do that?

OL: Not much longer, to be honest.

JS: We would love to have more than three weeks, but it's just purely a financial thing. You have forty actors rehearsing; we rehearsed 'Alice' in three weeks and there are thirty-three different rooms. And then in some rooms, there are five different scenes in those rooms. So, it's amazing that we covered it all in three weeks. But then when you go into the venue, we probably have three weeks in the venue as well. Rehearsing for that long with forty actors and seven stage managers is an expensive thing. If we were millionaires, we'd probably do months and months.

JB: Is that the first contact with real audiences then, in those previews? Is that the first time you get to actually push people through the show?

OL: Yeah, they're like early friends or/

JS: /yeah, friends, and probably crew. We probably had about a hundred people work on 'Alice'. Designers, carpenters, painters, a costume department of ten. After that you start getting friends and family. And then after that, cheaper tickets for other friends and family of 10, 20 pounds. And then, you know, it goes from there.

JB: It's a huge logistical undertaking; the show itself is a huge logistical proposition. How do you finance these shows? How do you get them off the ground when so much work has to be done before anyone ever purchases a ticket?

JS: As a company, we fit in kind of a strange place in a sense of sometimes we do shows that are funded by the Arts Council England (ACE) and subsidized. Others, we fund ourselves from using money from other shows that have done okay. But 'Alice' was a massive leap for us – the capitalization was 600,000 pounds, so we had to raise 600,000 pounds. The most we've had to raise before that was probably 60,000 pounds. And then suddenly, we had to raise 600,000 pounds. We needed someone to come on board and help us with this, which is why we co-produced it with Emma Brünjes. And it was a good collaboration because Emma is quite commercially minded and came from, I guess, the right-end side, and we were, you know, quite left-field in a way. And we met in the middle. We learned a lot from Emma, and Emma learned a lot from us. But she was very used to going out there and raising the West End way, which we'd no experience of. But we committed to raise 300,000 pounds each. Emma had raised 300,000, and me and Ollie raised 300,000. But that was very, very hard. We were still raising on press night! We weren't in the West End kind of mode of, like, knowing, having a little black book of investors that you just go, 'Hey, doing this show. Do you want to invest? And if it goes well, you get X. And if it doesn't, you lose it'. And people are, 'Yeah, love a punt.'

OL: That would've been the end of it.

JS: And I'd like to say it was slightly easier in 2017, but I don't think it was. Because the show improved; it got bigger and better; the capitalization was higher. It was almost a million this time, so we had to raise 500,000 each. As a commercial producer, that is quite tricky.

OL: Equally, there are other producers that could raise money all day but can't necessarily make a show. We're sort of the opposite. You know, we're producers through necessity.

JB: I was going to say, when you're working with IPs and with institutions, have they invested a baseline amount that you can then sort of start from and build on?

JS: It depends on who you're dealing with the IP. With the Sherlock Holmes show, that was different because it was in their building and they put the investment in, so we didn't have to raise any investment for that particular show.

JB: It's more like a commission then?

JS: Yeah. But with the Dahl Estate, it was a collaboration, but we still had to raise the money ourselves. Commercially raising *is* what big shows do, and West End shows do, trying to raise money from investors or other producers. And with large-scale immersive shows, that's the same as well.

OL: We're working towards building a partnership at the moment which will hopefully make it a lot easier for us in the future. But, yeah, up until this point, it's never been easy.

JB: Secrecy is a really big part of immersive theatre. How do you manage that sort of balance of not really giving too much away but also giving enough away to get people through the door?

JS: In 2015, we decided we're not going to give anything away, and we didn't give any, like, pictures, drawings, limited drawings. But we made the decision in 2015, nothing. But in '17, we were like, 'Bugger it'. Everything. And we put so much out there, all the pictures. And we were lucky/

OL: /I think, you know, secrecy is now less important. I think the fact that Secret Cinema advertise all their shows. People are more concerned with knowing what they're going to get and if it's worth their time and their money, I think. It's more like prestige. It's more like getting the exclusive experiences more than it is the secret experiences. They're a form of each other, but now, it's not just about bragging rights, it's about your Instagram photos as well, it's about, like, being in the best place, as opposed to, like, necessarily the secret place.

JB: I call it 'elusivity' because – I think you're right – it's that mix of secrecy and exclusivity, but in a heady mix.

JS: Everyone likes to feel special, that they've discovered, you know, a restaurant that no one else has discovered, that is an amazing restaurant. They have the best food, and it's a bit quirky, and a bit cool, and, you know, no one else has discovered it yet, and suddenly, it becomes a sensation. And, you know, everyone loves that kind of feeling with a film. And I think that plays into this a little bit.

JS: Yeah, the word is experience, isn't it? That's what it's all about, it's the experience economy, isn't it?

JB: During restrictions, you've been able to make a couple of different pieces that were digital, that were online. And I wondered if you could just talk a little bit about *The Prism* (2020) and *Sherlock*

Experience (2021). And how it's been engaging audiences in an immersive way through digital engagement?

JS: *The Prism* was in the summer last year, and that was obviously as a direct result and a consequence of theatres being closed and it was a call-out to the general public. It was very much our show, but it was also their show because people filmed themselves and sent it all in, and then we were editing all these things. It was kind of a community project.

OL: And it was the response to what was happening. But also, it was trying to give people the opportunity to be able to make stuff. For us, we knew it was important to be able to continue making stuff.

JS: Ollie found a website called *Eko* (2018),[6] those choose-your-own-adventure books. You watch a video and then, at the end, you choose left or right, and you go to another video. It's like a spider web. And that's a little bit like how our shows work. And then when we started thinking about: okay, we want to do our own show now, and we thought which show lends itself – that we'd done in the past – to being an online experience and blurring the lines between game and experience and show, that was very similar to *Game's Afoot* (2016), which is a show, but it's also an experience – it's a kind of a game. And we thought, well, that would be a good thing to put online. And finding *Eko* helped us think, actually, we could do some of this. The main thing that we wanted to do with the Sherlock show was put a live element into it. We wanted to make it on a platform that people were used to, which was Zoom. The planning of it, doing an audience route through the show was very similar to how we do normal shows. It was just, you know, the audience do this, then they do this, then they go here, then they may get a choice here or here. And that was planned exactly how we normally do a show. So, in many ways, it was very similar. But in many other ways, it was not. You've got a barrier here, of course, and immersive is all about being in a world. We knew we're going to do a scene, the crime scenes, on a 3D camera, the audience could look around the room by moving their mouse and see this vase. If you want to click on it, then the vase would come really close up. Thankfully, it worked out quite well.

OL: The same as everything, you know. Experiment and just try things out, and get it wrong, and then keep going until you get it right.

JB: And it's just more accessible, isn't it? You know, the cultural location of traditional theatre, especially West End theatre, feels inaccessible for so many different reasons to so many young people. Not just young people either but across the board. And I think because immersive often happens, like you said, in the gaps between, and in communities, and in found spaces, and in dark cellars, and in the woods, I think people feel less like, 'I shouldn't be here', or 'This is not for me'. I think it's more inviting in some ways.

OL: Yeah.

JS: Yeah, inevitably, when you're at a cast size of forty, and you've got fifteen people backstage and a hundred people working on the show. The economics are that you have to charge quite a bit. But we really try and keep our prices very, very competitive, some tickets are 25 pounds, which is rare. We really want to make sure that it is accessible for people who come see it.

JB: The term 'immersive', how do you feel about it? Where do you locate yourselves against that term?

JS: It's a big question. Do you know, in 2015, when we were doing the show, we banned that word!

OL: We were quite snobby about it.

OL: But I think the thing is, It's just so wide. I actually think the word immersive is not necessarily the problem. What we need to start doing is differentiating between immersive theatre, immersive experiences and immersive drinking and immersive games, you know. Immersive is not the problem. The problem is immersive what? There's a lot of things that call themselves immersive theatre that aren't theatre.

JB: Immersive what? And I think theatre is a really particular thing. Performance, again, is a really particular thing. And they have histories and lineages and all. . . .

JS: I think that word is a buzzword, and I think different companies and corporations have jumped on it because companies have come to us, and gone, I want some immersive, but they didn't even know what it means, some of them. But they just heard this buzzword.

JB: And why? It's back to that – why?

JS: We're a theatre company, so what we are making is immersive theatre, whether critics say that it is or not, or people say that it's not, we make immersive theatre. We make stories. We have scripts. We have a beginning, a middle and end. It just happens that next year, we'll do a show onstage, and we'll also do an immersive show.

JB: Yeah. And I think you're right. I think you very, very specifically make theatre. And I think you put audiences inside the stories when you make work like that, rather than them being on the outside of it. And I think that is very clear. I would very distinctly say it's theatre. And I think that's at the heart of what you do, it's that theatrical storytelling, whether we're inside it, or the other work that you do, sometimes when we are on the outside of it. Les Enfants' work is very distinctly theatre, but I think there's lots of work that isn't and that is something else. And I think you're right. I think it's starting; I think we've got to the point now where we can start to draw some of those distinctions about some of those forms. And I think holding on to that idea of theatre, I think very much what you do, I think, is a powerful and useful tool. Because that's also what we have to remember, the word 'immersive' is also useful for people finding us and finding the work and connecting with work in some ways. And I think total abandonment of it would be foolish.

But it's just holding all those things at once, isn't it? But, like you said, it's always theatrical for you. My very final question is, what one piece of advice would you give to young theatre makers who want to make immersive theatre?

OL: Why? Not just why do you want to do it? But why do you want to make it immersive? You know, it's like what you just said, why this form? And what do you want your audiences' experience to be? And are you sure that's an experience they're going to want?

JS: Yeah, we always think about the audience. Why is the most important, as Ollie said. Definitely. Two or three years ago, there were loads of immersive shows popped up, and a lot of them were great, but there's some of them, you were looking and going, guys, why?

OL: Why would we want to go to that world? I would prefer to have the distance that a stage gives me because I don't want to be in that world, you know. It's so simple, and it's the same piece of advice I give them for a piece of stage theatre. It's the same piece I'd give them for, you know, anything. What is the story? And what is the best way to tell it?

JS: Always think about your audience. Think about, I said before, giving them a role and a reason, for being there, an objective. What is their role in this world? And a reason for being there.

OL: Yeah, because if you're making a piece of immersive theatre, then your audience is part of it, so you've got to treat them as such.

Notes

1 The Latitude Festival is an annual music festival hosted in Henham Park, near Southwold, Suffolk, England. First held in July 2006 and every year since, apart from 2020, when it was cancelled due to the Covid-19 pandemic.
2 The Edinburgh Festival Fringe is the world's largest arts festival, which was established in 1947 and is hosted across Edinburgh every August.
3 Edward Sharpe and the Magnetic Zeros is an American folk-rock band formed in Los Angeles, California, in 2007. The group is led by singer Alex Ebert.
4 *Alice's Adventures Underground (2015, 2017 & 2022)*.
5 The Vaults is London's home for immersive theatre and alternative arts, situated in the tunnel system underneath Waterloo. It was established in 2014.
6 https://video.eko.com/v/zr7a3A?autoplay=true

FIGURE 3 *Image features Christopher styles and Zoe Flint performing in* For King & Country *at the COLAB Factory on 9 December 2017. Photographed by Owen Kingston.*

CHAPTER 2

Playable worlds with Owen Kingston from Parabolic Theatre

Speaker key:
JB: Joanna Bucknall
OK: Owen Kingston

[This conversation was recorded over Zoom on 6 August 2021.]

JB: Parabolic was forged out of a confluence of aspects, so I wanted to just dig into those a little. I know that you've been hugely influenced by the work of Punchdrunk and specifically *The Drowned Man: A Hollywood Fable* (2015). Could you talk about the ways in which that's consolidated your desire to shift from working in more traditional theatre to making immersive work, all those years ago?

OK: I decided I wanted to be a director when I was very young, when I was sixteen. It's been a lifelong obsession for me. The thing that drew me into wanting to work in theatre, was Brecht originally – political theatre. And it was really about wanting theatre to be a more viscerally engaging experience than it commonly is. It's the boxing match analogy (Brecht 1964: 233–46), wanting the audience to be that invested in something. When you look at Brecht and you see his ideas taken up by Boal but developed in a different context; seeing audiences actually get involved in playmaking through the forum theatre process, I'd always found that very exciting. That's always been kind of lurking in the back of my head – some of these European practitioners who play around with the use of space and the actor–audience relationship. When I was at university, I remember reading about Grotowski creating integrated performance spaces, where the audience were integrated into the set and therefore in some way part of the world of the show – but Grotowski probably wouldn't have used a phrase like 'the world of the show' – that sort of thing stayed with me. At university I directed a production of *Romeo and Juliet*, with some people who have also gone on to work in immersive theatre. A guy called Lee Ravitz who's acted on a lot of immersive shows, Sam Booth who's done a lot of stuff with Punchdrunk. We made a version of *Romeo and Juliet* that blurred the lines between the audience and the actor space. It didn't directly involve the audience, but there were beginnings of that there. So, I've always been interested in that.

Seeing a Punchdrunk show for the first time via Sam just blew the doors off my mind in terms of what was possible. I came to Punchdrunk quite late with *The Drowned Man: A Hollywood Fable* (2015) – I'd always been too busy to catch their shows before that, and I must admit I'd been sceptical. I'd never really wrapped my head around how you could scale the idea of the audience being intimately involved. Seeing hundreds of people moving around a vast space yet having intimate moments everywhere was hugely inspiring. To see that the audience had the agency to go wherever they liked, there were no boundaries, the boundaries were so far away from conventional theatre boundaries. For me, I think was kind of a light bulb moment of, 'Oh, okay, this stuff can really work'. What really lit my fire was the one-on-one experience that you get within Punchdrunk shows. It was Sam who introduced me to that side of it as well. I'd let him know I was going to be in a particular show, he said, 'Come down to the basement at the start of the first loop and find me. Get in as early as you can' – so, I did that. When he spotted me, he did his entire loop with me, all of his interactions. I was so grateful for that because that more than anything else, he just lit a fire under me for the possibilities of interactivity. He gave me my first one-to-one – for those that know, the oranges one-to-one. That is still probably the single most intense theatrical experience of my life, probably made more intense by the fact that I knew the guy doing it. I remember the moment he said, 'Do you trust me?' And I was like, 'I have known you for a long time, I definitely don't trust you.' *(Laughs)* But I said yes because I wanted to know what would happen next *(Laughs)*.

In terms of the start of Parabolic, it was those ingredients, those final ingredients going into a mix that had been brewing for twenty years; suddenly, the potion was ready.

Then it was a question of trying it out practically because I had a theatre space I could play in, there were friendly actors around and people who I knew would be interested in this. I got somebody to come and see *The Drowned Man* with me. So, it was like, 'I want to make something that works a bit like this. I want to play with these ideas.' And so, we were able to then start experimenting, really.

JB: And that was very much within the cultural backdrop of Croydon, wasn't it, in the Croydonites Festival?[1]

OK: Yeah. A lot of stuff happened in Croydon roughly ten years ago. A big milestone was the riots. We'd already lost the Warehouse Theatre[2] in Croydon by that point, that had gone in the aftermath of the 2008 financial crash. Croydon Council were absolutely desperate to renovate Fairfield Halls,[3] God only knows why, because it's a terrible idea. I've been saying it's a terrible idea for ten years. And now, it's completely failed as a project.

But in the aftermath of that and the riots, I was introduced to a visionary guy Saif Bonar, who founded Matthews Yard Café.[4] He wanted to make a performance space in the back of the café using some of their spare space. Somebody put him in touch with me through mutual friends knowing that I'd been involved with the Warehouse and so, he asked, 'Do you want to help build a theatre space?' So, I did. We installed all the tech for him, created a performance space. I managed that for a couple of years; having that as a 'petri dish' for our own projects was great. I put on a few different experimental projects there, playing around with immersive theatre concepts and ideas. There were a couple of early versions of Parabolic shows that we did using that space. But also, with the support of the Croydonites Festival, which was another grass-roots thing. One good thing that Croydon

Council did was they employed someone (Paula Murray) to enliven Croydon's artistic offering. That really helped us in the early days, and it enabled us to use Croydon Town Hall as a performance space, particularly the underground tunnels, which is where we did our first show as Parabolic, as part of the Croydonites Festival. That all came along at the same time. The space to play, create and experiment. Space to work in, in the first instance, and then a bit of funding to enable that to happen.

JB: Do you think because it's the low-risk environment initially, that you were working within, that gave you a bit more freedom to be riskier, to play and to trial things?

OK: Yes. Yeah, it did. Absolutely. That stuff's invaluable. And alongside that, what was really important was seeing stuff. After seeing *The Drowned Man: A Hollywood Fable* (2013), I wanted to see anything and everything that called itself immersive, that used that word because I was so excited, I just wanted more of it.

I started looking for other things. And the *Punchdrunk Lovers Facebook Group* became my 'go-to' place to find out about other things going on. I realized there was this rich world of this kind of performance that had been going on for ages, but that I just didn't have a connection with because I didn't know how to find out about it.

JB: You have to be in the know, don't you? It's one of those/

OK: /You do, yeah/

JB: /I've been thinking about this quite a lot recently, the role between secrecy and mystery.

JB: You have to have the same kind of mindset and productivity as an audience member to find the work as you have to have when you're in the work.

OK: Felix Barrett, particularly, was very prescriptive of about how he thought audiences ought to encounter it. He was really against people putting material online. He wanted it to just be a complete mystery and he wanted every audience ideally to have that same experience.

But as an audience member, I was like, 'Fuck that. I want to encounter it on my terms.' My terms were, 'I want a map of the space', you know. I spent that entire first show just exploring the space. I missed most of the/

JB: Yeah, I know. I'm/the same.

OK: Because the way my brain is wired, I need to know where everything is. And I can't really relax until I've sorted that out in my head.

JB: But also, there's a few little things like when I went to *Masque of the Red Death* (2007) I did spend a good forty minutes trying to find the loos.

OK: Ah! *(Laughs)* that's it.

JB: And I know that sounds really bad, but just kind of like/I really need the loo!

OK: /Where they are. Things like that are sort of like red flags that crop up in your mind and as an audience member they are really important. Because if you don't deal with them, they're going to stay there and they're going to distract you from anything else that's going on.

I guess the other thing I learnt through seeing immersive shows was how inspired and how obsessed audiences can become with work that they feel that they're a part of. You realize if you can capture the hearts of some of these people, they will champion your work, and that will help you grow.

I was like, 'We're going to go to these people and see if we can capture their hearts by offering them something that they're going to love'. It was all based on that, my experience as an audience member. That's what we set out to do with those early shows.

JB: I just wanted to circle back and pick up one of the things that you mentioned earlier, which is this idea of politics. Your work on the surface doesn't present explicitly as political, but I know that politics drive how and why and who you make your work for.

OK: I think to address that issue of it not looking like what it seems on the surface; I had an epiphany moment, I don't know how many years ago, where I came to the realization that I was not content with making work that merely causes people to think, I had to make people *feel*.

And that was the most important part of it for me. I just realized that was what 'juiced me up' about making theatre, was the emotional response.

A lot of political theatre does run the risk of becoming very dry. If you look at Boal, Boal does successfully engage feeling, but I think it's baby steps in terms of forum theatre (Boal 1985).

Forum theatre, you know, it jumps across that line of 'let's get the audience to do something' but doesn't really go very far with it.

Theatre practitioners are obsessed with risk when it comes to involving audiences, the minute you invite the audience to contribute in any way, everything becomes about mitigating that risk. It's only by embracing that risk you move forward. If you want to make a show about current events, you need to find some kind of mask, some kind of/

JB: /vessel?

OK: I think going out to theatre should be enjoyable. We shouldn't just be beaten over the head with a moral stick every time we step inside a performance space.

JB: When shows are hard to experience, that's a problem. There are very few people like me that will be drawn to that. I'll go to that, because I'm an academic, I like difficult and challenging things. But the reality is, it's part of my job, I wouldn't take my friends to it.

It's not okay to just make it hard, uncomfortable and awful, which I think some of the historical acts from the '70s, like *the Living Theatre*.[5] Some of the things they did to audiences, and audience did to them are horrifying! That used to have a really problematic attachment to audience participation/

OK: /And that baggage has been carried over into/

JB: /Immersive.

OK: Yeah, absolutely.

JB: Some people are like, 'Oh, I can't come with you. I can't imagine anything worse being made to do something.'

OK: I live in a very working-class area – I live on a council estate. My immediate next-door neighbour is a lovely guy. He would never go to the theatre unless it was a pantomime because that's just not what he does. He just doesn't feel like that's his place. But he watches loads of films, and I thought, with Brexit going on and people talking about Churchill all the time, and Britain having this sort of historically revisionist view of the war, maybe we can send some new people into a theatre with a wartime-themed show. You see, my wife is Dutch, and her family's experience of the war is completely different to mine, in the same way that the continental experience of the war was completely different to the British experience of the war. Britain was never invaded, but every other country in Europe at some point was invaded by one side or the other or maybe even both. So, continental Europe has this shared experience of living under occupation, and my wife's family, well most of them were killed in the Holocaust. They're a Jewish family. So, her inherited experience of the war is a horrible, depressing, frightening thing. Whereas my inherited experience of the war, because my dad lived through it, my mum was born in the last couple of years of it, is triumph. And that's how the war is universally presented in this country – a British triumph – so there is a mismatch with everybody else in Europe. I think that is one of the things that underpins this British exceptionalism that has driven Brexit, this idea that we're better than the Europeans somehow, because we didn't get invaded.

So, I thought, 'what if you could create an experience for British people of being under occupation? Of invasion and disaster – of the war not being this triumphant victorious thing, but a narrative of needing our European allies and neighbours and being in the same boat as them? How would my next-door neighbour engage with this?' So, we created *For King & Country* (2018), which is all about Britain being invaded by the Nazis. This for me encapsulates where theatre sits within the political sphere, where it has always historically sat, as a means of helping people engage with societal issues. But whether or not you can actually ever meaningfully change people's minds, I'm really not sure.

We've seen this with *Crisis? What Crisis?* (2021). We had the political editor of the *Daily Telegraph* come, gave us a glowing review, but said in his review that the Conservative Party should send as many people as possible to our show because it would teach them why a Labour government is never going to work. Completely the opposite intent that we had in making the show!

JB: But just offering sometimes a chance to live through or be in a different role or position has potential/

OK: /That's what I think the magic of immersive theatre is. I think the thing that immersive theatre does better than anything else is in enabling people to empathize.

JB: Yes.

OK: It encourages empathy in a way that conventional theatre maybe does do, but not to the same extent. Because it's one thing to watch a story play out in front of you, but it's a completely different thing to actually be put in that situation for yourself, and as yourself be asked to make decisions. There's a whole new level of empathy that comes to that. I think forum theatre touches on it – that's part of the magic of forum theatre, is you bring somebody into the situation, and you say, 'How would you change this for the better?', and particularly magical if you allow the person to play the role, but I think within the work that we're making, that is the experience for every member of the audience from the word go.

We don't actually assign a character to somebody in the way that you might in LARPing,[6] but we give people a real reason to be present in the world of the show, a real function within it, but to do that as themselves just in a different situation. I think that's where the magic happens.

OK: You see it in *For King & Country* (2018), with the parliamentary debates. That is a realization of Brecht's aim to make theatre like a boxing match, because it gets real spicy, you know?

You say to one group of people, 'You are the Conservative Party. You need to argue the position of your party.' And you say to the other group, 'You're the Labour Party. You need to argue the opposite position', and they are able to do that at arm's length – playing the role of party member, but then, you allow them to vote according to their own conscience. What that does is, it allows you in arguing with other audience members that shield of, 'I'm just playing the game', so you can go at it with gusto.

JB: So, we talked a lot about kind of the ethics and the drive of kind of why you make, let us talk about kind of the 'nitty-gritty' nuts and bolts, could talk a little bit about the way that you've developed sort of mechanics for marshalling that and for kind of keeping it driving through?

OK: It is genuinely a lot of freedom. The first show we did that really embraced that was *For King & Country* (2018). I remember that feeling at the first night of that show. I've never felt so scared I don't think. *(Laughs)* We were about to give our audiences an unprecedented level of control over our show, and until we had tested that properly we wouldn't know if it would work or fall apart completely.

I've played a lot of D&D, [Dungeons & Dragons], and I grew up playing role-playing games. So, that's partly where that came, that idea of pivoting a story to the direction players want to take it.

JB: D&D and RPG [role-play games] are the same, aren't they? They have really tight mechanics. They unfold within a very specific kind of set of rules and tasks that have to happen.

OK: They do. But the golden rule with those games is always to make sure that everybody is engaged and having fun. That is not always best served by pulling people in the direction you want them to go in; those games are most enjoyable when everyone inputs. That was part of the foundation of it. And I think the other part of the foundation of it was a desire to ensure that people really felt like it was real.

I played *Revolution*, which was one of Joe Ball's shows – *Exit Productions*, earlier that same year. I really enjoyed it. The mechanics for it were great as you would expect from Joe. He's got a brilliant mechanical mind. It was very, very tightly constructed. *Revolution* (2017), essentially, it's set in the future in a post-apocalyptic world. And there are three factions vying for control of London. They have this lovely little Euro game-style hex map of London with all the different boroughs. And the idea was, you have to try and take over as much of London as possible. There were all kinds of tasks that you would do to further that aim. If you completed the tasks, it essentially meant more points. The mechanics were all on display – you could see how it all worked.

But there were things that you did that felt very theatrical, like you had to argue your point about particular things, you had to negotiate agreements and deals with other people. You had to design the flag of your faction and present it and explain what it all meant. It involved the audience in a lot of fun ways. But, you know, this all took place in the COLAB basement. There was no set really barring some tables and chairs; it was just the basement. You knew you were playing a game, you know?

I was like, 'Well, what if you took that, but you really went to town on the design element. What if you really made people feel like they were there?' It raises the stakes, and it buys deeper investment. And what if it wasn't a competitive thing? What if you're all on the same side? In coming up with *For King & Country* (2018), *Revolution* was in the back of my mind, but what we were trying to do was make it feel as real as we possibly could on the budget that we had/

JB: /You embed, you manage to hide the mechanics, the nuts and bolts and the gameplay in some respects. And you do that very well. How do you do that? How do you/

OK: /It frustrates gamers sometimes. We have people who love MEGAgames[7] come to our shows; they want to see more of the mechanics because that's how their brains are wired. And we're like, 'Well, if we do that, it doesn't feel as real.' Part of the reason we put so much effort into the characters and generating character content is we want the world to feel as alive and convincing as possible.

So, that is one step for burying the mechanics, making the world really interesting, making set design as good as you can get it, then bringing to life the characters. They start as a function within the room – they start as an archetype. With *For King and County*, when I was coming up with the show plan for that, we had a list of archetypes – for example the RAF officer, and then a couple of lines about him being a bit of an arrogant twat basically.

The army officer who was shell-shocked, quite timid. The WAAF, the Women's Auxiliary Air Force, officer who was quite stridently feminist. There was a little character hook, and then the function within the room. And then we rely on the actors to turn that into a living, breathing person.

I remember seeing Squadron Leader Muir, which is the RAF officer, come to life for the first time when Eddie who played that role was in rehearsal and said, 'I'm just going to try something.' We were 'hot seating' as a way of trying to get these characters' voices and personalities to come to life, and suddenly, Squadron Leader Muir was sat in front of us. He named him Muir after a mate of his who was a bit like that. *(Laughs)*

I remember seeing that character come to life for the first time being like, 'Yes, that's the one.' Since then, we've done a lot of work on trying to break down how performers interact with audience members and trying to categorize types of interaction. And we've got so far with it, there's a lot of work to be done on it still.

We came up with four broad categorizations, which we equate to playing card suits as a means to remember them. So, you have seduction, the characters that are seductive in some way or another. Not necessarily sexually but sometimes.

You just want to be close to them because they're charismatic. Then you have characters that are very authoritative, powerful and directional – that just dominate you. And they are the two more extroverted types – the red suits. That's the hearts and the diamonds for us.

Then you have the characters that are quiet and don't necessarily say much, but somehow capture your attention because you're just fascinated by what they're going to do next. They intrigue you, and you're just curious about them. You want to follow them around; you want to know what they're doing. And finally, you get the characters that just make you want their approval. They're not necessarily attractive characters. They're not necessarily nice people. But somehow, they just make you want them to pick you and give you their approval.

Muir is one of those characters. He's horrible to everybody. But he'll pick a few audience members each show – 'You're the ones I like'; 'You're the special people'.

He builds a little circle around him, and by the third act, they'll just do anything he asks. *(Laughs)*

That's our first line of defence against the mechanics – is to make the world as interesting as possible to make the characters as interesting as possible.

JB: That's why it's theatre and not just a game. And that's why it's theatre and like it's not LARPing. That's why it's theatre and it's not RPG.

OK: Yes. And that's why the performance spaces are a character as well to some extent. The bunker in *For King & Country* (2018) is a living breathing character.

If you come and see the second part of the show, set in 1944, when you return to the bunker after four years you realize that the entire set is essentially the same, except it has been redressed with Nazi paraphernalia. We specifically designed it so that you couldn't look in any direction without seeing a Swastika. It feels like squatters have moved into your home while you've been on holiday – that feeling of violation/

JB: /Invasion.

OK: Yeah, that character and story stuff needs to be front and centre.

In *For King & Country* (2018), burying the game mechanics was critically important because the core game that everything else must support is that you are an MP in 1940, and you are trying to save the country from being invaded by Nazis. So, everything must build towards and support that core game.

If you've got stuff that undermines it, then the whole house of cards collapses. So, the second layer of defence against mechanics is how the actors facilitate the gameplay. We avoid any language that sounds gamified.

There are no points to be spent, there's no tokens to be moved, you know? We'd always talk about it as real people and real lives.

When they're looking at the most game-driven bit of it, which is the map, if they ask, 'How many squares can that unit move?' The answer will always be to point out how far that is in miles.

Because, yes, it is squares on a map because the map is full of squares, but you're moving from, you know, Surrey to Croydon. That's going to take/

JB: /Time/

OK: /thirty miles. Obviously, we do compressed time within the show.

There are things we do to try and obfuscate that as well. So at least it still has an illusion of reality. The big 'no-no' with the cast is, you don't let an audience member give an order, and then immediately feed back to them that it's been completed. Something else has to happen in between. It may still get completed in a completely unrealistic timescale, but we try our very best to give the illusion that time has passed in between.

There are no clocks in the room for that show. It is much easier to get lost in time that way; you're always distracted with something else then come back to feel like time has passed.

That's a huge part of hiding the mechanics really, misdirection. And always talking about things in terms of the 'real world', not in terms of the mechanics of the show.

JB: The audience are so central to your work. How do you ask that? How do you run something, trial something, rehearse something when the biggest character isn't there?

OK: You can't, is the honest truth! The closest we can get without any audience present is what we would call a 'dry run', where we go through the motions of doing a show, but there are no audience. 'Dry runs' always end up with the wildest things happening in them because we just get carried away and lost in our own world of fun.

We put *For King & Country* (2018) together in a week. The first version of the show had one week of rehearsal. That's all we could afford. Once we'd got the characters and we'd run through the mechanics of the show a few times, the very first run through of *For King & Country* (2018) was with the father of one of our performers (Zoe Flint, Artistic Associate). He'd come down to London to visit her for a couple of days, and we got him into rehearsal. We had a bowler hat, we stuck it on his head and he was the prime minister. *(Laughs)* We got him to essentially make all the decisions for an entire audience just to see how it would work. We got some really interesting feedback from him about things that didn't work, which set us back a day or so because we weren't expecting that. We had to make a few bold decisions of, 'Well, that didn't work for him, but that doesn't mean it isn't going to work for a real full live audience'.

We tested that show on just two or three people before it went live for the first time/

JB: /Which is terrifying/

OK: /Absolutely terrifying. The actors were terrified as well. I've lost the list of people who were in that version. I'd love to talk to them again now because it worked, but it wasn't as good as the show then later went on to become. But I think it taught us what we needed to add to it.

That first run was immediately prior to Christmas. It was two weeks before Christmas. It didn't sell out; it barely half sold; it barely made its money back. We then added a third week after Christmas that we were going to do after we'd made some improvements because we really believed in it.

I was just going to abandon the concept after that, but Eddie who played Muir came back and said, 'You cannot do that. There is some genius lying in the heart of this. We have to make the show on a bigger scale because it'll find an audience.' He runs his own conventional theatre company, *Bedouin Shakespeare Company*. He put 10 grand into it. He was like, 'I'm going to pay to get this thing up properly.' From that, we had a run that extended, and extended again. And we ended up running for like three, four months/

JB: /Could have gone longer/

OK: /It definitely could have gone longer. And that's when it completely took off. So, if it hadn't been for him, it might have just died in a ditch, because I've always been very down on my own work. I will see the flaws and won't see the good stuff. We barely survived it financially. But you can't rehearse it.

    I think if I invited most people to come and see those first runs, they would think Parabolic had lost the plot! They're going to make a stinker of a show, it's awful. And then they'll go and tell people it's awful. And then they'll be . . . and then they won't come back because they're like, 'Well, I had a horrible time. I'm not coming back to that.' You know? So, those first couple of times, we're only going to get people in who know that process, have been through that process, who trust us enough to be like, 'No, you'll be fine, guys, but this was pretty bad because of x, y and z.'

    What that taught me was if you're going to make something that's interactive and invite the audience to play with you and invite them to do unexpected things, where an unexpected thing happens, it is not a problem to be solved, it's an opportunity for you to do something cool.

    To embrace it, to bring it in, to make it part of what's going on, and then to create something out of it/

JB: /The mechanics, they're not rigid; they're an elastic band/

OK: /Flexible/

JB: /Something pushes against it, it should be able to absorb it/

OK: /This is one of my problems when I hear people talking about writing immersive theatre. What is writing immersive theatre? You've got a script? What is your script? How can you script an audience's response? You can't. You don't know what they're going to say.

JB: No.

OK: You can script what the actors say. Fine. But there are a lot of problems with that. I've routinely seen immersive shows where the actors are very clearly delivering a very eloquent script, their level of verbal dexterity is up 'here' somewhere. As an audience member who's new to this world, who's just come to see the show, no prep, no nothing, my confidence to interact with somebody whose verbal dexterity is up 'here' is right down 'here'/

JB: /It's intimidating.

OK: Yeah, it is. It's very intimidating.

The only people with the confidence to try and match the verbal dexterity of the actor's written lines are drunks and assholes. As an ordinary audience member therefore, I think that in order to play in this show I have to behave like an asshole because I'm watching assholes interacting and that's being met positively, therefore, I'm being trained that, in order to interact, I've got to lose my inhibitions and become a complete wanker for the next couple of hours. And either I will do that, or I will just ball up into myself and not interact but just watch. Then if I'm the producer of that show, I'm left wondering, why does everybody behave so outrageously in my show? Well, that's why.

Because you've trained them to. For me, one of the big things that helps to mitigate against that, is not scripting what the actors say, not giving them hugely beautiful verbally dextrous lines because if they are essentially improvising on the fly, they may say things in a similar way, most times, but the dexterity of their speech is lowered more into the range where I will comfortably just have a conversation, as opposed to feeling like I've got to somehow perform alongside them in order to meet them where they are. I have to fight for this every day, as actors want lines to learn!

JB: Of course, emotions, objectives.

OK: And writers, want to write lines.

Yeah. So, one of the battles I have within the company is, 'No, don't write down what you're going to say. Make it up on the spot.'

For King & Country (2018), for example, we had a period of couple of weeks where Eddie couldn't play Muir. He said, 'I know somebody who would do it fine.' We got this guy in, with all the same stuff I'd given to Eddie, but he came up with an approach to the character that was very different, but it still worked, and it worked just as well because it was authentic. It had come out of him.

JB: Isn't it as well to do with the function because that character also had that function?

OK: As long as you fulfil that function, the character detail layered on top of that can be entirely their own.

JB: Would you say that function replaces that very cliched actors' question, what's my motivation?

OK: For me, that's a real battle in immersive theatre generally, how we define roles and what the roles do. We put a lot of effort into that; we're still learning it. Particularly in terms of how a show is created, you can break it down into several different roles and those are very distinct from staff that you see in the conventional theatre world. I completely stopped talking about a writer now. I don't think we'll ever talk about someone having written a Parabolic show ever again. It's just really unhelpful.

We've replaced the term writer with two terms broadly, 'architect' and 'world builder'. The 'architect' is the person who essentially designs the structure of the show, the mechanics and how it's going to work practically. The 'world builder' is the person who fills in all of the details of the world of the show to make it feel like a living storytelling space.

JB: It puts flesh onto the bones.

OK: They are distinct roles, but they can be done by the same person, or different people can do different bits of the same role. In Parabolic we have a great core team of creatives. Nowadays, myself, Tom Black, Zoe Flint and Chris Styles divide most of the creative stuff between us, but we also work with others alongside – but at the start it was just me doing pretty much everything. I was the architect, world builder, director, producer, the whole lot – but collaborating with others, dividing those roles up between different people, definitely helps keep you sane!

JB: *(Laughs)* One of the other things, well, two of the other things actually that you use as a mechanic is adaptive narrative and structuring.

OK: In the years before starting Parabolic, I did a lot of filmmaking, mostly short films. I've learned a lot about narrative structure from the film world. It's horrifying really how little attention is paid to it in the theatre.

I would subscribe to the idea that structure is writing; the exact words you put on the page are largely inconsequential because if it's well structured, it's going to work. We applied that to our shows right from the beginning but when we really stepped into letting the audience drive the show, the thing for me that was really important was to make sure that it didn't just descend into complete chaos. For me, it was all about marrying together that really high level of audience agency with something that nevertheless felt like a story that had been well told. To get to that, we needed to adhere to a structure that people would recognize instinctively.

If we're going to have let them have this much control over the course of the show, they need to nevertheless, leave feeling emotionally satisfied by it. They need to feel like it was, that it wasn't just anarchy.

JB: So, you wanted to hang on to that theatrical thing actually which is at the heart of a lot of good drama, Catharsis, isn't it? The achievement and the fulfilment of that narrative and having been through it?

OK: Absolutely. And for me, wanting to primarily cause people to feel rather than think, but if they think as well then that's great. That's a huge part of it.

There is really strong narrative structure in all our shows for that reason. In *For King & Country* (2018), we essentially broke it down into a five-act structure which I modelled quite closely on things like the classic film three-act structure. Those structures are designed for films, so you've got to adapt it a bit. You've got to make it make sense for the theatrical context and for an interactive theatrical context. *For King & Country* (2018) has a series of story beats that play out across five acts. Each of those five acts corresponds to a turn in the game mechanics. We talk about 'turns' and 'acts' interchangeably because really, it's the same thing.

Those beats always need to fall in a certain place. With *For King and Country* (2018), we kept it more on rails than I would perhaps ideally like by making sure that the show always ended in the same manner. It's a little bit of a cheat, but it meant that those narrative beats were really strong and contributed to the advancement of the story. No matter what the audience did, at a certain point they were going to discover there were spies in the room, and in the end the bunker was always going to get to the point of being overrun. The war game was unwinnable. The choices they made were meaningful because they had a moral impact – save these people or those people, sacrifice this unit or that one. By playing well they could hold things off longer, but it was always going to end tragically.

As a narrative structure, it meant that the audience definitely had the feeling of agency and the stuff they did in the room did really matter and did have a tangible effect, but it always led to that carefully structured ending which felt really satisfying.

The challenge after we made the original *For King and Country* was to try and deliver a sequel that had that same dramatically satisfying experience but with more variation – particularly to the ending. So, when you arrive at those narrative beats, you know that a certain type of thing has got to happen at that point in the show, but precisely what it is could be different depending on the decisions the audience have made up to that point. We could have a few pre-planned options that it could be and then we slot the right one in at the right moment, and if the audience have come up with something themselves that could fit, then we slot that in instead and potentially make something really cool. But we've also got fallback options in case that doesn't emerge.

JB: It's that function again, isn't it? Everyone can play within that structure because the things you do on a minute-by-minute basis do have obvious knock-on effects especially in *For King & Country* (2018).

OK: A huge part of that is having the show live-directed. The actors are great, and they can coordinate, and they can do loads of things within the room, but having a brain outside of the room that can make responsive decisions holistically with all the information in front of them is truly magic. Each individual actor has their area in front of them; they have to concentrate on that. Having somebody who has got an overview of what has happened, who can pull all of that information together and then can make an intelligent decision about what happens next. You can't automate that. You need a person. We did tests to see if we could automate it. Tom built an incredible spreadsheet to manage *Crisis? What Crisis?* (2021), and it's a fantastic tool; it collates all the variables built into the show and has flexibility to track new variables created on the fly as well, then spits out possible scenarios that make sense of the collated data, but it can't make decisions for you. You still need a person who can read the room and make the call as to what is going to tell the best version of the story that makes most sense to the audience in front of you.

For example, sometimes *Crisis? What Crisis?* (2021) will end in a military coup. That's one of the endings we've pre-planned – the army rise up and decide that government's gone completely off the rails and essentially trying to bring a Communist state.

They will push back; the vote of no confidence is abandoned. We get a completely different very serious ending.

There are conditions that we look for to make a coup possible. There are mechanical conditions that exist in the room that without them being fulfilled, it wouldn't happen, and the spreadsheet tracks those just fine, but we still make a human decision as to whether we do it or not. Just last night, for example, we had an audience in, who had pushed most of the buttons that normally would trigger a coup, but we thought with this audience, actually, a much more satisfying ending for them is if they manage to subvert that, then go on to actually have the vote and maybe narrowly lose it. So, we're reading the room at that point and figuring out what is the story that is going to feel most satisfying for them, which is something you cannot determine on pure mechanics alone.

JB: But interestingly, I have a theatre background but also live art experience and live art training. And this is one of the things that's actually particular to live performance art is the *act* of things that happened in the room; that's where live art and performance art claim its integrity and what makes it distinct from theatre. In immersive, some of these things merge and then come through and like you said the film influences, the gaming influences, it's a very interdisciplinary approach.

OK: Many immersive shows are built on a very rigid decision tree. It's how you write a computer game, or choose your own adventure novel, but the reason those things, like *Bandersnatch* (Slade 2018), have to work like that is because they are all forms of recorded media. But in a live performance context, the ability to make decisions on the fly is the one thing that computer games and novels and TV shows don't have – the live actor responding to the participant in front of them is unique to live performance.

Through Parabolic we've really tried to inject that idea into the broader immersive conversation – to embrace the audience's potential in collaborating with the performer in the telling of a story. To place them right in the heart of it – they are the central characters. They're the protagonist. In order to give them that agency and in order to make it meaningful, you can't just tell them that they're the hero; you have to actually make them the hero. Their decisions must be meaningful, because a hero is only a hero if they could potentially fail.

JB: Let's talk about money. It's just one of the shrouded areas; I don't know whether it's a very British thing. It's very hush-hush; 'let's not talk about the money. It's vulgar.' Owen let's be vulgar! How have your shows been facilitated financially?

OK: Oh wow – that's such a big topic.

JB: And you can tell us as much as you're comfortable telling/

OK: I will tell you everything I can think of because I think it's important that this stuff gets aired actually. I see all the time among immersive theatre makers and conventional theatre makers how everyone wants to pay people properly and is very vocal about that. I never met anybody who doesn't want to pay people properly. Why wouldn't you? You'd have to be an asshole to not want to pay people properly. That's a no-brainer – we're all on the same page with it.

However, there are plenty of companies who are just starting out or maybe at early stages, who have decided they will only make work when they can pay everybody at full equity rates. What that means is they don't make very much work. *(Laughs)* That's what it means. That's the fallout from that. Now, I know plenty of actors – I love actors. I don't think you can be a director unless you love actors, and I'm constantly trying to fight for actors to get work. I think there are very few actors out there that would rather have no job than have a job that maybe doesn't pay equity minimum but still pays them something decent. Maybe there are some and that's their prerogative – I don't blame them at all because everyone wants to be paid the proper rate. But the reality is there is just not enough money in the theatre industry to go around. There just isn't. There is not enough subsidy, and that's been the case for a long time.

It's not going to get any better anytime soon. So, it's all very well sitting there and saying I'm not going to do a show until I can pay people properly but that just means you're going to waste years of your life not making any work. So, one of the things I decided really early on was that we were going to pay people as much as we *could*, but we were going to be financially responsible. We were going to up the rate as far as we could without essentially causing ourselves to get bankrupt. That we would always prioritize paying people for stuff but that ultimately, if it meant that we couldn't pay £500 a week, then we'd offer £400 a week or £350 a week. And if people were able to work for that, then fine and we would make it really clear why we were doing that and be really transparent about it. That's what we've done. We haven't always been able to pay equity minimum for the work because, of course, we haven't got a magic money tree. *(Laughs)*

JB: I've spoken to a lot of people over the last five or six years who feel really strongly, You shouldn't do it if it's not going to pay but I'm a hungry little goldfish with my work. When someone says can you make the show, a little one-on-one for 60 quid in the next two days, I'm like, 'Yes!' I take the money but I'm just responsible for me because I make one -on -one. It's usually just me and some help from my partner. But I don't feel ashamed about that because it's either that or I don't make any work.

OK: You look at one of the largest immersive theatre companies. They make one big show every, what, five years? *(Laughs)* We've done two to three shows a year, every year for the last five years. We've made a lot of work; we shock most people in terms of the amount of shows we made. We've made more shows than some companies who have been operating for far longer.

JB: There is a bit of a fine line, because I have a lot of issues with some companies. I won't mention by name, who take huge Arts Council grants. But everyone involved is doing it entirely voluntary, but the company make millions of pounds! That never seems to either make its way back into paying people properly.

OK: That's the other end of the spectrum but yeah, I know, yeah.

JB: When you build a monolithic reputation on the back of/

OK: /Yeah, it's outrageous. And I would agree 100 per cent with that. The philosophy we've gone for is we'll pay absolutely as much as we can afford to pay and that's what we've done. And the first show we did, I ended up paying for a lot of that out of my own pocket.

JB: I was going to say you have literally staked the work from a personal perspective to get things off the ground.

OK: Yes. So, the only reason we could start Parabolic was because my mum died in 2016 and my dad had died back in 2002, so both my parents are gone now. I'm an only child, so when my mum died, she left me everything that she had, which included a house and quite a bit of money. So, for the first time in my adult life, I was financially secure. I could take the risk of ditching all of the side jobs and side hustles, put everything, all of my energy and enthusiasm and anything I had, into making a new company work.

I was still doing some filmmaking stuff when we first started Parabolic. That had been one of the side hustles – I made a kickstarter video for a friend who was making a board game. He paid us for that, and that money went into the Parabolic bank account. That's the first thing that we paid into the Parabolic bank account so a couple of grand to start, seed money essentially. I have a couple of company directors who are old friends who are, both of them quite a bit older than me, who are good businessmen, and they essentially helped me learn how to run a business.

So, that was the seed money that got us through our first show. And we got a little bit of money from the Croydonites Festival to do that first show as well. Not enough to cover the cost of it but just to sort of help. I've always been grateful to Anna [Arthur], who runs that for giving us that first gig and enabling us to get such cool space to do it in.

We sold a lot of tickets, and that was the start of it. From that point on, every show that we did essentially was made with the profits of the previous show. So, anything that was profit went back into the company and so it went on. I didn't pay myself from Parabolic for two and a bit years at all – not a penny. For me, Parabolic was never about getting wealthy; it was about making theatre. *(Laughs)*

JB: I think if you want to make money there is much easier ways of making money than being in a theatre *(Laughs)*/

OK: /Oh yes, absolutely. But I mean this story does highlight how privilege is still kind of necessary to open the doors to making theatre. I wouldn't say I'm the most privileged person in the world but essentially; if my mum hadn't died, I wouldn't be doing this which is horrible when you think about it.

Yes, I could have taken that risk looking back in retrospect, but it wouldn't have been a responsible thing to do for my family. I've got two kids and a wife and to have taken that risk without the financial cushion if it all goes wrong . . . I've got to have something that will catch me.

JB: Inevitably, I want to talk about that term immersive. The word, the very word itself, how do you feel about it; do you think it's useful?

OK: I love it and I think it's fine. And it is less useful than maybe it could have been at one time because it's been abused.

I've never been more annoyed than when I saw the Bridge Theatre[8] advertise *Julius Caesar* (2018) as immersive. Because you've got a theatre that has got a director who is a former artistic director of the National Theatre, A-list celebrities in the show – they need to use that word less than anybody else. They shouldn't need to use it at all and yet, there they are.

There they are robbing us of the things that make us unique – that really made me angry. Because I'm sorry, sitting on a stage does not make something immersive. For me, to be immersive, the audience needs to be part of the world of the show/

JB: /Not part of the set/

OK: /Not part of the set.

Not in the same space as the actors. But part of the same world as the actors. I was sitting people on the stage at university for heaven's sake. It doesn't earn the right to use the word 'immersive'. If you've taken the audience, if you have immersed them in the world of the show to the extent where they are part of the world of the show for however long the show lasts, if the audience are vital to whether the show is able to function at all – then I would call that immersive. Anything less than that and it may as well be a themed bar.

I think that's my hallmark for it. I've had people come and try and define it for me. I remember having a chat with a lovely Italian fellow after a performance of *For King & Country* (2018); he tried to tell me it would be more immersive if there were things to smell and things to taste. And I was like, that's great mate. I'm glad that's how you're doing immersive theatre but it's not what this is. But it doesn't have to be because the audience is still an essential and vital part of the world of the show.

JB: There is a smell in the basement; it smells like war rooms. It smells like bunkers.

OK: It does, and that's great, but I think people get very hung up on very specific definitions of immersive theatre because they apply those definitions to their own work, hence the smell, taste and touch stuff. But that's the broad one for me – whether or not you're inhabiting the same world as the actors, you're part of the world of the show and you are fully immersed in that. That's immersive theatre for me.

When we first started making immersive theatre, there were so few structures to hold immersive work. The main thing that you saw all the time was what I would call the 'carousel' where you go from room to room through a series of scenes. And then another group of audience comes in behind you doing the scenes you've just done.

I just find it boring. I mean a show that works like that, it better be really, really good to keep my attention.

The more structures that we can invent to create that sense of being part of the world, that keeps for me, the interest and excitement of immersive theatre. I think one of Parabolic's big contributions is just to create new structures. It's absolutely lovely. I remember going to see *CROOKS 1926* (2019), and essentially, Bertie borrowed most of the structure of *For King & Country* (2018) to make that show. And I was like, 'Yes', seizing on these things and borrowing them, putting them alongside other things, because there's loads of stuff in that show that's come from Bertie's old work as well, he mashed it together and made something new. And that's what it should be about. We should be creating new structural vehicles to hold each new experience. Not just rehashing the same old thing all the time. We need to shake off the tyranny of throughput and give our audiences something unique every time.

JB: So, on that note, what advice would you give to people starting out who want to make this work?

OK: If you can do anything else, do that instead. *(Laughs)* Because you won't make much money and you'll have a lot of frustration. And it's really hard to do it well. And not everyone is up to that. And you see conventional theatre makers dipping a toe into immersive theatre, making a hash of it because they think they're smarter than they are, or they think that the work requires less thought than it does. It's really hard. Brace yourself. But if you can't imagine yourself doing anything else, run at it full force and don't stop for anyone. And don't let anyone tell you can't. And there'll be lots of people who want to give you advice, but nobody knows anything really. It's like the early days of Hollywood. Nobody really knows anything.

We're just scratching the surface of what you can do in a live space with interactivity and there's so much more to be discovered and learned. Immersive theatre has had its silent movie phase and now we're into the 'talkies'. I can't wait to see what comes next.

Notes

1 Croydonites is a festival of new theatre and performance for Croydon, London, that was established in November 2015.
2 The Warehouse Theatre was a professional producing Victorian theatre in the centre of Croydon, England. The theatre closed in 2012 following withdrawal of funding.
3 Opened in 1962, Fairfield Halls is a Modernist arts, entertainment and conference centre located in Croydon, London.
4 Established in 2011, Matthews Yard is a non-profit community and cultural venue next to West Croydon Station. It consists of Platform 2, a multi-function events space, a café with vegan kitchen and regularly rotating art exhibitions by local artists and a lounge with couches, board games, table tennis and an N64.
5 Founded in 1947 by actress Judith Malina and painter/poet Julian Beck, *The Living Theatre* is the oldest experimental theatre group in the United States.
6 LARP is a type of role-playing game in which participants physically act out scenarios, typically using costumes and props.
7 'A megagame is an interesting combination of different game elements encountered in other places. They involve role-playing, simulation, and social interactions. . . . A megagame is a large-scale game that contains different elements found in other games. Those elements include (but are not limited to) role-playing, simulations, social interaction, economics, and politics, which are combined into an overarching narrative. This combination takes place through other, smaller, interlocking games that occur concurrently within the megagame' (Eng 2020).
8 The Bridge was founded by Nicholas Hytner and Nick Starr in 2017.

FIGURE 4 *Image details a live public performance of* CROOKS 1926 *at the COLAB Tavern on 2 February 2020. Photographed by Matthew Kaltenborne.*

CHAPTER 3

Gamified experience with Bertie Watkins from COLAB Theatre

Speaker key:
JB: Joanna Bucknall
BW: Bertie Watkins

[This conversation was recorded over Zoom on 1 July 2021.]

JB: Could you speak about the way in which COLAB Theatre's approach is born out of the frustration with existing immersive forms?

BW: I realized now, it was the gamification of narrative that was frustrating me, and even though immersive theatre promised, back in those days, a lot of agency for audiences, consequence to actions, they didn't actually provide that. Which is what I found frustrating and now, however many years on, feels centuries later, immersive theatre is getting into quite an exciting field now where gamification and narrative are being married much better. There's a much better understanding of it: I think it used to be, Punchdrunk were the only – well, there were many other companies – but they seem to be the forefathers of it. To a lot of people, immersive theatre meant Punchdrunk, but it is nice now that people are understanding that it's not just Punchdrunk that do immersive, and that's quite good for us!

JB: I think you're right, there was an expectation, wasn't there? They became synonymous with the form. There was a lot of talk about agency and, of course, your feet have agency and you can move around the space. Reality is though, you're like a ghost it carries on whether you were there or not/

BW: /exactly, there's no consequences.

JB: No, no. You couldn't impact on the 'thing' itself.

BW: In a way, you could choose how you experienced it in/

JB: /The story would unfold in the ways it was designed to unfold. I didn't even realize there was a story. I thought it was just this incredible scenography. What drives you to make experiences, rather than theatre?

BW: It comes from, well I don't know if I should admit it, but it's kind of a childlike excitement that you get from wanting to be in the middle of things and wanting an hour of just feeling special and wanting an hour of being able to play. We're told to grow up the whole time, but immersive theatre for me is a couple of hours where you can sort of be a child again and have the feelings, the imagination of a child, and I think it mostly came from that. And that idea that for those two hours you can be more than just your cell phone and you can be doing these really fun experiences that you normally wouldn't be doing unless you find yourself in an apocalypse or something. What's nice about it is everyone wants to experience what it's like to be a cop and robber kind of thing, but you don't actually want to be a cop or a robber.

JB: I think you're right: play is something that is stripped out of adulthood in day-to-day life completely/

BW: /completely. It's really sad that we're told to not play, and the only time you can express a playful thing is when you're drunk or have some sort of inebriation that takes you out of what society is telling you. You're allowed to be a bit childish when you're drunk because you're drunk, and it gives you the approval to be silly.

JB: It is funny because we know that for children play is central to their development.

BW: Why can't we just play together? That's where I come in, because I find that a real desperate shame in society. It should be the thing in society that we should try and change. Going to the theatre, watching a film and watching a narrative is not so exposing as, you know, playing a board game with strangers, which is a bit stifled anyway, because we can't undo centuries of social influence. I think slowly people are going to want to do more interactive experiences, rather than just get smashed together.

JB: There's been a few art installations that have had adult-sized play equipment, at the TATE,[1] I can't remember exactly/

BW: /I met the artist that did that. They were in Zurich and we were talking. We're just told not to play ever and as soon as you give toys to adults and say, 'You're allowed to play', there's a lovely moment where they just sort of let go and you can see them crossing that threshold where they realize *what* they've been given and it's really lovely. Kind of why I do it is that moment where they go, 'Oh, I can play! And it's really fun!' It's usually because there's an actor in front of them, who is also an adult playing, they're going, 'Come on, come and play'. It just means that they get comfortable and then hopefully enjoy the whole experience because they've just been allowed to play essentially.

JB: When I went to Sweden for a conference a couple of years ago now, one of the things I found joyous were these swings, makeshift swings, in random places. It felt like a social activism statement, but they were all over the place; I was like, this is amazing! You can just take a minute, sit on it, then carry on your way/

BW: /that's really lovely.

JB: There's something about that, it's the invitation and the permission. To do it and the swings had signs or someone had scribbled on the wall next to them to invite you/

BW: /To just use it. The ironic thing is that a lot of people go, 'Oh it's not for me' and shy past it, when really you know they want to! So, it's breaking the eggshell of social inhibition. It takes that little bit of a push to get through but when you get through, it's lovely and it should be everywhere. We should always be playing.

JB: There always needs to be, because it's prohibited for adults to play within our culture, especially Western culture, a moment or an invitation, a way to pull someone in, to give them permission. There has to be something that makes them feel comfortable very swiftly. I know that you have always been fascinated with different narrative genres and that kind of pop culture references.

How have they influenced the development of your practice because in some ways they are something safe and familiar which gets people to cross into it to a place of play?

BW: We spend our lives being envious of actors on screen doing cool and exciting stuff, living an exciting life. And I think it breeds obsession with celebrity because we're wanting to do those things ourselves. What really helps immersive shows a lot is those sorts of tropes that people already know – it's already downloaded; you know what they are. If you put it in front of audiences, if you're a gangster you know what you do, if you're a policeman there's all these codes across the board that everyone already has in their back pocket they can get out because they've been watching it since they were a young person. They know exactly how to act, and that, on top of the narrative, allows them to be 'in world'. Existing within it is so much easier; it gives them that licence; it allows them to explore the world without having to expose themselves too much. They can be themselves within this sort of genre; it just gives them enough ammo to be able to experience the show.

JB: I think your work is very specifically theatre because of that relationship like you said to narrative tropes. Your work is very much about pulling audiences inside a story, situation or a series of acts, but inside the story, and I think that's something that keeps it theatrical.

BW: Story is the thing that can drive people. What's lovely about the stuff we do is that kind of middle ground, where you can gamify but also have quite a rich narrative within it, we call it the 'meal of theatre', which I think people do expect when they come and see theatre. I think you just emotionally invest more when it's a narrative you connect with more because you've got that downloaded tropism which fast tracks emotional connection. With narrative you sort of see the human side of characters more, rather than them just being there to guide you through an experience. You see them as another human being and seeing them go through some sort of challenge within the narrative makes you connect with them way more, which all in all makes the game better. Because then you care more and then have a better sort of cathartic experience from the whole thing. So that's why we try to balance the narrative versus the game.

JB: I was going to ask you about how gaming has impacted on the development of your work, and you have, of course, in the past used plays like *Romeo and Juliet*. Do you think that's to do with the playable nature of it or the story, or do you think it works on different levels? Do you feel the familiarity with those stories perhaps draws people in and the ability to be a part of that story?

BW: Being able to influence the narrative, that's what was really exciting about *Romeo & Juliet*. It's that choice as an artist, the whole way through, you have to go, 'Is it worth gamifying this or was it worth not gamifying that', if it is a game, not 'crowbaring' in the result. There is always a big balance, there is like a 'golden egg' somewhere within this middle ground that really can be found, and I think our practice now, very much tries to hit the middle ground. If we did do *Romeo and Juliet*, again, I think we would probably gamify it a bit more. Even though we gamified it quite heavily, I'd take a lot more script out because people know the love story, that's why I called it *Montagues and Capulets* (2017), because my fascination was the war between families, that big entrenched, tribalism kind of thing. The fight was really lovely; we started it with people bashing each other with pool noodles – 'You've got in your tribe, and then you met [the other tribe], and you did the first scene'. It was that kind of playing, it took a moment for people to sort of be like, 'Oh, we're actually involved'. It really worked that way of gamifying it because, again, people were more invested.

I think everything we do now is very gamified as much as we can in a way, but without taking away the narrative; it's more that the game feeds the narrative. Which works slightly better than a narrative well, obviously chicken and egg, but it starts with a narrative that you then gamify, if that makes sense? I think *Gatsby* (2019) was one of the only pieces of immersive theatre that I've seen that is pure narrative with some interactivity. That kind of works because of the environment and the thing it was selling was to be in a wonderful painting of the 1920s. That was enough for people to have that 'meal', it was pure narrative, and it was good writing as well.

JB: One of the key things about games is they often have a payoff. Do you think that element is carried across into your work, that idea of what's the payoff? What do they work towards?

BW: Yeah, that has to be everything! We don't think there was one game in *CROOKS* (2016); there were lots of mini games. Don't gamify it if you're not going to have a payoff. It was like that in *Romeo and Juliet* as well, for example, we made three endings because I knew someone would call out and tell Romeo that Juliet's not dead. It happened quite frequently; you can't ignore that! Suddenly, you have to go with that, and if you are gamifying something you have to be able to have the outcome and make it meaningful in several different ways. For the actors, the people doing it every night, to be able to open up potential like improvisation essentially on a game, like a game master you would know the binary choice would come but be able to finesse it, to keep that audience feeling like they actually impacted.

JB: Do you start with the IP or the narrative or do you start with those structures? How do you develop the mechanic and the narrative, the process of pulling all that together?

BW: We went through these workshops; they were quite revealing because we started on a feeling; we don't actually have a rigid way that we usually go. It usually comes from a feeling that I want to *feel*, like with our spy show, for example. It was more from a childish thing that whenever I was walking down the street and bored, I would pretend someone's following me on the tube or something like that.

JB: *(Laughter)*

BW: *(Laughing)* I was like, 'Oh, this is great fun'. I was like, 'This would be a great show', then just went from that to an entire show. It's those little things and it's stuff like, well, with a gangster stuff I do like obviously like Guy Ritchie films, a heavy influence of *Peaky Blinders* (Knight et al. 2015), you just sort of go, 'This is such a fun world'/

JB: /It's more like the completeness of it, rather than the actual gritty/

BW: /It is that 'Camp' gangster I really love to exist in. Then a show comes out from those. So that's our key starting ground and then buildings were really influential in our stuff because it all comes down to what building we can get. Like *CROOKS 1926* (2018) came because I saw the pub almost two, wow yeah, two years pre-pandemic. Then researched the history of that building, saw that there were actual real-life gangsters that were around. Originally, I was like, that'd be quite a nice springboard, then that develops the games from that kind of tropism. You sort of go, 'what do you do if you're a spy?' You know you're going to listen to someone; you're going to find something and do that drop. You think about all of those kinds of mechanics and then you go, okay cool, what kind of exciting games can come from exciting types of characters? We always start with a protagonist and antagonist which I think is always our narrative basis.

Narrative, play and game mix really nicely because that is the basis of all of it is, that there's an antagonist and protagonist and what happens is drama or game. So, I think about what fun things can come from those types of characters, we make the protagonist and make the antagonist. If it comes from history like CROOKS 1926 (2018), it was really handy because it is all there, all the history is already there. We just read our history and we're like this is brilliant! We just need to tell this. And really handy when you've got a script like Romeo and Juliet – it's the same with when you have an IP; it's a lot easier to pull apart that relationship between the two driving forces of the show. Then it's, 'What's the point of the audience being there?' – that's the next question that we ask. How does the audience fit in? If they don't, then we usually move on and do something else. Audience is almost like a third character, so you have the third character who's not necessarily a driving force but like the sea, the sea that the protagonist and the antagonist exist in. If that doesn't mix into the bowl, it doesn't work; they just stay still.

We then go okay, we've got all of these people, we've got a crowd within these two driving forces, where do we go from there? What stories do we get from that? Usually, without going into all of the specifics, you know the shows become developed. Like for Hostage (2015), for example, it was making the audience very much the point of the story, but for CROOKS (2016) it's slightly more relaxed, but they're still very much a predominant part of the story.

JB: Audiences were different sizes/Hostage (2015) was what 12?/
BW: /Yeah 12/
JB: /that wasn't a huge, it's bigger for CROOKS (2016)/
BW: /Yeah, 80. Even if we did 100 or 200, we'd still be very intrigued in keeping that amount of interactivity and making sure the audience are as involved as they can be.
JB: Who writes the scripts, do you work with different people for every project, or is there a core?
BW: Usually Ben Chamberlain our associate artist, he worked with me for CROOKS 1926 (2020), and we've done quite a few bits

since, like *Flicker* (2020), the Halloween one. He's a really good content maker as well, which is always really great; he's banging them out!

When you end up with loads of games there's loads of different avenues that you have to go down. Danny Romeo is the new one; he started as an intern. He's an American guy, came over here and now he's putting on his own show at the pub. And Charlotte Potter is our producer who is also an artist in her own right, everyone really is like, no one is solely/

JB: /just one thing. How do you work, is it quite informal, is it getting everyone in rooms together and sort of pushing ideas back and forth?

BW: We just sort of hang out/

JB: /and play? Play is probably a big part of/

BW: We do, we play a lot, and especially over lockdown, we spent most of it coming up with shows; we've got a good sort of five in our back pocket. When we can open up again, we want to be able to make the shows as best they can be. We've had loads of R&D time to develop the shows and write the shows, get loads of content for them. It takes almost three days of play and then there's suddenly a day of 'right let's do this!' It's difficult to say where it comes from, but it's usually I come up with a narrative and once we have got those elements all together, we start with space; we start with a feeling.

We think of the genre, think of the space, we think of the mechanics and then we, then kind of unless there is a script, mush them all together. Put them in a bowl; sort of mix them around together. We think of how the audience might interact with stuff, weirdly I know it's really annoying for you, but the idea comes from that. Then we talk about different characters and how they can interact, what they're doing and what are their intentions, then come up with the script and start storyboarding.

We start storyboarding from point A to point B; what they [the audience] go through then if we need to pull on standard narratives-type stuff, we pull on the gamification of it. What happens and where that antagonist starts struggling along the way. Then from the storyboard we usually get it into the rehearsal room, then script it once the actors are involved. It is very much just bullet-pointed, this is happening right, it's quite an interactive rehearsal process where it's like, 'This is one of the games', and sometimes we can just say this is a game that we're thinking about and work with it with the actors.

JB: Do you have a formal casting process because obviously they have very clearly a quite a collaborative role in the development of that?/

BW: /Yes! We've been struggling recently getting the type of people that we want because it's usually the same cast that are applying. We're trying to diversify as much as possible.

JB: /there's very little immersive training/

BW: /Really yeah, it does take a very specific type of person to be good at this type of acting. It's a very specific type of acting that needs to be trained, so we do sometimes find it difficult to find people, but we do have a rehearsal process. We are trying to teach it, like an audition process that's good for immersive and develop those kinds of techniques that are going to be, hopefully, used by everyone. It's really hard to find actors; you can't just get them to do a monologue. Having a character that's good at facilitation, it's quite a tricky process and usually, sadly it's down to their personality, the type of person they are. Which is difficult, you can't do that on a casting call, but it's good to do that in an audition process.

JB: You don't have the third character there, which is the audience.

BW: Yes, exactly! You can't tell anyone, that's why one of our main things that we call 'dickhead audience', where we play a purposely difficult audience member, and we see how they facilitate it.

JB: Do you hold workshops to cast your?/

BW: /We don't call them auditions; we call them workshops. Our plan now going forward is to do two a year, get as many different people into a room as possible because, and then play with each other, see how they're interacting with other /actors and us.

JB: /to build like a pool of actors and that you can draw on for different projects?

BW: We're trying to build a database for immersive actors, and we've got about a hundred on there now. Which are people that either we know of and know are good or people that are recommended to us. We are trying to get as rich a base as possible, adding to it regularly going forward. We're trying to change things a bit, but we usually don't have any notice that we're doing a 'thing'. It's usually like, 'Oh my God, these buildings become available; we got to get it on in a month'. We don't have time for a two-month workshop and R&D and a process where we have to audition actors over a certain amount of time, so we're quite keen to just do it anyway and keep adding to the database. This last round of auditions we got twenty new actors.

JB: You workshop and collaborate; then how do you test it?

BW: We have a minimum of two weeks of previews where we're continuously changing the show. For *CROOKS 1926* (2020) we did one R&D show a month away from the next R&D show which was then two weeks away from the first preview. When there's games involved, you just can't not have audience in it, because it's pointless rehearsing it because you have to go through all the different ways the audience come in.

JB: In some ways, is it learning all the different possible permutations of the rules of engagement?

BW: Yes/

JB: /Making sure that the actors are comfortable with those/

BW: /Yeah.

JB: There are things you could never have anticipated.

BW: Exactly, I don't ever want to stifle that. Obviously, it's money again, if we were really lucky to be able to do one month in a space, we do a month between shows, I don't think anyone could ever afford that. It was only because of filming in our space that we had some money. It's a luxury. I think it's really important to get the audience in front of the show as soon as you possibly can and just let them know that it is obviously a test and not the real thing. You can't make a show with audiences and give them freedom, and agency without testing it. I think a lot of shows have suffered drastically from not doing that.

JB: Space is such a big thing, and I wanted to ask you about COLAB Factory. You had just got into it when I first met you and you felt that it would be temporary, but you are still there over five years later.

BW: It was free back then as well, free for three months, lovely!

JB: The Factory has become really central and significant in helping out some other companies to get a foothold with their work. How did you come about getting the Factory in the first place and what have been the benefits holding on to a venue for a couple of years rather than a couple of months?

BW: Happenstance! I just happened to cycle past it when the old owners were leaving and they had a son, who was also like an 'arty' person. They were like, 'Oh, let me put you in touch with new owners and blah blah blah', and it snowballed into getting the space. There was also a film location company that was looking at the space and willing to pay a lot for it, and we were really lucky that they just chose us, because they just liked what we were doing more. The old owner, I don't know if it's true, when selling it put it into the contract that it had to be used for something interesting. Then it just kept failing at planning permission, but again, that really helped us; it meant that we could carry on. We eventually had to renegotiate rent though because it was free at the beginning. It meant that we could balance quite nicely, support smaller companies.

JB: You have a Tavern now as well. Is that going to be more long term?

BW: Yeah, that's just a normal lease. The Tavern is going to be a constant place where people can come and watch something great, and we can have two shows happening there at once and we're developing the outside space to be able to take more people, and so it's becoming a bit more like the Factory in that regard. Yeah, we got that for five years, so we were in for the long term.

JB: Can we talk a little bit about money – how do you make shows pay for themselves?

BW: We raise it all from previous shows. We always make shows that are appealing essentially; I think that's the simplest way to put it. In whatever sort of genre, you're in, or like or what type of person, you are we, I always try to make a show that people are going to want to come and see. My test is, would I want to see this and if I don't want to, I don't put it on.

I try to put our social issues very deep within the play and within your narrative and you don't notice it, but there is always a little message at the bottom that says something about society, but you wouldn't notice it. I feel that's the best way to do it because it is entertainment, first. It should be entertainment first and then social values later or your message as an artist second; otherwise people won't come see it. IP is such an easy way to get people to come, which I think is the genius of it, and why certain companies are desperate for IP, buying everything under the sun, but you should try and put a message in. But it just needs to at least be entertaining or appealing so that people bloody come and watch what you're putting on otherwise, what's the point?

JB: The bar is a central part of the funding model/

BW: /it's 40 per cent or so roughly now. I did have a meeting with the Arts Council because it is the shame of immersive that we rely 40 per cent on our bar income/

JB: /wow/

BW: The shame of it is we have to structure stuff around a bar. *Hostage* (2015), for example, we probably couldn't do again because it was all cheap, free space where it was out in the street as well, but that venue was free and so we couldn't really do that again if we were paying for space.

JB: There is no space for the bar.

BW: It's a shame that we're sacrificing the artistry for that need of a secondary income, to be able to get everyone paid properly rather than the Arts Council and others filling that gap which is probably their responsibility. In my view, even though they are trying, so many new immersive companies are relying on bar income, often sacrificing the art, for a bar.

JB: It's interesting actually that you mentioned the Arts Council, because I know that during some restrictions you've developed a series of workshops, which I think is really interesting because there is a lack of access to training and the sharing of knowledge. Everyone who makes this kind of work has ten years' experience of working in these ways, and at the moment there's no formal way to share. But I've noticed in the last year that a few of you have started to do these workshops. How have they been important to consolidating your practice?

BW It's all the little things they do, I realized actually it's because a lot of people don't know what they're doing! No one really knows; it's a new art form. They have their construction elements, like the mechanics, and they construct elements like scripts but on top of that – its audience. It's nice being comfortable enough as an artist to say, 'I don't know what I'm doing'. I'm just trying to see if it works and that's fine. Development takes mistakes. So, we made the workshops to share what we do know. It was really nice to actually sit down and think about our process.

JB: You need the space and the support to let those exciting things happen without necessarily knowing what the end of it will be.

BW: But it is important to be honest to be what you'd call established enough, I guess, to say, we can R&D a 'thing', and not necessarily know. But it's a shame that all the young companies that haven't gotten the financial backing or background won't ever get Arts Council funding because they're never gonna say, 'Go on, let's have a punt on this random person'.

JB: *(Laughing).*

BW: They're never gonna do it; that's a shame, because that thing could be amazing!

JB: I think the Factory gave a space for that in some ways.

BW: It did yeah because it was quite cheap.

JB: A place for people to try things out and it be a 'car crash'.

BW: Yeah.

JB: Or be amazing and no one come or/

BW: /Yeah exactly, it is that we are trying to help with the Tavern, that's what we are trying to do with the space. Make it cheap to get a show in a space that makes the money. I think, the more we share, the more companies talk to each other; the more that we are honest with each other, the better. Obviously, have your trade secrets if you need trade secrets, but I think with such a young industry, immersive theatre is going to massively growing across the world as well, so it's/

JB: /Global/

BW: /it's not like one audience member that goes to see one immersive show will not come to the other immersive shows.

JB: It's not one or the other, such a bizarre attitude/

BW: /I'm really thankful that *Gatsby* (2017) is actually a brilliant thing because it's like an immersive light. Once they've come, they/

JB: /Might try something else.

BW: Exactly, and it was a really good steppingstone for making people get interested in this kind of work. I think everything like I commend the success of Secret Cinema for that reason.

JB: It's a gentle induction, isn't it?

BW: Exactly, yeah, we call it immersive light, but it is that.

JB: It starts to open doors; it creates a bridge/

BW: /Absolutely, it bridges all the other audiences, and it works!

JB: I was going to ask you about international work, so what we, you know, we've seen Punchdrunk, we've seen Les Enfants Terribles, take work to Singapore. We've seen other companies take their work to the USA; is that something that you're considering for the future?

BW: Yeah, definitely we're in talks currently about touring *CROOKS 1926* (2020) – I can say that.

JB: Let's talk about the term 'immersive'.

BW: I think the problem with immersive as a term is that it's not necessarily a practice term. I think Punchdrunk made it a practice term as they started it. They sort of hijacked it to frame their practice as immersive theatre. I think, because everyone is making so many different types of immersive theatre, it's much easier to say it's a design term.

JB: It's an umbrella term, isn't it? That's what's so difficult about it because it refers to a state of being for the audience rather than the practice *per se*. When we call something immersive theatre, what we're talking about is the role of the audience within it rather than *it*.

BW: Exactly and that's what kind of ended up happening. I got really frustrated because, if you're trying to program a 'thing' for the Factory, you just want to say, 'What are you?' Which is why we made our definition grid.

JB: Do you find that the term 'immersive' is useful for you, in terms of marketing getting audiences in and so?/

BW: /Yeah definitely. What's quite nice about the term is that now when it comes up on things, you know roughly what it's going to be like; as an audience member, if someone says, 'new immersive experience', I know roughly if you're using the word 'immersive', what I will get. I do think it's really important for us to try and find the next level of definition though. It's nice that some people are being brave enough to say immersive game now as it adds definition.

JB: One of the problems I have is when people call everything immersive theatre, and I'm like, well lots of these things aren't even theatre.

BW: I think it is good that people are worried about calling immersive games, games, because there's less of a live game audience than a theatre audience. You can just appeal to people that play games, which is one of the biggest industries in the world at the moment.

JB: Most people who, like immersive theatre, like it because of the potential gamification or agency that comes/

BW: /the more people that watch it, the more they realize games are where the special bits are. It's not just voyeuristic watching of stuff; I think, eventually, it will mould into a more gamified industry. Which I'm really excited for.

JB: What advice would you give a new or emerging artist? If you have one salient piece of advice to people who want to make this kind of work?

BW: Good luck! Get in touch and because usually it's about space, everyone wants a bloody space, and they want it for free. Be realistic with what you want to put out; I think a lot of people try and do too much. Sometimes, if you do a bit less but better, you actually get a better process and a better show and it's an enjoyable process. We're quite adamant not to charge too much for our tickets ever and we've still not gone over 30 quid. If you can make it accessible, people are willing to take a punt; people are willing to take that risk on your show. You want to make it as appealing as possible, and if it's a cheap show and it's a good show, then they'll probably come back. My advice would be work within your means and be realistic with your goals and make stuff that is appealing. Realistically, at least at the beginning, you have to do an appealing thing and then, if you hopefully make some money out of that you can then try and do your 'arty thing'. No one's going to come and see your thing about your own experiences too early on, you have to do that a bit later on in your career. Then it can be brilliant, because you've learned all sorts of things. Then do your Magnum Opus.

Your first show is going to be shit no matter what you do; someone won't like it, which is the hardest thing to realize.

JB: The best thing drama school ever gave me actually was resilience, being able to make a fool of yourself and be okay with that and failure; failure is such a big part of what we do in rehearsals/

BW: /and in games, part of a game is to fail. The origin of game is that you fail and try again, and then you succeed. It's like that's what games are and that's what life is. It is life advice, you've got to take time, you know you won't be good straight away and that's fine, more than understandable, but it's okay to fail.

Note

1 The Tate is a Modern Art Institution that was founded in 1897 by Henry Tate.

FIGURE 5 *Image details* Love: Inc *at Rose Bruford College of Theatre & Performance, featuring performers from the BA (Hons) European Theatre Arts programme with lighting design by Jeremy Jason. Photograph by Michael O'Reilly.*

CHAPTER 4

Socially engaged interactions with Natalie Scott, Joseph Thorpe, Antigoni Spanou and Joe Iredale from The Lab Collective

Speaker key:
JB: Joanna Bucknall
NS: Natalie Scott
JT: Joseph Thorpe
AS: Antigoni Spanou
JI: Joe Iredale

[This conversation was recorded over Zoom on 29 July 2021.]

JB: You started making work in 2008 but really began developing your very particular approach to interactivity in 2010. So, can you talk a bit about the way that *Matador* (2010) and *Bull Pen*

(2010) really shifted your approach away from physical theatre to a more audience-engaged dramaturgy?

JT: We've always been interested in tangible experiences rather than more internal processes for both audiences experiencing the work and the performers who create the material. From something like *Inches Away* (2010), where we were exploring real experiences through physical acts of pain and endurance on stage, we were really interested in that kind of realness; we quickly realized we were interested in working more closely with audiences and developed *Matador* (2010) and *Bull Pen* (2010) at Theatre Souk. We had two different strands that we really wanted to examine: one which was looking at structure, which was with *Matador* (2010), and the other one was to look at game play, with *Bull Pen* (2010). *Bull Pen* (2010) was developed first.

NS: We realized that the audience numbers were really limited for *Bull Pen* (2010), which we had developed based on a game called Liar's Poker[1] – a stock market game that's played by traders. It was really great fun, but it was also exhausting for the performers because we would be doing show on show on show every night, up to six iterations of it, but it also really limited our capacity. We wanted an additional show, a one-person show that meant we could have more audience in the space and by alternating them, make sure that we could provide proper breaks for performers. Just jumping back quickly to what Joe was saying about coming out of drama school and exploring our practice; we started making in an epic recession and as freshly graduated humans, we very much felt that we weren't going to be able to go down a traditional theatre directing pathway because there had just been huge cuts to Arts Council funding, the economy was collapsing, there were no jobs. It was all very intense and really that was the inspiration for *Matador* (2010) and *Bull Pen* (2010), it was a response to that crisis, and we realized, I think, that it affected everyone so dramatically that to not share that conversation didn't quite feel right. That is also where the desire to develop the interactivity came from; we want to share in that dialogue; we wanted people to talk about it – it felt important.

JT: For the first time we started thinking about shared responsibility in society because at the time it was very – I mean we still agree with this – banker-hating. Actually, there's a huge responsibility in which the whole of society shares in accepting or resisting these kinds of movements of capitalism and we wanted to address this through performance. In *Matador* (2010) we started to look at a very simple invitational mode, so it was very much 'Are you with me?', 'You're my favourite' – using these statements to pull people through. Something we identified with Neil Connolly [Previous Lab Collective Creative Associate] was audience complicity – he asked each audience member to put their toe on the line (he was in the centre of a ring in the space); then the idea was to see whose foot was still there at the end. If their foot was still there at the end, it showed a level of engagement, and he would call upon them in world. Looking more at that kind of inherent invitation, we were like, 'OK, I understand this'. But for *Bull Pen* (2010), interestingly, Natalie began to work on a structured way of documenting and scripting the piece. This was the first time that we started looking at flow charts and at how the movement of the story or narrative elements evolve. It's important how pathways can create constantly unique and different changing theatrical stories.

JI: I was an audience member, and I think something that was relevant there and relevant in the work afterwards was about us joining the villain side to expose difficult ideas, which I think has come through in a lot of the work as well in the individual shows. But within the interactive low-scale immersive it's very subtly done – you don't even realize that you're sliding into the right or the left or the wrong side; it's about how easy it is to be led by someone who's so charismatic into making difficult and dangerous decisions.

JB: And in that group context it spreads across the audience. It's infectious/

JI: /That's how it grows.

NS: That's part of the game play because what both of those shows had in common was the system and the personal wrapped in together. For example, at the beginning of *Bull Pen* (2010), you were asked to write on a piece of paper something that you would be willing to bet with, something personal – your health, your child – and people take those things super, super seriously. They would start writing them down, putting a lot of thought into it and then interestingly just chuck it in the ring, like it meant nothing to them – and it wasn't really until the end when (if they had lost) we collected those up and read out the winnings that people were like, 'Oh God, actually that's really challenging'. There is that kind of personal provocation and then the provocation of the whole show and a reveal, an ethical reveal. Even with *Matador* (2010), if the person who had their toe on the line had a one-on-one moment with Neil where there was this intimate whispered conversation between them right at the end. That loop from charisma, charm, hardness, into intensely personal lets people feel a mixture of a lot of things in those moments.

JT: That moment of personal accountability then became prevalent, and we started to become interested in that type of idea. That last person with their toe on the line then became the Matador and took on the mantle to continue venture capitalism and neo-liberalism into the future. Taking it to *Latitude* and seeing a 12-year-old go up was repulsive, sad and meaningful at the same time. I think we said to each other we would never ever have imagined that that would happen and if we did, it wouldn't have happened in a million years. That spark of the spontaneity of chaos actually then pushed us through into the other work that we started doing later on.

JB: Politics has always been, even in that early stuff, more implicit. The next iteration, which was *Pinestripe Trilogy* (2013), I think the politics were much more foundational, much more explicit could you talk a little bit about how that has been drawn out/

NS: /*Pinestripe Trilogy* (2013) was really interesting because it moved from people's very personal relationships with politics, or like the private kind of sector and where they sit in the landscape, into a comment on absence of government. In fact, all of that work was about privatization, a lack of willingness to engage with the collective social good and how we're serving our young people. *Pinestripe Trilogy* (2013) was composed of three half-an-hour shorts: *Matador* (2010), *Bean Counter* (2012) and *Trust Fund* (2012). Two of those shows had already been developed, so we'd already done *Matador* (2010), we had already done *Trust Fund* (2012), so that was part of *Bush Bazaar*[2] in 2013, and *Bean Counter* (2012) was the last piece of the trilogy.

JI: It was just scratching the surface of it, wasn't it?

NS: Yeah, it was. It was starting to bubble up, particularly with Starbucks. A lot of our design was like a Starbucks cup with the *Pinestripe Trilogy* (2013) logo on it that was offered out to an audience. But it was all about what does that mean for us as a society if we're unwilling to pay to participate in it and kind of serve the most underserved in our communities? Then *Trust Fund* (2012) was about how that affects our young people? This idea of not only privatizing all education but actually thinking of education as more of a sponsorship deal where you get sponsored to have the best of the best then for the rest of your life you're paying that return off. You're paying off interest but not through your wages necessarily but through all your income in perpetuity. Adults and parents signing their children up to that without consent. It felt like these pieces were really, really connected. *Matador* (2010) was the foundation for that and for that dystopic timeline. We were interested in the presence of people but the absence of central government/

JT: /The absence of shared responsibility/

NS: /Shared responsibility/

JT: /There is something about the prophetic nature of looking at political work which I think all four of us are very much interested in, not what is the conversation now, but what's the conversation tomorrow?

NS: That's also reflected in how we listen to experts. When we make something like that, the research that we do is looking firstly at all points of view, regardless of whether we agree with it or not. That's a really key thing, going, 'We need to see all of these disparate points of view and listen to those people, even if we find it quite grim'. But in all the work we make, listening, researching that kind of future thought, thinking about how it relates to the work we're making and how we're translating that into something that's digestible, interesting, interactive and meaningful is really important. And ultimately it has impact on audience; that's the key thing.

JB: I wanted to ask you in more detail about some of the nitty-gritty of how work is made, how you start to develop that. I know that one of the big things that you've spoken about in the past is the way the core desires and psychology has been central to the way that you construct experience for audiences and the way that you anticipate and manage those experiences for audiences.

NS: Core desire tapped into this during an exercise where we were asking performers [during training] to sell us a concept or idea of a product that in some way was reprehensible. We were asking them to help us as an audience buy into these things and if the 'audience' were starting to be convinced by someone's pitch, they would raise their hand. What we really identified in that exercise, or articulated maybe more clearly, was this idea of core desire, what do people want? Is it sex? Is it money? The things that aren't necessarily the best bits of us but that we desire regardless. We want to be comfortable, we want a loving partner, but we also want loads of great sex. All of those things are core desires, and what we articulated was, 'How do we utilize that idea of core desire to provide the audience with either ethical dilemma or with choices?' It's that idea of seduction that we talked about a bit earlier, the charismatic person and the things that this can represent; ultimately, there is a tension within an audience of like, 'Here is a core desire, here is the cost or a price of it, how am I using my agency to make decisions as an audience, and where is that leading me?' We're using core desire. Tapping into fundamental wants and needs is a really great way of stimulating dialogue and of providing provoking or challenging ideas for people to get their teeth into.

AS: What's really interesting about the idea of core desire is the fact that as humans, we guard them. We don't fully express them. It leaves us vulnerable, which is I think a concept that makes people think, 'Oh, I'm weak', when actually, it's completely the opposite; it is courageous to be vulnerable, to express your core desire. I think the audience has this idea of, 'If I express my innermost desires I will be shamed or judged for them'. So, it's creating that safe space for the audience, creating those boundaries where both performer and audience come together; then you create what I call 'real interaction'.

JT: We're all interested in certain or different parts core desires. I'm interested in those darker desires: 'I'm a Liberal, I'm a Socialist, but God, I want to be rich! I do want to have real nice things and I want to consume'. That's OK to activate and talk about because it's important for us to open up these theories, these thoughts. Some of the work is about, 'OK, there's one core desire but how does that affect, or how does that activate somebody else's core desire?' It might be my core desire to say that 'you are absolutely 120% wrong and I hate everything you're talking about' as well as the desire to feel brave, the desire to stand up, the desire to fight – is also a massive drive to many of us, particularly those who may feel unable to do so in their everyday lives.

AS: On exactly that point of how brave you choose to be – because I have a background in science, I cannot get rid of my science brain! Looking at social studies, they can measure how brave you are, by how vulnerable you decide to be. I found this idea of creating brave space interesting, of how brave you can be with what you have to say, your opinion, how you express your innermost desires.

NS: Core desire is one thing. The reason for that core desire is something else and for me that's where the vulnerability sits. So, my core (I'm going to just keep talking about sex) desire is sex but the reason for it might be because I crave intimacy. Tapping into that core desire is one thing but recognizing the reason for it – even if it's just an internal thing – is powerful. It may be something that an audience has revealed to you, ever, but it might be something they think about is, you know, really important going beyond the surface. Like Joe was saying, 'I just want to say that you're really wrong', but why you might want to do that is because you want to feel brave or speak out or feel empowered, you know, is the next level that sits underneath core desire.

JI: It's the manipulation of the arena which you give them to play; it's about trying to draw out different elements of that core desire. For example, if you're bringing some audience members into a room, the person that's brought them there leads; if they have a disagreement, you're already suggesting that it's OK to disagree. You can construct a healthy argument. That's something that we've worked on; how to put in those mechanics and those parameters to have a safe, brave, space.

JB: It's informed, isn't it? I know you used psychology, you do lots of research into behaviours, and so I wanted to draw out a little bit more on how you use those things to create those spaces and to sort of – I say 'manipulate', but it is in some ways, it's manipulating/

JI: /Coax/

JB: /Coax, is a good way!
   (Laughing)

AS: Facilitate/

JI: /It's making those key decisions; we're talking about manipulation, but when we use the word 'coax', then we're changing the narrative, we are being the British news media, you know what I mean? We're putting that overtone, not undertone.

NS: For me that has to do with intent. To manipulate has a negative intention. To facilitate, to coax in a direction, to unfold something, is very different because the purpose is not to embarrass or humiliate or to get something out of someone because there's consent. I think manipulation implies lack of consent and for me maybe facilitate is correct.

JT: I was going to use the word 'create'. We're trying to create these spaces for people to express, but it's also recognizing those moments, that language, that behavioural language. How does someone step backwards, how do they step forward? Who's the first in the room? Who's the last in the room? Inherently, people like to talk, a lot! One of the things that we train into our actors is to allow people to talk, because they will either back themselves into a corner or they'll say it 200 times better than we could ever say it because it comes from an honest place. That's part of that behavioural psychology. We understand that some people want to be in that limelight, so we let them be in the limelight. Let's let them have their time, but let's be clear – we will not tolerate, or platform hate. They're here to be – I think Sarah Morris says this – a hero in some way, but the audience don't necessarily know which side they're fighting on until they've already done the action. Developing on from *Matador* (2010), we were looking at that simple interaction and invitation of a question 'Are you OK?', 'Yes'; 'Are you with me?', 'Yes'. It's picking those people that you can see that are engaged. Taking back from 2010 and going 'that single thought of open your eyes, performer; look out, performer; keep your focus on others, performer'. That's something that has grown throughout the industry into something much more inherent in all training of the work. But these things were developed back in 2010 with those simple interactions, not long or big conversations, just reading the body language of somebody, being able to have your focus outwards. It's also important to not just be about the psychology of the audience member, it's also about the psychology of the performer and their removal of ego, removal of internal focus and beginning to look outward facing/

NS: /active listening/

AS: /When you're looking at performing to a group and you have this crowd psychology in the group, you use it, go with it and build on it. You can identify crowd characteristics; like the sense of de-individualization and lack of sympathy and anonymity that people hide behind in a group. Being able to identify these characteristics, for example if somebody is leading something and is being conductive, is creating the situation, pointing out an audience member by name breaks that down.

JI: It's either you stoke the fire, or you throw water on it, trying to gauge their attitude and their instigation. In our kind of performance, a lot of the time we're saying to performers that 'you're not the show, you're an important facilitator in the show, you're part of the subtext' and I think that's maybe what we were trying to get to a bit earlier. This is your scene but you're serving a higher function, you've got your own text but it's not about you, it's about the audience's experience and you're facilitating that. You are the shop assistant to the show.

JB: It's worth recognizing, this is a big shift away from traditional performer training which is often about those internalized things. The cliché of 'what's my motivation?' becomes 'what's your motivation?', to the audience. You have to think, how do I facilitate that, how do I either combat that, like you were saying if it's being troubling and it's going to break something, or how do I kind of stoke that and pull that out of you? It's well worth recognizing that is such a shift for performers.

NS: Because what we're really doing is saying, 'You may have that lovely dramatic monologue that we've worked on', but equally you might have to throw it away if the audience is moving you somewhere else. We use the idea of herd mentality a lot in training and in how we put together our performances. We also recognize that this doesn't exist within a binary. They might be pushing one way or another way but there is always a third way, a fourth way, a fifth way. The performer needs to be OK relinquishing their material and giving in, to lead and facilitate the audience so that they get something meaningful from their experience. You are relinquishing your performative ego to serve that audience in a totally different way, and I think that that's a really hard thing for performers to get their head around. Because what they want is to be 'and now it's my moment' but 'actually, now it's *their* moment'.

JT: It's our moment/

NS: /It's our collective moment, and we have to embrace it, or we will fail.

JI: If A is arrival and E is exit, the performer knows that they've got to hit B, C and D but that might happen in any order depending on the energy of the audience. That's the importance of improv skills, actually listening. It's important to find the realness but also, it's not getting too lost. You've got to get a little bit lost to find something new, but you can't just leave people out in space.

NS: That's where the skill comes in, bringing people back into a structure. I think performers have that same thing when they don't know what to say or do, they rush you onto the next bit, the next point that they have to get to, and I think it can be very challenging for an audience. That's often when bad behaviour ensues, or when they become very challenging.

AS: Just a small asterisk here: what performers need to learn first and foremost is to relinquish part of the control and hand it to the audience. Be brave enough to travel with the audience and discover what happens in there and that's OK. Don't overthink about what your motivation is; discover what connection you can create with this person, in this space, in this time, in this very moment. Not pre-empting it because you can't pre-empt a human; you never know what you're going to get.

JB: Your work is only activated by people being in it. People are what your work is made out of, so that understanding people is useful.

JT: Yeah, the harder that they play, the more fun you can have, which sounds really obvious but actually during a lot of shows, oftentimes the hardest players are actually punished by being gotten rid of, being sent away mostly because; 'you're a problem because you don't fit my structure' and they get sent away. We get very frustrated with this as a concept and have spent a lot of time thinking about how to reframe that engagement, going, 'OK, well we need to reward people'; as Natalie says, it's that reward/

NS: /Praise, rule, ignore/.

JT: /There you go. It's that monologue that you have developed, that's your gift for your best player. That's something you reserve for that lovely moment when you've found somebody who's really in with you. You're going, 'I'm going to give you the gift of this thing. This thing is full of absolutely everything that my character is about, or everything that this experience is about; I'm going to give it to you because you're really engaging'. Also trying to develop the ideas of, if you are going to send somebody off on a random thing, how do we make sure it's meaningful?

NS: We're not denying your agency and obviously we want to avoid anything that's hateful, anything that is discriminatory; that has no place in our work. The idea that it connects more to inclusivity of going, 'You might be challenging or perhaps don't understand this content in the way that we have intended it, but we still can absolutely 100% explain and wrap you in'. So, for small issues, we use things like praise, rule, ignore when people do something that might be challenging, you know? Let's say somebody has stolen something; it's finding the good in the negative action: 'wow, you're super sneaky. I didn't even see that happening'. Rule, so you're going to give them a new rule: 'I need a second-in-command; I've got a special job for you' (this also means you can keep a close eye on the audience member); ignore the negative behaviour so that you're not punishing. I think the idea of punishing in interactive immersive shows is really challenging because often it drives people further into the desire to be disruptive.

JT: Or worse.

NS: Or worse. A lot of our technique sits around going, 'We see the disruption and we catch it before it becomes destruction', before it starts to ruin the experience for other audience members, nip that in the bud. There is a lot of behavioural understanding and analysis that we train performers to look for, techniques for them to use to catch that disruption. An audience member might have had a terrible day: they might not want to really be there; they might not understand what's going on and to push audiences away, especially if they might not be traditional performance goers, can actually turn them off from the form; it can turn them off from performance and it's not an inclusive way of working for us.

JB: You have an extremely robust and rigorous process for how you capture that, how you marshal it and how you run it? Mechanics, flow and feedback loops, how does gaming leak into the practice? How does that inform the way you design those experiences?

JT: Something that I enjoy about mechanics is that they're dry. They are boring, dry things. They're extremely logical; they're based on rulesets, tasks and goals. But what they can do for people is where it becomes interesting, where they are the facilitator of other things. When we're playing generally – when we play anything – there's always inherent rules that I kick around and rules that get developed along the way. My favourite core mechanic that most 3-year-olds play is 'I win now', because now, suddenly the rules have changed. So that is a mechanic, in itself. It's a chaotic no-rule mechanic. But if you looked at something like a betrayer mechanic, in its essence, somebody in the room is working against you, find out who it is, which in itself you could walk around and go, 'Is it you?', 'No'; 'Is it you?', 'No'; 'Is it you?', 'No'; 'Is it you?', 'No'; 'Is it you?', 'Yes, it's me'. 'OK, great'. What it actually does is create a psychological feeling of absolute paranoia. It turns people both towards and away from each other, it makes people read every single physical movement, every single behavioural trait, every word which they say, and it makes people go into extreme statements of like – I think my favourite one is – 'if you're the betrayer, I'm never speaking to you again!', this came from my best friends!

NS: A really good example of this is a game we use in training called 'dark handshake'. At the beginning of the game, we give somebody the dark handshake, when they move around the space and tickle someone's palm, that person 'dies'. Nobody in the room knows who has the dark handshake and it immediately creates the betrayer mechanic. We have planted a betrayer in the space; it creates an atmosphere; it generates emotion in the players, in the participants and creates a dynamic in the relationship between people. And then beyond that it can create meaning. Part of the game is that collectively you have to uncover who has the dark handshake. Someone points at someone else and accuses them and if everyone does that to the same person, that person is accused. If they are guilty, yay, the group has won, well done everyone. If, however, that person is not guilty, you've killed an innocent person. So, what you start to see is this tension, this ethical tension of like, 'Am I sure? Is this right? Is it OK? I don't know'. What you start to get is meaning. You can expand that game even further so that whoever is making the accusation has to explain themselves and justify it, they themselves might have the dark handshake. Suddenly through a really simple mechanic is an entire experience for the players to participate in and question what they're doing and why they're doing it and if they think it's OK.

JT: Often we set up the game and then tell everyone to ignore the game. We're really interested in going, 'OK, here's the game to win; now which one of you will do anything to win and which one of you will question those people?' For instance if you look at *Incoming/Exodus* (2017), the game is set up like, 'we must get these groups of people into our society, we have numbers, we have rounds, we have collective decisions, we have a voting system that you decide but we set up these game rules to begin with'; actually you rarely get through to the next round because audiences are too busy talking about the things that interested them.

Because that idea comes back to the ego again but the win conditions. The drive for people to win something, they want to win, they want to be the best at that experience and that game, which can be all-encompassing to some people and actually the removal of that core desire, or the heightening of that core desire, can push back the moral and ethical elements of a human being. That's something that we're hugely, hugely interested in. Even in the idea of structure, it is important to be able to understand that there's more than just the game. The game is just facilitating the rest of the meaning.

NS: A lot of the time people don't know they're playing. We work really hard to hide the mechanics so that people don't feel like they're playing. They might sense there's a win to be had but they can't quite identify what that is and actually what that does is free them up to just make the choices they want to make. There is always this fine line in game mechanics in relation to performance, which is like, winning isn't necessarily hugely important; the process of how you get somewhere is though, and I think that really sits under our work.

JT: I think that's in design.

NS: Yeah, in design. Mechanics as a tool to create structure and extract that meaning – it's really important. It's quite fundamental to how we construct a piece.

JI: When we've pushed that more into the performance world rather than just in the training world, we create a filter system on it. Within our world we might have a small hierarchy, so your first interaction you interact with someone, maybe one of our less experienced performers, but from there, they're identifying potentially positive players, potential bogey players. Then that can get passed through the system, as they go higher up this filtering system, we can tailor the experience to not lose anyone, to not let anyone go way too far down the rabbit hole. We 'hyperize' it within the world in which we've created and then if there is an issue or a moment, we have an in-world character that can try and tackle this, unless it's gone way too far.

JT: It's interesting Joe talks about this because, you know, using dice is a mechanic, having cards is a mechanic. Here what we're trying to do is place the performers as a mechanic or the management structure as a mechanic. The idea of the 'pit boss' as a mechanic is about safeguarding, yes, it is about keeping performers and audience safe but it's also a way of actively directing and moving pieces around on the board, getting things to continually moving forward. We can influence the game as makers; we're not just kind of letting this all go to the audience because ultimately as we said before, it's *our experience*, not necessarily your experience or my experience.

NS: That's where the role of the stage manager is important because there is a certain amount of creative licence that stage management teams have within this context. Just to clarify what Joe meant by 'pit boss'; this is a person in the space who I suppose traditionally would be stage management, but in an interactive context they are at the top of the tree in terms of safeguarding that space, making sure everyone is OK and heading things off at the passe. But they are also there to oversee that the mechanics are happening, to pass on messages to performers as well, so that we know where everyone is at, and there is a certain amount of creative licence that comes with that/

JT: /Oh, there's a huge amount, a huge amount of creative licence.

NS: When we work with traditional stage management, it can be really challenging to begin with because it's like, 'Is that OK? I just made a decision' and it's like, 'But we trust you to make the decision in that space because you've seen that the audience are really enjoying that moment, they're getting loads from it and to push them on now would feel wrong or disingenuous or disrupt the flow'. So yeah, OK, we add on a few minutes there and we steal a few minutes from there, and that 'pit boss' is the person who bridges the communications between everybody.

JT: I just want to clarify that, oftentimes the 'pit boss' and the stage manager are two separate people. I just want to make sure that's clear, because it's often our most experienced, most trusted performers are the ones that sit in those 'pit boss' spots because they are ultimately directors of the space at the same time.

NS: That position will have a characterization or persona, a role within the overarching world. You won't necessarily know they're a 'pit boss' but they might have a higher status and they seamlessly fit into the world. It's one of two things: they're either the higher status character so they can talk to people individually, move them away and negotiate or unpack if something isn't quite right, or they have the lower status of the space and are invisible almost, but ever-present.

JT: Because this is part of a game mechanic, there is something to be said about where this developed from. We were doing some work in 2013/2014 and looking at more commercial spaces and floor manager kind of concepts. What we found when we were moving into Boomtown[3] etc. in 2013 is that it became important to develop an idea of 'what does it mean to have a performative hierarchy to keep people safe when you're working in extremely chaotic environments?' Different companies are using different words, different things but our concept of the 'pit boss' is very specifically about, the pace-maker, the 'safeguarder', the director on the ground rather than a captain performer or somebody along those sorts of lines.

JB: I think one of the things that strikes me very much about this is, how do you rehearse this? How do you know before you get that audience in/

JT: /We don't!

JI: Like a comedian doing their set, the best comedians are doing it for two, three months until they've got the first performative draft. A lot of it is finding the needs within your experiences, those mini 'get out of jail free cards' – what text phrases do work, if they're down, if they're high, if they're excited, which angle can you come in at? That is all, fail, fail and fail better. Every time you don't do it as well, you learn what might be effective next time. You're always getting it less wrong.

AS: It's intrinsically linked to the training. You're probably going to fail and that needs to be drilled in your brain. You shouldn't have fear of that; you should just accept it. So how do you learn to recover from that in the moment? How do you bring it back? How do you move on? How do you find something else in that moment? Really getting that ingrained in your brain so you know as a performer in that moment what is best.

JB: Practically do you do this with each other initially before you encounter outside/

JI: We're all pretty good at being the best audience – the audience that you want, and the worst audience. Depending on the stages of their careers, the stages of the show, you come in as a good customer or a bad customer. As the show is getting closer and closer, you play more devil's advocate to test how strong they are within their structure. But at the beginning you're coming in, 'Oh, this is going to work fine' but then you start bringing your red herrings with you, dropping them to try and pick out the loopholes. That's why coming with a solid structure is so important to us.

NS: What we have identified is almost like audience archetypes, so different kinds of audiences that will offer different things. When you start playing out your interactions or you start playing out your structure with each other, you quickly realize, straight off the bat, there are things that you'll just get rid of immediately, like really, really, early on. Then the more you play with those different modes, with those alternative outcomes, the possible kinds of humans that you might meet and what they may bring to the table, it creates deeper and richer interactions. Things will happen. You will meet people that you never would have dreamed of; in the moment, 'how do I reframe something for this human?' is super important, but the more you rehearse that interaction and the different modes of audience, the easier it becomes. We go through so many stages of development. With *Incoming /Exodus* (2017), we went through at least three and it was a year. It took time to develop the work and learn.

JT: If you're a maker, leading other facilitators or other performers, it's not up to them to come up with all of it and this is a really important point. When we design a show, the four of us, in each of our different ways of working, when we create work, we come in with something that is a structure. We come in with a plan, we come in with a way in which we think functionally the piece is going to work, with the understanding that we're going to burn that. We turn to our performers, and we say, 'Draw down a structure first, because I want you to burn it afterwards', because again it's about identifying that you're going to fail but you must have something to start working on.

Thinking about *Incoming/Exodus* (2017), you're looking at the concept of rounds. We went into rehearsal thinking of it as a tabletop game to begin with; there are rounds and there are mechanics and there is an outcome. We just looked at the structure of what those rounds are, before we've got to rehearsals, before we start talking to the other performers. There's a responsibility as makers to start that process as early as you possibly can. You've got to go, 'What is the structure of the piece that we're going to be talking about?'

Using this shared language of flow, of feedback loops and everything else, I can draw this on a board and stick it in the middle of a room and people that we've worked with or people that we are new to work with, start to understand what that means. Performers can start using it themselves and sharing it with each other and passing things over to each other; we're all using the same visual language throughout.

NS: It's so useful as a rehearsal tool; you can just keep on track of things. You've been devising for ages, you know, your structure has changed, you've got a shorthand, you can doodle it down, you've got a record so that when you come back to it, you know where you're at, so you don't forget.

JT: And it's all in light pencil or in dry wipe; it's never in full pen.

JI: As that develops or as we try and get to a harder part or a more challenging part, that's when we think about the physical environment. You will be in smaller rooms to make more difficult decisions. If there's something that we really want audiences to think about, I like planting a seed that I have to water, because it just gives that time of nurture; it's a suggestion of something, we want to nurture the answer. Or the space has become smaller and closer because we're talking sensitively, you know. It's the things beyond the words, so if the structure doesn't quite serve it, then the world echoes it.

JT: We talk about choice of words and Joe spoke earlier about getting the right question. That's something we work on a lot, what happens if we change one word of that question or just change the tense slightly, it might actually get closer to what you want. Oftentimes we take the first game or the first idea that a performer comes up with. We celebrate it and then we start pulling at its threads, challenging it and then create a new game. That new game will have elements of the old game inherently inside it but we will start to hone and hone and hone and hone until the task and the meaning starts to emerge from the mechanic.

NS: We do ask our performers to do a lot. Not in terms of making the structure and making our work for us because I think that is really important to stress. Like Joe was saying, we come to the table with something really clear, with really clear audience objectives and meaning that we want to extract. But the rehearsal process is also the honing and development of the many brains that the performer utilizes. The kind of outward-facing self – that's presented and the outward characterization, but also beyond that – the reading of the audience, the active listening, the thinking; underneath that the structure itself and the strategy that they need; underneath that the very technical elements of like/

JT: / 'What time is it? How much time have I got?'

NS: The experience of the performer needs to be held in a way that, firstly they can get a sense of their own boundaries but also a sense of trust between us. It's our duty of care to listen to that and respect it.

JT: Everything's a draft. Going into the show is a draft. The last show is a draft; everything is a draft; everything is a rehearsal. Everything. And actually, you should always be prepared, even straight after a show, to go over to that white board and wipe a big chunk of it out, recreate another one because, again, the most important thing for us is the lasting legacy of the audience's agency on the work. So, if they do something that absolutely surprises us and we go, 'Oh that's better than we could ever think about', then we take that and incorporate it, because it's now part of the show – they have affected it in some way. So, if they return, they have a new experience. As a group, we all must have that understanding. Us as directors, performers, technicians, stage management, everybody has to have that feeling that we could go over to the white board at any point during the show, during the rehearsals, wipe something out and draw something else in.

NS: And we think we really lead by example in that: we are not overly precious about that kind of collaboration; we have to do what we ask the performers to do; we have to let go of our ego and our attachment to certain things. And in doing so we also know how hard that is.

JB: One of the areas that is a bit of a mystery is finances. How have you been able in the past to fund work, to facilitate work? How do you get work to sort of cover its costs?

JT: Everyone goes quiet!

(Laughing)

NS: Three main ways: commission, so being paid by an organization, a venue or a festival to develop a piece that's bespoke for them, or a piece that isn't bespoke that can be transferred that we can use again elsewhere. If we can do the second one it's great because it means that that piece is already made, it's part of your body of work, it's transferable and it can continue to generate funding for you as it can be produced elsewhere. The second is through partnerships. Institutions and bodies like universities: developing those kinds of partnerships that often create research-led work but again you often will come out with something at the end of it that might be transferable. It might not, it depends on the IP; it depends on the other organizations involved. Thirdly through – well, there's two more – public funding, applying for things like Arts Council England or Trusts and Foundations, generating funding that way to make work. And lastly through use of capital. The way that we first started, we went to work with Theatre Souk,[4] we put in a lot of hours, there were a lot of hours that were free, but at the end of it we paid everybody, apart from ourselves – that came later! We weren't a charity at this time but at the end of it, after we'd paid everybody there was a small pot of money. With that money we could reinvest it in other shows and then refill the pot after everyone had been paid. So, you're sitting on a permanent amount of capital that you can keep investing in your shows, really what you want to do is break even or better. Building that capital so that you can scale up your shows. From the commissions that we've made, we keep 10 per cent or 15 per cent behind to add into that pot, so what you're doing is building something that is viable. We're not for-profit; we are a charity. Our aim is to break even or better. If we can do 'or better', the money goes back into the pot; it doesn't come to us as makers necessarily. We might go, 'OK, I've spent loads of time on the accounts' or 'We are developing this thing and we need to spend a bit of that capital', we have to go to our board of trustees to get that signed off. The idea of it being for-profit can't be a model for us.

JT: Because of charitable status as well, it happens to align with the rest of our ethics. We can't take private or commercial investment.

NS: We can take donations.

JT: We take donations but again, we can't take investment that offers a return to people. We are very much interested in public money; the way in which we work is geared towards that. Research and development is a similar concept; you're constantly looking outwards to pass out the things you are learning rather than holding and hauling inward. Success is driven not by the profit margin but by sustainability – that's been the drive from the start. What we are doing is affecting a group of people and what we are doing is developing more practices, opening that out, training and passing it outwards into the industry.

JB: That's what you've always done, isn't it, with Lighthouse? You've always had that ethos of an open space, building a community, building discussion, building dialogue and building relationships that have a broader impact than just the bottom line of making a profit.

NS: Yeah, it's also important to clarify that by being not-for-profit does not mean that people don't get paid. I think sometimes people get really confused by the idea of not-for-profit. Since the beginning everyone, every performer, every maker, is paid for their participation in a project because that's part of the costs of doing a project. But what isn't part of the costs of doing a project is then taking whatever we have at the end after being paid and dividing it amongst us.

JT: Or investors.

NS: Or investors. We feed the company like we feed ourselves. We think of it as an entity that requires resource; it means that the company can be enriched.

JT: I think the next step of that is to then consider how the core company can be supported in a more sustainable way. That's something we're working towards now.

NS: Jumping back to the Lighthouse for a minute, the idea of resource sharing is not necessarily cash either. Resource sharing can also mean, like when we had the Fly Pit,[5] we had this space that was particularly suited to interactive, immersive work, and we were interested in that as a resource for people to use to show their work, share their work and get feedback from industry professionals. But also meet people from cross forms. The nights weren't just interactive and immersive, there were always two interactive or immersive pieces but then there was also live artists and spoken word artists.

JT: And keynote speakers talking about sustainability, the way they run their companies or model their careers as artists. The Lighthouse was about sharing, openness with each other and because you're working with people from other disciplines, a painter, for example, their experience is actually hugely valuable to me as a performance maker, as I am to them, or to this other person or to this mechanic who's turned up.

NS: Originally, the Lighthouse concept came from the idea of a salon, like a nineteenth-century literary salon where you have a theme or a keynote speaker or a human that you're particularly interested in and exploring their work in whatever shape that takes. What we did was take that idea, and instead of it being solely discussion based, we built the whole thing around the 8 o'clock slot, which mirrored the overwhelming theme of the evening. Then different forms could engage in the spaces in an open flow in different areas of the space; there would be drinks and live music. It was almost a salon; it was very salon-y focused and it had that feel. It was still quite structured but also really free-flowing. In terms of feedback, we asked artists, 'What do you need? How do you want that delivered?' For a lot of people, they don't want discussion, they want a big noticeboard, or they just want to circulate in the room for like fifteen, twenty minutes to talk to people. So, it's really going, 'What do you need and how can we facilitate that in this structure?' The Lighthouse was a really great way of diversifying away from just this form, to embracing knowledge exchange, form exchange and wrapping in ideas from elsewhere. Because we're very insular, this industry is really insular. It's very self-focused and actually we can learn a lot from other art forms.

JT: And other non-art forms.

JB: Yes, absolutely. Well, this kind of leads me into the question that I ask of everybody which is about the very term 'immersive' and I know that from the very beginning have really described your work as interactive work.

AS: I think it's a trend, for sure, to hear the word 'immersive' and it's become a selling point. I've seen pieces of theatre that I think, yeah, this has been advertised as immersive, but it doesn't really tick that box for me. There are specific elements that need to be fulfilled for the work to be described as immersive. Personally, I would avoid using the term. I don't care how trendy it sounds or if the producer wants to stick it in there because, if it's not really that, you lose trust with your audience if you're not delivering what you're promising you're delivering.

All theatre has the capability to be immersive. But to be completely immersed as an audience, to lose the sense of time, of space; it's elements like these that need to be ticked in order for me to experience the work as immersive.

JI: I think the trend of immersive started with Punchdrunk – they did 'total immersion' really well early on, and they were pioneers; everyone tried to follow that format. That's created a certain kind of idea of what immersive is to lots of people, but I really think we need to break that down because is it immersive design, is it immersive interaction? You've got big companies showing a movie with a world that's loosely around it, or you've got younger companies trying to do a full immersive experience on a budget that just really can't tackle it – then the thing is you're creating a price point of 40, 50 pounds, which *seems* acceptable and is one of the things that brought me to immersive performance as an artist. Now we have different price banners, often starting at quite a high price ticket, going to an extremely high priced/VIP ticket, and when you get new audiences coming in and feeling dissatisfied – they've been burnt two or three times, because of that buzz word 'immersive'. You're creating an elitist audience rather than an inclusive company. We really need to break down what type of immersive different shows are. If immersive is going to become a recognized style of theatre, it needs to be broken down into what it can be because that's how all other genres of art and theatre have developed, existed and been fair to its audience.

JT: I think there's something in there and I agree with Joe on the difference between form and brand. The brand is what is currently being pushed and heralded. I think that it is becoming more elitist because the group is getting smaller and smaller at the top that can afford to stick to the immersive brand. They're going to continue pushing that branding – I've been quite unpopular in some of the ways in which I've expressed this – but I do think that there is space for that particular style of brand. I work in a lot of that, I make money off that side of the industry by using either management skills or build skills or sharing knowledge.

NS: /As a freelancer/

JT: /As a freelancer/

JT: /We are definitely not immersive, and I think we're very, very happy to not be that.

JB: But it's part of the broader creative cultural economy, isn't it? I do think it's very swiftly consolidating itself as an immersive industry.

JT: I love immersive shows, I love running around and being playful, but I am very much aware of where they're coming from and where they've been.

JB: And the cost as well, it's pricing lots of people out but even just getting hold of a ticket in the first place before they're just gone, regardless of the cost of them, is also a huge problem.

NS: From my perspective, there is also cultural capital that sits there as well as different kinds of exclusivity. Let's run around and have a great time, let's have some interesting and weird shit happening. Great, I'm on board. But I do think when there is that very polarized approach, and I think that's why audiences who go to see things like *Wolf of Wall Street* (2019), may not have gone to see SHUNT.[6] I consider ourselves to be interactive makers; there are immersive elements to our work. We do things that are held in common with immersive making, such as space, world-building elements of design, elements of technology, you know/

JT: /Structure. Training.

NS: /Structure, game play, playful elements, training. We can't deny that there are immersive elements but interactive is where we sit. Whether that's how we identify in marketing copy, probably not. Again, it's audience expectation.

JI: I was going to say, we invite people to immerse themselves in the world.

NS: Yeah. 'Immersive' is a really challenging term because it is seductive, it is fluid, it is unfixed, it can be whatever you want it to be and that means it's a slippery form that people keep trying to grasp. No matter where you go and how hard you try to hold on to it, there is an element of dissatisfaction. That's why people keep going back because they're searching, they are hunting down that thing, that seductive, charismatic, indescribable, intangible thing that makes it immersive, and often will be disappointed but will then be like, 'Well there's more!'.

JT: I also think in connection to that, that audiences want it to be what it was the first time they went. So, makers are constantly looking backwards trying to be the same as all it was ten years ago and actually what that means is that the brand of immersive isn't moving forward, it's just trying to be Punchdrunk.

JI: It's the super-fan isn't it; 'this isn't immersive. I know what immersive is', so immersive means something different to all of us.

NS: But it taps into the cult of the individual. Like, 'here is your tailormade experience, here is your thing'; therefore, it is a self-fulfilling prophecy that, in designing for an individual, it can't be meaningful for everyone. There is ultimately a refinement to be had, but also, I don't think people want a refinement of it. I think they just want to see it all and be a bit disappointed sometimes; then at other times feel like their life has been changed. For a lot of people that's what happens when you go to an immersive/interactive show, that they go and feel impacted and they're hunting that down, again and again – but it's an expensive risk.

JB: Our ticket prices are nothing compared to the ones in New York, for example for equivalent performances it is three or four times the price of what they are here. Right, I am going to pull all of these threads into the final question to ask you about advice. It's always tricky isn't it, but if you could give a piece of advice to emergent practitioners who want to make interactive work, what would you say to them?

JT: Buy a bigger sledgehammer, be braver and if you go around tapping walls like you're putting a picture frame up in a rented house, you're not going to find the radicalness, you're not going to look further forward. Take that sledgehammer and smash into the bathroom/

NS: /You're so destructive, Joe!/

JT: /I know I am. But it's that thing of not being scared to experiment, to be wrong and to learn, but you've got to take that risk. I saw you shaking your head I think; it just makes me lack confidence in what I'm saying. *(Laughing)*

NS: No, no, I'm not.

JT: Yeah, it's putting yourself out there; don't be afraid of being challenged and doing something difficult. But I think ultimately look for the question – not that you're interested in now – but what you think might be the question tomorrow and that's the socially activated interactive work that you maybe should be looking at.

AS: I come from a very specific point of view; the intimate-interactive form. So, for me I think when you are approaching this type of work, my advice would be, be willing to relinquish control, to expose parts of yourself, to let go of the fear and do not ask your audience to reveal things that you're not happy to reveal about yourself. I have loads of rules, loads of advice, but I think those are key, especially in interactive one-on-one work.

JI: Ask, 'Are you actually saying anything? Are you making entertainment or art, what is your subtext, what is the thing you're not talking about?' What are you posing to your audience members, to the people that are paying your bills? Are you showing them a good time? Because both of these things have their place, but don't get them confused, because that's what's happening a lot. People are putting on TV shows left, right and centre, or movies, and there is a space for that, but with this form, I think art can really question, really change people's motives. Talk about what you know.

NS: What's really interesting about all these pieces of advice is they all represent a lot of our work! My advice is, it's really important to engage in radical tenderness, radical generosity towards each other and towards your audiences. Create a brave space where that sledgehammer can fall but not hurt anyone. We are in a position in our society right now where without these discrete elements of care, bravery, a little bit of destruction, knowing what you want, who you are, what you're saying and doing it in a way that is generous and with love is so important. Because we are at quite a fundamental turning point in who we are as a society and my question is – Who do you want to be in that? Who do you want to be and what do you want to say? Really embracing the people that challenge you and who you find difficult and sometimes a bit abhorrent but embracing them too and doing it with care because ultimately, we, as makers and artists and as a group of individuals, are really challenged right now. Think hard about who you're reaching and why; are you just reaching one group of people or are you trying to reach beyond who you already know?

Notes

1 Liar's Poker is a betting game often associated with Wall Street traders. It involves wagering on the frequency of digits appearing in the serial numbers of US paper currency.
2 For three weeks in 2010, 2012 and 2013, Bush Theatre and Theatre Delicatessen held a 'bazaar' of audience-centric, theatrical experiences. Many different companies and artists offered small-scale performance experiences. Audiences could choose from the various 'stalls' and pay what they felt the experience was worth.
3 Established in 2009, Boomtown is a British music festival held annually near Winchester, Hampshire, on the Matterley Estate in South Downs National Park.
4 Theatre Souk is an experimental theatrical model first developed in 2010 by the London-based theatre company Theatre Delicatessen. It was conceived and curated by Jessica Brewster and co-produced by Roland Smith. The Theatre Souk model is that of a performance marketplace where emerging theatre companies showcase their more experimental work in an immersive theatrical environment governed by the principles of exchange and barter.
5 The Flypit is a performance venue housed in the historic and beautiful Stanley Halls and until recently was the home of The Lab Collective.
6 SHUNT is a theatre company that was established in 1998 by ten performance companies as a collective to explore interactive and immersive performance.

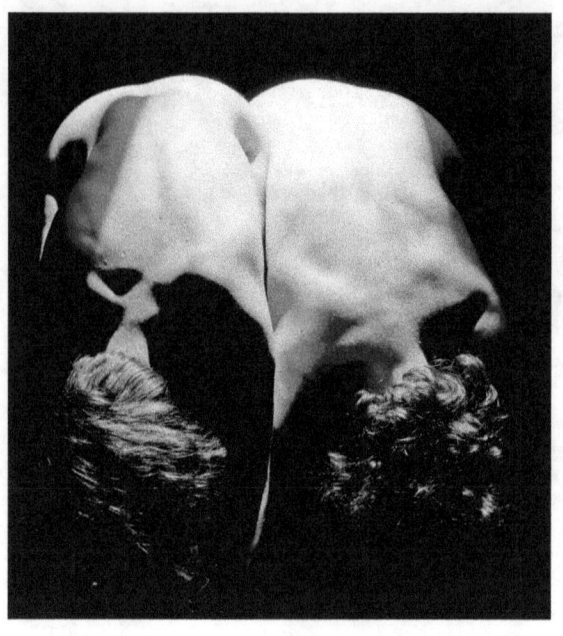

FIGURE 6 *Image details performers Billie Beckly and Ruth Cross of Meridian by Cross Collaborations at Battersea Arts Centre, 12 December 2014. Photographed by Camilla Greenwell.*

CHAPTER 5

Intimate encounters with Ruth Cross from Cross Collaborations

Speaker key:
JB: *Joanna Bucknall*
RC: *Ruth Cross*

[This conversation was recorded over Zoom on 23 June 2021.]

JB: Ruth, can we start at the beginning-*ish* by discussing *Post Present Future* (2009). It's become a defining project that you're well known for and it's been a big influence on the work of other artists in this field.

RC: *Post Present Future* (2009) I began in 2009, more than a decade ago. I never thought it would be such a longstanding project when I began it. It's a letter project where people write a letter to their future self. It began in Dartington College of Arts,[1] when I was graduating. Dartington College of Arts had just announced that they were going to close, so the staff and students in the college were mourning. There was a real sense of loss, as this very unique, very progressive learning environment, not just at Dartington but many of the other alternative arts institutions across the UK, and across the world were starting to close down. I felt like I wanted to find a way for people to really remember the uniqueness, this sense of creativity and exploration that grew out of these types of settings. That's where the seed of the idea came from, for people to write a letter in this moment that they would receive in five years' time: to remember the magic of Dartington College of Arts.

Maybe another thing to say is that simultaneously to these ideas, I was in a flea market, and I saw this beautiful writing desk, and it was 50 pounds. I didn't have 50 pounds. So, I said very confidently – I distinctly remember the moment – I said very confidently to the guy, 'I am going to pay you £10 for this writing desk'. He looked at me aghast, and then said, 'Okay.' I became this very proud owner of this really beautiful, antique writing desk, that from that moment on became the site of *Post Present Future* (2009). I've carried this writing desk with me in my car, up and down spiral staircases/

JB: /Which I'm assuming was heavy.

RC: Yeah. It was. There was a certain position that I used to carry it in, so I could manage it alone. It became an installation-based piece; the writing desk had all of these tiny drawers and little slots for the envelopes. I could pack the entire installation into the writing desk itself and then take it away to all of the different festivals or art centres, gallery spaces that I/

JB: /Where was the first place that you carried it to?

RC: The first place that I took it after Dartington was the Battersea Arts Centre in London.

JB: Which is where I came across it – that's the first time – which is the one-on-one festivals that they did, which must have been around 2009/2010.

RC: I did it in the Battersea Arts Centre several times; in fact, I celebrated posting the first ever batch of letters after five-year by creating a retrospective of the project in the Battersea Arts Centre, so that must've been 2014 that I took over one of the rooms. I did an exhibition of letters and several letter readings and performances. Then we went to a promenade walk from the Battersea Arts Centre to the closest post box (which happened to be in Asda!) with all of the audience and did a very celebratory 'post back'.

JB: Must've been incredible, that first moment when everything was being posted out rather than just coming in. It's been one of those projects that's been going for more than a decade now, and it wasn't something that you anticipated. What do you think gives it such longevity? Why do you think it's a project that's continued its life way beyond what you anticipated?

RC: I need to give some thanks to the Battersea Arts Centre, as a place where young artists and makers can develop work. I feel like that was a real springboard. Because while I was there, the very first time doing this project, many producers and festival organizers were there also and came to write a letter. There are many layers really; one aspect of the project is that I had a conversation with people before they wrote. I introduced the invitation of sitting down at this writing desk and having some time to think about what it might be that you want to receive. What would you write in a letter to yourself that you knew you were going to receive in five years' time? I think the provocation itself; people find very curious. I would have a conversation with each person, I saw it as a piece of dialogical art. I've had thousands and thousands of conversations with individuals across Europe. From meeting a few different festival producers, I got invited to the next place and invited to the next place. I've never actually applied to take it anywhere, it's always been this project that people say, 'Oh, yes, *Post Present Future* (2009), you want that in the opening of this gallery or in this festival.' There is something about just going back to the conversation, I think that there's so many intimate and quite unique experiences that happen along the project. The festival, this conversation with a stranger– I was so privileged. I feel like it's really shaped me as an artist to have these conversations with people.

It was a huge one-on-one performance in a way for me to meet and step into the lives of all these people, to meet so many strangers in quite an intimate way. Because they also, at that time, were reflecting on what their hopes, fears, dreams are, what they might want to write; they're preparing. Then they sit down at the desk, and they see the red-embossed writing desk pad, and they can choose which type of pen and what envelope, and the colour of the paper that they want to write on. So, all these details, the aesthetics, I feel were very important. And then they would write a letter to themselves.

Some people would take ten minutes, other people several hours. And then they would post it into a little post box that I would carry around with me. Obviously, there's this very intimate experience; when the letter arrives five years later, people are very sort of taken aback: 'This is my handwriting on an envelope.' That's another one-on-one performance, that happens with you and you. You receive this and then start to realize, 'Oh, it's a letter that I wrote to myself!' I just imagine people; they're making a cup of tea and sitting in their favourite chair or going for a walk maybe and finding a bench that they like to sit on or somewhere that they feel it's special for them and opening this letter that they've written to themselves.

JB: I got it sent to my mum's house because I know that she wouldn't move around in the way that I do. One of the times that I visited my mum, she's like, 'A letter came for you but it's your handwriting'. And I really remember that moment, taking it off her and scurrying off to find a space to be by myself. Because as soon as I saw it, I remembered but I hadn't thought about it much since I'd posted it and left it behind. When it arrived, it was this little moment of joy. A really intimate experience but with the self. How do you prepare for those conversations? Do you have a structure or a process that you go through, or do you just respond in the moment to the different people that you encounter?

RC: Over the years my process has evolved. I found it an incredibly humbling experience. I'm quite intuitive anyway and I see it as, I see the conversation as art. The conversation feels like a dialogical or a socially engaged experience, the conversation itself.

JB: That's a political act in itself, isn't it? It's a choice to have a dialogic exchange rather than having a transmissible exchange which is the usual in theatre. I think even that decision to do that is charged; it is potentially transformative and potentially radical because of those things.

RC: At one point, I experimented with writing instructions. It felt dead I have to say; it deadened the experience. There is something about having a quite intimate conversation with a stranger and then sitting on this writing desk knowing that thousands of other people have also sat down at that writing desk. All of that is the preparation for writing. Sometimes people said, 'Oh, why don't you develop a website where people could just write? It would be so much easier, you wouldn't have to have thousands of stamps, you wouldn't have to store all the letters somewhere. People could just write an email to themselves and then the programme can send it back to them five years on?' There is something in me that was like, oh, I'm so interested in spaces where we can counter the capitalization that is so often happening with this kind of immersive or intimate experience. Yes, we could do it online but then everything is happening online, even our bills don't arrive to us anymore through the letterbox, they come online.

I love that there in the UK, the post office, or here in Spain where I live now, Correos,[2] I love that you can put a stamp on an envelope, you post it. Then it gets touched by so many people on this chain; it goes on its own experiential performance. And then it's always struck me as such a magic process when that actually arrives in the post box of the person who's receiving it. I love writing letters anyway, the art of writing letters in my day-to-day life, so there is something about really focusing on gifting that. It felt like a gift. It's a gift to other people so that they could take a moment in time to gift to themselves. I saw myself enabling people to take part in a time capsule project but allowing them to give the gift to themselves, facilitating that process somehow.

JB: There's a generosity there. I used to write a lot of letters because I was at boarding school when I was little and my parents lived in another country, so did all my friends, and so letter writing was a really big part of my childhood. Then with one of my very good friends, when I went off to university, we were both in different places, so we used to write each other letters every week, but we'd include tapes. We used to record both sides of a cassette for each other and that would go in with the letter. There's a real joy and something really generous about receiving that hand-crafted *thing*. There's a generosity of time, of giving that and in receiving that. Something very intimate and beautiful about that. That's maybe something that the project taps into because we don't have that in our daily lives; I think the art of letter writing is something that has very much slipped out of general cultural practice and so I think there's something very incredible about that.

RC: The quality of presence and the attention to what is being written changes. If people were invited to write an email to themselves, there's a real sense that you can delete a part, you can copy and paste something; if you can't remember how to spell something, you look it up online. When you're sat with a pen in your hands and a piece of paper, it creates attention to detail. I got so curious about what people were writing, the scenes that came up in a moment and how people wrote. The pressure that they were pushing on to the paper or whether they drew little details in the margins or they put arrows from one part to another, or underline something. There is something about the quality of writing that changes as well, and the detail is very alive as a process. You asked me before if I prepared about speaking with people; and I have this memory of a moment where I met a young boy who really wanted to write and I was going through a very basic explanation of the project, and he said, 'Great. Oh, it's a bit like my diary project that I write to myself every day, I've got'. I was totally taken aback by my own judgement that he needed it explained in a particular way but instead he was so accustomed to the idea of writing to himself. Going to the other extreme, I spoke to an older woman who must have been in her late eighties. She was questioning whether she would still be around in five years' time to receive the letter. She sat down to write and afterwards she said to me, 'It was so hard to write'. 'Because of this concern?'. I asked. 'No, no, it was hard for me to hold a pen. I'm so used to typing.' This is why it was humbling because it helped me to notice the kind of prejudice or the interpretations that I was making on other people; it was almost like I would sense energetically how the other person was responding and what sort of information that they needed rather than by what they were wearing, their age, how they were dressed. It helped me as an individual. It probably prepared me for some of the work that I would make later around migration, seeing and stepping into the life of other people; it was a real preparation for me.

JB: You made a documentary about the experience and did get to hand-deliver some of the letters, to experience that intimate moment of receiving themselves.

RC: In 2012, I was invited to a Theater Aan Zee,[3] a city-wide festival in Ostend, Belgium. I didn't actually take my own writing desk with me, but I sent very specific descriptions of the writing desk and we went to find one in Belgium. In 2012 I collected letters, and the writing desk was on the end of a pier looking out over the harbour. It was a very beautiful setting. The festival happened all over the city of Ostend with lots of different kinds of pop-up or walkabout performances, and installations. Five years later, in 2017, I was contacted again by the festival and invited to do something to celebrate the five years of the posting back. I decided to collaborate with filmmaker Ayla van Kessel, to make a film of hand delivering – like you said, going and knocking on the doors of the people in Ostend who had written a letter five years earlier.

It was an incredible experience because it really enabled me to witness this moment of people reading their letter if they were willing to. Some people didn't want to but lots of people did. I am often surprised by how open people are to share something very intimate. People would invite us into their houses and make us a cup of tea or a cup of coffee. I would have a conversation with them so that they would feel relaxed and ready for Ayla to put the camera on.

One moment stands out from that whole experience; it was tremendously moving. The experience, in a particular house, when we knocked on the door and a woman welcomed us in, and we had two letters for that address. One for her and one for her husband. And since 2012, her husband had died, and we said, 'Please don't feel like you need to read this out loud, it's such a powerful, intimate, very vulnerable thing'. And she said, 'No, no, I'm really happy. I'm really happy to. It would be a pleasure to read it out loud.' First of all, she read her own letter. Her daughter was there; I remember her daughter. She was in her late fifties I would say or early in her sixties. And her daughter in her twenties was crying already when her mum read her letter. And we were all crying actually. And then she opened her husband's letter; it was a very short letter. But so much in it. He wrote about how happy he was to be on the end of the pier, watching his grandkids jumping off the pier like he used to do in this very place where the writing desk just so happened to be, that he used to do as he was a child, jumping off the pier. And he felt that he had so much love for this place. Some of his favourite memories were swimming there as a child, so to watch his grandkids he felt like he'd come a full circle. He wrote a line as well saying, 'If by chance I'm not here in five years' time, I want you to know that I love you so much, my dear family.' And then she closed the letter and slowly explained that exactly on that pier where the letter project had happened was where they scattered his ashes.

We were all in tears. But this type of thing has happened many times within this project because often people are together with their loved ones or they're writing about a parent who's ill and then who isn't there.

I also had an experience of two people who had written their letters to each other; the man had written, 'In five years' time I want to be marrying you.' And then four years and a half after this, he'd remembered that he'd written that in his letter and he contacted me saying, 'I know it's slightly early, but could you send me our two letters because I really want to, on our wedding day, just after we get married, give her the letters that we wrote together. To show that, look, we did it in five years and now we're here married.' And that was beautiful as well because he sent me photos of them opening their letters on their wedding day.

And other times it's very mundane what people write, which holds its own significance. The key themes that have come out often are family. It comes up in a lot of letters, people writing about yearning for home, yearning for belonging. Like discomfort in sense of self or place. Belonging, family and place comes up a lot.

Often people write something that's very touching, something to themselves, that maybe they wouldn't necessarily say out loud, a sort of secret like a personal sort of motivation. 'For all your faults I love you and I'm very proud of you.' But, often it's kind of like a criticism and then a compliment; we're used to signing off a letter to a friend or to a loved one, we put how much we love them, but to ourselves it's much more vulnerable to say that.

JB: Not having consistent support for the project, how do you practically facilitate it? That's a lot of responsibility, to hold those letters, especially when they keep building up a well because a project is ongoing, do you have help?

RC: I do and I wouldn't be able to do it if I didn't. I wanted to say a big thank you to my mum. I moved to Spain six years ago and have been living between the UK and Spain, making work in the UK and making work in Spain. It is impossible to travel between two countries with 5,000 letters, and it was a big responsibility. I take it very seriously – I have to say – the responsibility of making sure that these very precious items get delivered successfully. My mum is kind of a secret artist. She's an amazing woman, I am very grateful that she offered to help me. We've put all of the letters in plastic boxes so they can stay safe over five years. They're in her house. We've got a 'post back' plan, we have to be very organized because if not it becomes chaos. Cross Collaborations, quite literally in this case, is me collaborating with my mum. I'm very grateful for that support.

In terms of finance, each time I do the project in the different festivals or theatre spaces, I would ask for the price of stamps. People would commission me so I'd get a fee to do the installation, they will pay for my time to be there and then also the extra of the price of stamps. It's interesting because sometimes I've had to make up the difference of the cost. I've had to find ways to find funding from other projects to cover the cost of stamps.

After a few years of running *Post Present Future* (2009), I got so curious about what was inside the letters that I added in another element which was if people wanted to leave their envelope unsealed then they could do, which gave us, Cross Collaborations, permission to read their letter, to make a scan of it and to work with it as a creative stimulus. In another strand of the project, we made a performance in the Barbican Theatre in Plymouth in 2011, and also in a space called the Fire Station in Bristol in 2011, which were immersive theatre performances where audience members went in one at a time to different rooms and they would meet a character that was created from a letter. In each room you stepped into the life of a stranger that was represented by one of the performers that I'd work with to create these immersive worlds based on the content of letters. That was another way sometimes, that I could get funding to support the core project.

There's been all of these different strands and it's helped me to find a way of seeing this as a more integrative project; I've been able to use many different mediums or creative ways of exploring.

JB: Dialogical exchange is something that runs across all of the work that you make. I wanted to talk a little bit about another very impactful project which was *Meridian* (2014/2015).[4]

RC: *Meridian* (2014/2015) was an immersive performance piece that I made in 2014 and 2015. It was originally commissioned by Theatre Deli, and it was first viewed in a one-on-one performance festival in the ex-BBC studios on Marylebone high street in London. I had some initial ideas about the threads of what I was interested in exploring. I worked with artists and makers, Megan Nash, Billy Beckley and Annabie Daly to create the original performance and we got some more Arts Council England funding to develop it at the Battersea Arts Centre in 2015. Then toured it to a few different festivals including Latitude Festival in summer 2015. In each iteration, I worked with a few different artists and makers, but they were their core group that were part of the devising process with me.

JB: Can you talk a little bit about some of the threads that you wanted to explore like touch, intimacy and engagement?

RC: There were three main threads that went into the creation of the performance. I was interested in exploring how they would sit together. The first, like you say, was around touch. At that time, I was studying Shiatsu, which is holistic massage based on the five elements of Chinese medicine. Meridians are lines that run through the body, Shiatsu practices work with Meridian lines. There is a sense of gaining rebalance in the body through being in contact, so it heals and realigns the body, both physically, emotionally, spiritually. I was very interested in working with Shiatsu as an artist and the power of touch. It's quite taboo, touch, in society. But there's so much potential for transformation that happens through touch. Touch is something that is really based on a sense of creating a space of care. This piece was full of ethical considerations.

The second was the ecology of the body and linking that with the ecology of nature. I became fascinated by the body as a metaphor, the human body as a metaphor for the earth body. Those over millions of years, we come from the earth and we go back to the earth, the way the components of the body are made of materials that come from the earth. If we think about sedimentary rock that is deep within the earth, it's made up of bones, decompressed bones, so, I was really interested in looking at the metaphor of the skin of the body being the soil which is the skin of the earth and exploring how we can create a sense of ecological awareness through giving this sense of the ecological components of the human body.

The third links with some of the environmental activism work that I was doing at the time, so this was another strand. I was very influenced by Joanna Macy,[5] who's an eco-feminist environmental activist. She's been working, for many decades, in the US, focusing on opening and creating spaces where people can touch the vulnerability and love of this incredible planet that we live on. To connect people in this space with a deep sense of love and care, so that we can make more courageous ecological choices on how we move forward as societies. I am really touched and very motivated by her work. So that was another strand that was coming into I guess the ecological aspect but also thinking about human choice and that we are responsible for the choices that we make both in our own lives and as a society.

The final influence was a book called Fugitive Pieces by Canadian writer Anne Michaels (Michaels 2009). This book has stayed with me for many years; I found it incredibly haunting and metaphorical, very poetic. She's a poet as well, so the book feels like reading poetry. And within the book, it explores the themes of the holocaust and collective grief, but the main character is an archaeologist, so he's really fascinated in archaeology and geology. And so, all the way through the book, there's a digging into the underneath of the personal histories of the individual characters and a digging into the rock of the earth. That metaphor of entwining the earth history and our body history was so present in the book, looking at this intrinsic connection to place. We can never take ourselves away from where we come, we return back to the earth.

JB: I thought that really actually came through and it's one of the performance moments in my life that has stuck with me because I was so deeply perturbed by not recognizing the sensation of soil beneath my feet. Once I realized that's what I was experiencing. It's something that's haunted me, since that experience at Battersea Arts Centre and makes me stop and take account of things that I find touching my senses or touching me. I will take longer now if somewhere smells incredible or there's something I want to touch or I want to just remember, hold on to that moment, so that I can remember or recall that sensation later, back into my body. That troubling has changed my daily practices. For me it's a performance that I cherish. During that performance, I felt very cared for, and I think care, that duty of care is something that is really strong in your work. Did you have any difficulty in terms of sustainability? Having three or four performers and one audience member is a difficult financial model as well, isn't it? So, did you encounter any kind of push back against that from producers or venues or did you find that you could use that reputation you have to dissolve some of those anxieties I'm sure producers must have expressed?

RC: Yeah. Yeah, yeah, very much. Yeah! There were lots of questions from producers about the number of people involved, and the length of time because the performance lasted forty-five minutes, more or less. I think each iteration it had a slightly different timing, but that's forty-five minutes with four performers and one audience member. There were also concerns about the amount of people who would be able to come to experience the performance. When producers would experience the work, they would come out and understand why it needed to take so long and why there needs to be four or five performers because we literally, you know, we worked.

Maybe just to explain a bit about that. The person started blindfolded, the room was full of sand or full of soil, depending on which edition of *Meridian* (2014/2015). We would lie people down so we needed four people because we would support the weight of this human body. We would bury their body in sand, and then dig them out slowly.

Talk about immersive work, they're immersed literally, buried in sand! This morning I found my comments book, and it made me cry when I was reading through it, when I read some of the things that people have written and it makes me want to defend how important it is if you've got an idea and you think that it's worth doing even though it doesn't make financial sense, it's so incredibly important to keep going. Find cracks; find ways of doing things creatively because the feedback that we had for this performance was just exceptional. People said that they've never experienced anything like it. How could they have because it's such a rare gift; there was text in it; there was lots of song and humming; it was incredibly experiential. We didn't try to convey a storyline so much. It was much more about the individual coming into this space of deep care, deep connection, and then their personal history, their own sense of body, their own sense of their skin and their sensations of the body, the images from their memories that were going on inside them, that was the performance. We were just giving the sense of their skin being the semipermeable container, the membrane of the body, the weight of the sand and then these lines that we took from the *Fugitive Pieces* (Michaels 2009) that helped just to create that sense of layering of body going back into the earth.

Lots of people wrote about this experience of dying but without being in pain, of feeling so cared for that it felt familiar and completely ancestral at the same time. And of course, we couldn't create that with one performer.

I'm quite feisty in that way, if I have a vision and an idea, and we explore it, and if it feels like it's working, I'm happy to defend the artistic and the experiential because I do think it's a gift.

JB: I genuinely believe that using these kinds of approaches to create experiences that you put someone inside of or that you give them even just the space to think about their bodies or to think about their connection to something or to someone or to an idea, is far more powerful, transformative and potentially radical because of that. It's a potential tool for changing behaviours. This is probably the most powerful way that we could do that but again it's very slow, isn't it, because it has to be done with care, and it has to be done in intimate and considered ways. That slow, gentle change can have a huge impact, even if it's one person at a time.

RC: I have a real sense in me as a maker and as a practitioner around the need for art activism and change making being political. Being political not in terms of party politics but acknowledging that the way in which I live my life, the decisions that I make are contributing to change. We're constantly contributing to and shaping how our society is created. For me there's a responsibility within that as a maker to think about what is the work that I'm creating, actually *doing*, and how can that have an influence to give people the experiences either of stepping into, embodying and being with the lives of others. It's allowing people to have a sense of themselves as, you know, the human body and being human, as an essential part of the ecology that we live within. I'm not expecting there to be grand changes that are created from this, but I feel like my life decisions and the way that I live has been informed by the performance work that I've seen and experienced and particularly intimate one-on-one performances, where I feel like I've changed on a cellular level by the experiences that I've had. It's an experiential shifting of understanding ourselves in a more embodied way, in a more animalistic way, and I'm very interested in the power of that.

JB: I have a toddler and so he will also experience me, now taking more time to notice things and to feel things, and to be inside things because whenever he's with me I do that, and so I hope for that sort of more mindful practice, I think it's passed to him too, and that he takes the time to think and to stop, and to feel, and to be in, and to acknowledge and recognize, and let things sort of wash over him. It's not a huge or instant change but there's that potential for exponential transference because it's not a shift in thinking, it's a shift in being; it's a gentle recalibration.

RC: Oh, I mean, I love this quote. I think it's Gandhi: 'be the change we want to see in the world'. This is something that I've always been interested in. This kind of slow and gentle, full of care, recalibration, is allowing a kind of opening, it's like Shiatsu, touch is realigning the body so that it can be more attuned to the world that it's inhabiting. It uses the five elements: earth, fire, metal, wind and wood, as a way of helping the body to understand how it's imbalanced in any one of these so that everything is interrelated to each other. It's the same with the way that social change happens. Everything is interrelated. What I'm interested in is acknowledging our connection to where we come from and not considering the human experience as separate from or living above the earth that we are inhabiting. *Meridian* (2014/2015) was my way of being able to make sense of some of these things, like what happens when we try to slow down and connect more, and how can we create performance that offers others the experience to do exactly that?

JB: There are some key concepts that cut across all of the work that you make, and I was hoping we could dig into some of the more holistic aspects such as the work that you've done with the Schumacher College[6] because I know that's played a massive role in the direction that your work has taken and some of the ideas that are woven underneath that.

RC: I spent a year in Schumacher College, Devon, UK in 2013/14, and it was a deeply transformative time for me. I had just come off the back of spending four years working as a producer in Falmouth University, and I became really interested in the restrictions that I was experiencing in Falmouth as I was organizing work with students. I did a Post Graduate Certificate in Higher Education in 2012 and I became really curious about communities of practice. Always throughout my life, I've been interested in how change happens, so this has been a reoccurring question. But I came to this point where I was getting really frustrated with reductionist thinking and rigid structural limitations, being contained. I was seeing within communities of practice, a way of organizing where things were emerging seemingly out of nowhere, but it was emerging out of this space that was being co-created between all of us, taking part and participating. This sense of participation has been a really key question. I was full of frustration and lots of questions, when I arrived at Schumacher, with this real sense of being in a place that was a leading voice in holistic science. Very connected to Gaia Theory,[7] connected to looking at exploring complexity and living systems.

I went like a sponge to absorb and experience another more alternative way of thinking about how change happens. During this time, I learned a lot, about moving from this more linear, transactional way of thinking about systems and how systems occur in the world – to looking at living systems and looking at how nature works. How does it work in terms of the ecology of water systems for example? That there's constant movement in nature, and constant iterations in terms of how a fern unfolds, the pattern of how the original part of the fern is continually recreated in every other part of how the fern evolves and grows. That sense of looking at how everything is contained within the seed of itself. Through this time of exploring concepts such as radical amazement:[8] I remember being in the Schumacher kitchen and cooking for hundreds of people, slicing a cabbage or a broccoli in half and then just standing, just seeing all of the fractal patterns that exist in a broccoli, all of this amazing, intricate interweaving lines that happen in a red cabbage for example. Staring at it, and feeling, this *is* radical amazement. Just being with and seeing, somehow being moved, allowing myself internally to be moved with what I was experiencing.

I'm considering how performance can be a vehicle for talking about natural systems and complexity; how things relate to each other. During my experiences, I became very curious in this connection with living systems in the natural world and using performance as a way to bridge that into how social movements form, how social systems form. To think about how to create these ongoing immersive and transformative learning experiences, where people could connect in with, both the holistic science and living systems, and use performance as a bridge to bring that into an understanding of social change and how change happens in the world.

JB: Could you talk a little bit about how that experience at Schumacher College has shaped the ethics that have driven the work you've made, well, I'd say work, in the very broadest sense of the word, but in the interventions that you have devised since then?

RC: I'm working towards a fellowship with the Schumacher Society Research in Action community, so for the next four years, I'll be working in this very reflexive way, looking at my performance making, looking at living and social systems. For me the thing that I'm really interested in, in terms of ethics, is looking at how things are occurring in the world. A question that I return to often is 'whose reality counts?' This is something that expands very much into the work that I'm doing now with migration. There's a sensibility of being able to look at the plurality of lives that are being lived concurrently in any one given context. Being able to take the time, and that's the thing, it does take time – to really see, reflect, explore and listen to all of the threads of what's going on, and how change is happening or how action or organizing occurs. For me that's essential, when we're talking about the ethics of a piece of work regardless of the scale or kind of project. When voices, and ways of being, are excluded, or aren't considered in the 'making of' this is often related to the need to decolonize our thinking. Whether it's in terms of a local community project, or international development. For example, when European development projects take place in a country that once was colonized, and still to this day take colonial ways of thinking into their work, they often don't see the ways in which they are really intervening i.e. perpetuating colonialism. I want to bring these learnings about ethics back into the way that I work performatively because I think that these ethical considerations of being able to make work that speaks to not just white, cis, middle-aged men strengthening a particular patriarchal paradigm; it's almost given that this is *the way*, because so much of the way that performance is made and has been written about backs up this particular experience.

We need to remember that this 'particular experience' is a particular experience – and not 'the only experience'. The often-marginalized voices of people of colour, LGTBQI+ people, disabled people, people with a migrant or refugee background. If we don't give voice to, no, it's not even '*giving voice*' – this is not way to say it – it's almost like if there's not an acknowledgement and space allowed for all of these diversities of experience to be shared, then we're recreating, continually recreating this dominant culture. There's something for me, in the work that I'm doing in terms of looking at a diversity and racial justice; it's about working slowly; it's about listening and about considering whose voice is missing. What do I need to do as a white woman; where are my blind spots? There's a lot of self-reflexivity that's happening within the work that I'm interested in making.

JB: You currently work with marginalized communities and have been exploring migration, migration routes, and that work isn't necessarily performance work, is it, per se?

RC: While I was in Schumacher, I met the love of my life, my life partner and long-term collaborator since this point; she is Spanish, hence my connection now to working in Spain, María Llanos del Corral. She's got a background in international development, and I've got my background in performance making, in the arts. We came together with this sense of wanting to really explore how we can recreate some of these very transformative experiences. What we decided was that we wanted to try to bring this type of multidisciplinary practice that looked at deeply transformative, personal work that would also lead to deeply transformative social change or social action around social justice and environmental issues – using her skills in social organizing and mine in social arts.

Through the *Eroles Project*,[9] a learning for action space that we set up with other collaborators in 2015, we ran annual change-maker residencies, to explore and take action around 'big systemic questions' reflexively and creatively, in community. In 2016, we focused on 'Borders'. We spent three weeks living and working as a community of migrants, a woman who had worked in the UNHCR[10] all of her life writing communication on a UN level. We were joined by quite radical and anti-borders activists, scholars, artists and a Jesuit priest. Sixteen of us came together to share these different threads of ways into understanding migration: experiences, causes, integration and asylum processes, border politics, migration routes. All of this background research and collaboration which is very true of all of the other projects. For example, in *Meridian* (2014/2015), there is a lot of research that was drawn from very different practices or experiences, so this is I think something that I've brought into this other work which isn't necessarily performative. During 2016/17, we worked collaboratively to develop the vision created during this *Eroles Project* residency into Asociación La Bolina[11] based in El Valle close to Granada in the South of Spain. The project is a small-scale response to some of the biggest social, humanitarian and environmental challenges of our times such as food systems, migration and depopulation.

Villages that are depopulating, which is happening, it's true of where we're living in Spain, it's true of as we were talking about earlier, true of many countries across the world. Another phenomenon is that there's more and more people migrating into Spain, particularly from sub-Saharan Africa. Often people are arriving because of the way that state and border policy is at the moment, the legislation means that these people can't access legal work very easily, and so often are forced into irregular farm work growing in these mass greenhouses in Almería, called the *plastic sea*.[12] La Bolina is trying to create an alternative to this way of working, so people are working in ecological, agro ecology, in permaculture and getting a fair wage, working with dignified conditions where they're able to contribute to local development and intercultural activities.

Currently, I'm working on an art activism, film and immersive performance project in collaboration with artists from a migrant and refugee background to make visible what goes on underneath the plastic sea. We've been developing an anti-tour of the area. I'm very excited about the potential of what might come next. I've also been creating performance work with migrants, refugees and local people, that draws on Social Theatre and Theatre of the Oppressed (Boal 1985), exploring experiences of migration and belonging it's in the process that we get to be immersed in the lives of others. Through song, through storytelling, through dancing, through movement, and for me I've come to think this is theatre at its best. Because it's really engaging with the core questions of what it is to be human. I'm much more interested in making work for those who wouldn't have access to a theatre and making work with people who don't necessarily consider themselves as creative or a theatre maker. Often because people are speaking four or five different languages, Arabic, French, Spanish, English, Wolof, many different African languages. Though we have many translators that support the ongoing rehearsals and performance making, I really love using much more physical and embodied performance. It also allows a space for the people who are sharing their stories of migration, of being for weeks, waiting for the smugglers to tell them that they can get on the boat, who were trapped as slaves in Libya for years, who came across the channel, holding on to the underneath of a lorry, that they can share these experiences but using their body. This is the process that I've been using as a way of creating immersive performance journeys that then with an audience, we would move between in the different physical locations of a space, indoors, outdoors, following the performers – as if we ourselves are migrating with them.

We perform in village squares, and as an immersive walkabout performance at the social centre in the city of Granada.

JB: How have you been able to financially facilitate working in this way? Like you said it's slow, it's time consuming, it's very multidisciplinary, interdisciplinary as well, it doesn't really fall neatly within specific categories and I should think evades some types of arts funding. So how have you been able to make this happen?

RC: I've had to be creative and very strategic in the way that I've funded all of this work, in in a way it suffers because it falls in the gaps between many different kinds of funding criteria. But it also meant that I've been able to strengthen certain parts of the work to apply for funding that isn't coming from the arts because I think the work touches on so many things from environmental change to local community development through to intercultural, intergenerational work. There's been pockets of funding that I've been able to access, that are not arts based but they love the fact that art is being used as a way in, to talk about local community development for example. It's very inviting for people who are thinking about local community development to receive an application that's saying we're going to put on a theatre festival; it's going to be with migrants and refugees, sharing stories, local people are also involved. We're also going to be doing intergenerational work. I've had to get skilled at weaving in the different strands. Also, as a facilitator of these transformative educational programmes, we receive funding from the EU, so that's another way that it's enabled me.

JB: You've mentioned the word a few times. How do you feel about the term 'immersive'?

RC: I'm interested in unhooking, the word 'immersive' from immersive theatre and exploring what immersive is and immersion means. For me, I'm fascinated by immersive experiences. That would be particularly when there's a sense of real presence and a sense of a liveness and being enveloped in a particular experience. That could happen when we're reading a book, when we're watching a film, when we're on a walk-in nature, swimming in the sea – I think it happens in our daily life all the time. We find ourselves completely contained by, and stimulated by, and enlivened by, a particular moment. I'm fascinated in harnessing and working with these moments, so when people receive the letter, they're invited into this particular world, and they can have this connection with themselves. I'm really interested in experience, in the experiential, and so I would say maybe, I think the word 'immersive theatre' then has another layer of connotation. I find it very useful to orientate people, to say that I'm an immersive theatre maker. However, I think that I'm much more interested in going into the phenomenology, going into the experience of what's really going on in each piece to talk about my work in a way that gives more colour and more flavour, sort of distinct. Immersive theatre has the risk of being understood as a particular aesthetic and that it has a quite loaded way of working. I don't feel like my work that I create is associated with that.

JB: My current thinking is very similar to yours, it's the theatre, the immersive theatre, that can become reductive and a very particular container that has very particular expectations from audiences, from producers, from venues and culturally. The cultural currency of immersive theatre, it has a very particular face I think at the moment across the Anglo kind of speaking world.

RC: Yeah. With that Anglo-speaking world, there's something; this also came up in the dialogue that we had during the round table, that when we think traditionally about original theatre, about how people were coming together in their communities to/

JB: /Drink, dance, sing/
RC: /Storytelling, protest even. All the ways that protest has been used or coming – yeah, coming together to watch, you know, it's a bit grotesque, but coming together as communities to watch/
JB: /Hangings, beheadings? /
RC: Yeah. Community events or parades. I think these are true, not just the history of Britain and how theatre has kind of developed but across the world. Looking at ritual spaces and ceremony, how people participated in the retelling of the ancient tradition through the storytelling or through the participation in recreating these, yeah, these events and these rituals. That's immersive; that is the original form of immersive theatre. It's the original theatre. The fact that we went through so many years of people sat down, being separated from theatre.
JB: It was really the Victorians who did that to theatre, put it in this strange little glass cabinet, where it said, 'This is art, and this is where you observe the art'. Whereas the lineage of immersive goes back to the origins of theatre and it's really about coming together. That's what's exciting, that is what is at the heart of immersive. And I wonder if immersive theatre is what stifles that? But it's so interesting because every single person I speak to has issues rubbing up against that or fully accepting that. You can hear it in the roundtable discussion, everyone's collected under this fascination with this thing, which is actually coming together, the coming together of people to participate in an experience. Everyone has spoken, to some extent about that being the driving force in some ways of immersive performance making.
RC: There's a distinction, like the risk that's involved, the participation that's involved, the sense of belonging, the sense of togetherness, like you're saying, that stepping into either a fictitious or a speculative world. That these things invite us to become a character in a book; we dive in, and we can try on clothes; we can try on what it is to live another life. I guess my interest is creating those experiences where people can go, understand beyond their own limited habiting of what it is to be human in their particular context. But there's something about being invited on a journey, a physical journey when I'm participating, that I think has so much aliveness and so much potential. I feel quite fiercely, kind of adamant that we need

this word to stay broad and to stay pure and not reduce to one particular aesthetic. It needs to have different pluralities and strands available within it.

JB: What advice would you give to an emerging practitioner who wants to make work like you do, that is socially engaged, that is about experience and that has an ethics that really drives it forward? I know there are probably a hundred of pieces of advice you'd like to give but what solid piece of advice would you offer to them?

RC: The first one is, listen. For me this is crucial. Listening is such a gift in all areas of life to be able to really take the time to listen to someone else's experience and to use listening to transform ourselves, to reflect ourselves and then to gain a larger sense of what's possible. I think listening is really the key, to letting go of our assumptions of what we think we need to be doing and to open ourselves to be vulnerable and to be humane, and to listen, to be humbled by the world around us, because it makes us much more sensitive and much better at what we do.

The second would be about collaboration, for me it is essential to find support when we need it, to network, to be able to feel you're not alone. I've struggled a lot with being, feeling 'outsided', by the fact that I don't neatly fit into any one particular category. For those of you who are working in post-disciplinary, interdisciplinary and then liminal spaces between practices, find people to collaborate with, to have conversations, to find support and really, really feeling you are not alone. Even if you, you know, going out into nature and lying and being held by the heartbeat of the earth is a way of feeling a sense of a much wider connection.

Notes

1 Dartington College of Arts was a specialist educational institution near Totnes in Devon, southwest England, offering performative and multidisciplinary approach to the arts (1961–2010).
2 Correos is the Spanish equivalent of the UK's post office.
3 Theatre by the Sea – Theater Aan Zee or TAZ for short – is an annual ten-day multidisciplinary arts festival that takes place in midsummer in a range of extraordinary locations in and around Ostend, Belgium.

4 *Meridian* (2014/15) is a bespoke half-hour performance experience for one audience at a time by Cross Collaborations. Complete darkness. You lie encased in the landscape, experiencing your own body's intricate physiology and inner sensations. Then slowly the earth beneath you begins to shift away, your body falls. You find yourself enveloped by the vibrations of singing bodies wrapped in your arms. You arrive in the present, suspended in the fragile balance between ancestry and future generations. *Meridian* grew from a desire to reconnect the ecology of human body with the earth body.
5 Joanna Macy, author and teacher, is a scholar of Buddhism, systems thinking and deep ecology. A respected voice in movements for peace, justice and ecology, she interweaves her scholarship with learnings from six decades of activism. https://www.joannamacy.net
6 Schumacher College, near Totnes, Devon, was co-founded in 1990 by Satish Kumar. The first visiting teacher was Sir James Lovelock, best known for proposing the Gaia Hypothesis. The founders were inspired by E.F. Schumacher, the economist, environmentalist and development educator and the author of *Small Is Beautiful*. Schumacher College runs holistic education courses for people concerned with issues around ecology and sustainability, in which 'students are encouraged to develop a deep, participatory relationship with nature'.
7 Gaia Theory proposes that living organisms interact with their inorganic surroundings on Earth to form a synergistic and self-regulating, complex system that helps to maintain and perpetuate the conditions for life on the planet.
8 Abraham Joshua Heschel wrote about wonder as a state of mind that leads to radical amazement and gratitude.
9 Eroles Project co-founded in 2015 (by Ruth Cross and María Llanos and others) works to create the conditions for personal and political change towards a sustainable and equitable world, through building an active community of changemakers, designing complexity-responsive projects and hosting international residencies. https://erolesproject.org
10 The UN Refugee Agency.
11 La Bolina founded in 2017 is an intercultural regeneration project based in El Valle, Granada, Spain, working with people with a migrant and refugee background in ecological growing, rural development, education and the arts.
12 The plastic sea is the name given to the mass of plastic greenhouse used for intensive agriculture in Almeria, Spain. It is a model of agricultural exploitation of high technical and economic yield based on the rational use of water, plastic greenhouses and tens of thousands of migrant farm workers. This area produces thousands of tons of food for European supermarkets.

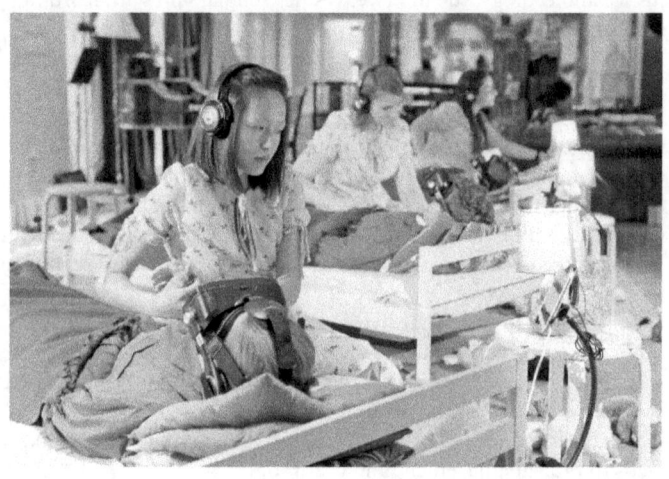

FIGURE 7 *Image details live performance of* Goodnight, Sleep Tight *by ZU-UK, taken at Gerry's Bar & Kitchen. Photographed by Ludovic Des Cognets*

CHAPTER 6

Post-immersive interventions with Jorge Lopes Ramos and Persis Jadé Maravala from ZU-UK

Speaker key:
JB: Joanna Bucknall
JLR: Jorge Lopes Ramos
PJM: Persis Jadé Maravala

[This conversation was recorded over Zoom on 23 June 2021.]

JB: Can we start at the site where your collaboration and your partnership was forged, which is *Hotel Medea* (2006–12). Could you start by talking about what brought Para Active[1] and Zecora Ura Theatre[2] together to collaborate on that project?

JLR: Absolutely. What brought Zecora Ura and Para Active together was this shared background of physical training and body-based practice; that was something that aligned values and areas of interest. But also, an obsession with the role of the audience. The fact that both companies had explored alternative spaces for years as Jadé usually says, because theatres wouldn't have us. Zecora Ura and Para Active, for different reasons, couldn't get access to stages and theatres and so we explored everything we had access to, and that was often public space or borrowed space where there was a garage, or a train, or a kitchen, or a toilet. The combination of the understanding of the depth of physical training, that joint appreciation of the rigour, combined with a real kind of desire to push the role of the audience.

JB: Where did you actually come across each other; when did your paths cross, so to speak?

JLR: I watched Jadé perform *Onion Bar* (2002) at Stratford Circus probably 2000/2001, and we didn't have a conversation, but it was an incredible piece of work, musically, physically. Audiences were very much guests in the bar and participating in a series of rituals including birthday songs and collective crying. And Jadé came to see a piece that I had developed in 2004 which started at the underground station Mudchute, with a man in a suit with a horse's mask that guided audiences, trying to avoid teenage abuse being shouted at us for just looking weird!

PJM: I think looking weird is a slight understatement; you had a massive horse's head over your head and a suit on and it just/

JLR: /and an umbrella, yeah, that was the first thing that Jadé saw.

PJM: Yeah, we saw each other's work. Because your thing was with Ian Morgan, who's a friend of mine, who I know from the Grotowski world. But I think what's probably really interesting about our meeting, is that we were just so incredibly different, almost opposite, but the one thing that we had in common was this background in physicality. For Jorge, the physicality aspect was more a vehicle for, well I don't want to talk for him, but for quality experience of the performance and of the performers. Whereas for me, my background in physicality was a little bit more rooted in perhaps more of a spiritual basis, or something that was a lot more grounded in ritual. Practices that were shamanic and very much connected to my own origins. And actually, for Jorge probably as well, being Brazilian, but I think at that point we were connected on an intercultural exchange level, without really knowing that. We didn't really understand that – we didn't understand how significant those practices were, in terms of who we were and how our lines were crossing. And so, those really important intersections between non-dominant culture practices were the things that could speak to each other. Jorge was much, much more, much, much, much, much more into progressive ideas. Whereas I had come from an extremely closed, precise, insular practice – he was really lateral, really spreading his wings! I remember one of the early tensions was that I'd be leading something in a very serious and very important way, to do with molecular levels of vibratory sound (or whatever) and being quite committed to the depth of that practice, and then he'd be like 'oh I've invited a couple of bods to come and watch the rehearsal'. And I'd be like 'what'?!

We were clashing all the time and I don't even know how we managed it. But I do think it was in that clashing that all the amazing stuff we did became really positive, like these two force fields just gave birth to this other thing.

JB: Jorge you've talked about that your work is quite horizontal and Jadé you've talked about it being vertical; I think maybe the thing that sits in the middle of that axis is probably audience and a relationship with audience.

JLR: And rigour. I think one thing coming from physical practices is that there is an appreciation for discipline and rigour that can easily get lost in cultures that over-celebrate collaboration and over-celebrate horizontal kinds of structures without considering the best format for an intended purpose. Even if it's a collective purpose. While we were clashing, we both understood in each other that we deeply respected each other's practices, or desires, or vision enough to go, 'No, hold on, this doesn't work, but tell me more', you know? Like, 'I'm listening but, no'! So, it was a productive thing/

PJM: I think it was a bit different in the sense that you were always making choices which were about getting us out there, and getting our work seen/

JLR: /And funded.

PJM: / I was always resisting that, and there was just something in that push and pull which meant that the work would just have to be so incredibly ready before I would be comfortable with people seeing anything – and that meant an incredible amount of training and an incredible amount of discipline. And hardcore rigour, which I think is sort of missing a bit from general theatre practice across the board. I'm really glad that Jorge and I went through a process that was very kind of, 'earn your stripes' – in which you recognized the value in just sheer hard work. I think sheer hard work is very unpopular right now.

JB: Graft, I think, isn't it?

PJM: Graft, yes, graft is controversial.

JB: I think that's very clear in the process that you went through with *Hotel Medea* (2006–12), it has graft *(laughs)*, kind of at the heart of all of that. I wanted to pick up as well a little bit on this idea of resistance/

PJM: Just to say that it's interesting, isn't it, because we both, Jorge and I, have working-class backgrounds; I think there's something about working classness and grafting that is connected.

I think that's what Jorge was really good at in terms of what you're saying about the resistance. His pushback was always making sure that the training never became just for training's sake. The training had to serve a production, it had to serve something, right?

What he was doing, and of course we couldn't articulate this at the time, we're doing that now, you know, years and years later, but what he was doing was like, 'Right all this fucking getting up at five in the morning and running across meadows and just doing your mental regimes! That's fine as long as I can see what this is all about, as long as the proof is in the pudding'.

JB: I wanted to pick up on this idea of resistance from venues and what role that resistance from the theatre industry played in the process of *Hotel Medea* (2006–12), because, like you said, there was so much scepticism about you can't do an overnight thing, you can't do this, you can't do that. How did that drive the way that you made that work?

JLR: I was the main person interfacing with venues on behalf of *Hotel Medea* (2006–12), at the time. So specifically in relation to *Hotel Medea* (2006–12), it was a massive undertaking. For you to approach a venue that either doesn't know your work or knows your work in the way that doesn't match this form that you're about to present; for instance, Zecora Ura had just completed a twelve-venue tour in the UK with a piece that went incredibly well and all the venues were happy and festivals were happy to book again on the same genre and same level. Coming to them, they were reticent. It was about finding those gaps and those people that would go, 'Yeah this is risky but have this little bit of space' so we just took anything that we could where there was space or support or mentoring, you know, anything, we just say, 'Yeah, yes please'. It would be a jigsaw which took six years of failed arts council applications and then successful arts council applications that wouldn't cover even 10 per cent of the cost. Festival grant or festival fees that again might pay for everyone's food and that's it. It was trying to square a model where, if you came from Para Active, which was a training-based model, everyone who was there was attracted primarily because of this training, the productions would be a vehicle for that process, that growth process, that human sort of growth process. So that model where there is a trade between training and production, which is an old model, and another model which was Zecora Ura, which is more of like, 'Oh everyone collectively collaborates; there's no money but then if there is any money, we share' mode. And coming together trying to figure out this very, very hungry beast. Just in flights alone between UK and Brazil. That's the one thing that came up from the intercultural training period, is that we were aware of so many ethically questionable ways in which non-Western work was presented on a Western stage that we did not want to do that; we did not want to fall into the trap. Despite the fact that I'm Brazilian and Jadé is from Yemen, we didn't want to just drink from that and then present to a white audience. We wanted to have a genuine UK/Brazil company who would work in Brazil and the UK for Brazilian and UK audiences. So, we kept going, travelling with this huge group with little or no funding just moving about and creating these structures where fifteen/twenty people would need to live and eat and be together. It was trying to square those models. It's just kind of balancing and who needs to be in the room, who needs to support us, who needs to be excited about this? It's me making up for the lack of a producer really because all the producers we'd worked with had not worked at all in any way; they just wouldn't get the work; they just didn't get it.

JB: Over those six years, were there interim versions; did it go through kind of a life of different presentations to different kinds of audiences in different spaces before it ended up how we kind of encountered?

PJM: I think it was more like seven years and it started, because it was a trilogy. I know that our first outing of it was in Arcola 2009. Is that right?

JLR: No, it was actually, well it depends how we call the outing, but the first full overnight that we did with audiences was 2008 at Salisbury International Festival.[3] In a converted cathedral, yeah, that was the first. But if we're still talking about resistance, I think *Hotel Medea* (2006–12) is just such a great case study for it being, like, it doesn't work on paper, shouldn't work, nobody actually thought it was going to work except for me!

PJM: He was encountering resistance from within the company, from me, and outside of the company as well. Completely all credit to him that it happened at all, his temerity in just making sure that he was going to have it be something that was what he felt was needed. Whereas for me, the way that I existed, because we're existing in resistance, aren't we? We exist on the sidelines; we exist on the margins; that's the kind of groups that we come from, whether it's about being an immigrant or refugee or whether it's about, you know, being a person of colour. Jorge arriving to England not speaking English, things like that, making sure that we're on the margins and then how do you sit in the margin, what is your mode going to be? I think for Jorge, his mode was just like, right, let's sort this out; let's bring this to the fore. Whereas I was very much happy to stay safe in that space that was not taking part in the mainstream, but also being able to kind of have some sort of weird stability by having an identity which was wrapped around outsider art and outsider/

JLR: /Underground.

PJM: It was very cult-y; it was just not mainstream; it was very cult-y, very underground. Whereas Jorge was like, 'No we can do this; we can get into', for a lot of us that was politically just a weird idea. For me it was hard to know what that meant, what did it mean to cross over into the mainstream? I guess *Hotel Medea* (2006–12) was an attempt to cross over to the mainstream while not negotiating our bottom lines and that's why it was so stressful.

That's why every artist who works against the mainstream ends up, you know, you can get into some really dark places when you don't have the same kind of support as other groups who are accepted. I was seeing at that time companies around Battersea Arts Centre, for example, other known places for theatre and they're just very clique-y. I cannot stress how left out we were, how that felt miserable. I'm sick of it being a romantic idea, because I think a lot of people talk to me and they're like, 'Oh yeah it's so cool'. It wasn't cool; it was fucking painful; it was horrible! You just were getting knocked back all the time and with *Hotel Medea* (2006–12), we were getting knocked back all the time. And it's not cool. It was really hard, and we didn't get any support. And that's OK, you know. It's not that anyone who has an idea should deserve some support, I agree that we had to put the work in, but I think that there were other barriers that weren't only about the work and those are the sort of barriers that we might come to later. Salisbury first and then it was a mess; I mean, it was an embarrassment.

What it was, was just pure energy, it was just energy, it was like going to a really choreographed riot, or a highly controlled mess, because we didn't know how to work with audiences properly. We just knew what we had come from, which were very, very audience-centric experiences, both in my Asian cultures and Jorge with his Brazilian culture. We knew there was a way of people being together sharing energy and that's a very English working-class thing as well. But this is what that early immersive stuff was trying to harness, kind of collective energy between audiences. We had come from that.

All the rituals and festivals in Brazil, even when I went to Brazil for the first time, one of the things that really struck me was that there wasn't so much of a separation between those who could do culture, that is, singing and dancing, performing, etc. and those who watched and those who couldn't do. There wasn't that in Brazil and that's what reminded me of growing up, when I was growing up we had these things called Gahambar[4] and they're kind of, like, sort of, like, parties but party isn't really the right word but more like – I don't know how to explain it – just meetings, encounters where there's loads of people playing music but the instruments are being passed around and the voice, you know, and who decides to sing and, like, and the closest thing to English working-class culture with that is like a singalong, like a proper singalong.

And it's harnessing that energy of the collective being in control of culture, allowing themselves to express through song and dance on a really simple level. And you can get that feeling at gigs, out in a mosh pit. You get that feeling in football: there's a lot of singing and chanting, even if it is very minimal and includes a lot of swearwords, doesn't matter. There's still this expression; it's still an expressive force, right, which is really strong. When we were making *Hotel Medea* (2006–12), we knew that we wanted audiences to dance; we wanted audiences to sing but we didn't quite have it worked out in the beginning. There's that whole space between the invitation to the audience member and everything that pivots around that invitation. What is necessary for them to feel comfortable enough to let their guard down? There was an idea in the beginning, wasn't there, Jorge, that like, 'Oh, Brazilian audiences are really up for it', because they were, and English audiences, oh we have to work in a different way because they're so fucking repressed and tight, and they've got something stuck up their arse. It was very funny being a Brazilian group working in England with the show because it was all about, but we didn't realize, it wasn't them; it was us! We just weren't doing it right, because with English audiences if you just unlock in the right way, if you give the right permission – boom!

JLR: Exactly, absolutely.

PJM: BOOM! BOOM! They're like all over it! I mean, it's like woah! There is no holding them back; they're just like 'yes'. We realized it was humiliation. English people do not like to look stupid in front of other people. One of the biggest things that we learned, and I think that immersive needs to know more about, is allowing audience members to feel safe, comfortable, not, and I don't mean safe in that kind of 'this is a safe space' kind of way. I mean like literally, 'You are perfect, and we have been waiting for you and here's your space, it's been held for you'. I've always worked on that principle. That was the same thread that has carried on since all of that in terms of making audiences retain the care, that kind of personalized and bespoke experience that was genuine as opposed to just really fake.

JLR: Completely, there's such a difference between the commercial idea of customization, which is very trendy, to the person feeling acknowledged as an individual at that time and that they belong there. When we talk about the care for each individual audience member, we don't mean encouraging selfish, self-serving, pleasure-seeking consumer desires. By saying, 'You can have anything you want, this is yours' and then trampling over the others around them, it's not that at all. It's about looking them in the eye, metaphorically or really, with *Hotel Medea* (2006–12); it was really. So, if there was to be one action, then that action had to be done with all 150 people it had to.

When Medea gives a poisoned kiss, it had to be done seventy-two times; it had to be something that not just a few experienced; it had to be an invitation for each and every one. People can decline the invitation, anyone can decline any invitation, but the space was there for them. In our work, when we do scale up to larger audiences it's about going 'how on earth are we going to make sure each individual feels held, welcomed, belonging and seen here and listened to, while at the same time feeling responsible. We make a temporary community where everyone's signed up to similar values and similar challenges; everyone's aware of the challenge they have signed up to.

PJM: The temporary community thing is very, very important because it was an overnight show, that was almost like a dare as well, wasn't it? Like a bit of a test that you dared to come and spend the night with us and something about creating not just any old temporary community but one that's spent the night together, which is, I think, just way more kind of permissive. There's something about spending the night with each other, like just the invitation already unlocks something in audiences. It's a bit like going on holiday where you behave a bit more permissively than you would if you were in your normal daily life, something about it being an overnight show. But much, much more important than that, it is something we're only just realizing now, which is that early immersive performance was our culture, it was actually a culture that came out of our racial and ethnic cultures. All the ensembles and collectives that I started in with Para Active in the late nineties, then Zecora Ura and Urban Dolls Project; they were all made up of people that came from the global majority cultures. We were very much 'off white'. We used to do these events that were overnight workshops, overnight trainings. It wasn't for audiences; it was for each other. And we would have people over – for me, that was what the real happening was – that was where the real work lay – not in the shows that we performed but these encounters in which we would perform with and for each other and so we created this space in which we could belong, and it was distinctly a non-Western, non-white space. It was intensely physical, intensively collective; the experiences were absolutely non-Western, both in the approach to the body but also in relation to the other. And then we used this approach and we extended it into how audiences engaged with one another. That blurring of the relationship between audience and actors by extension then encouraged audience to audience experiences, and not just creating temporary but creating genuine communities out of audiences. Because we weren't ignoring the relationships between strangers, we certainly weren't fucking anonymizing them by putting masks on them or whatever and we/

JLR: /I think what is so, so, so, so crucial here, as Jadé's talking about temporary communities, is that we weren't anonymising them and we weren't treating them as customers and trying to milk as much money as we could in the breaks. Because there were two breaks for about fifteen to twenty minutes, where we would provide tea, hot chocolate, biscuits, cakes at no extra charge, it was all part of it, especially the breakfast at the end, it meant that people could switch off from the show at that moment, which also didn't feel like a show, because it felt like a party, and they would just see each other and go like, 'Oh yeah'; we just shared that extremely intimate moment ten minutes ago. They wouldn't be thinking about 'how much does this cost' or 'do I get in line for this'; it would just be open to just for whatever was stirred up in them to continue. It wasn't cut through or interrupted. And we would hang around, I mean, those of us who weren't running in the background getting ready for the next bit, so there was no masking of what's going on behind. We're making this happen together, you and us.

What Jadé said about the events we would hold since the beginning, what would happen is: what we were asking the audiences to do was something we would do ourselves. There was no throwing the audience in a really difficult place, but we would know how vulnerable that was; we would know at which points it was harder; we would have some tricks ourselves to deal with going through the night and staying awake. So, the 'lived experience' of setting ourselves up for it before the audience meant that there was just compassion and empathy and understanding. We were able to talk from experience, like, 'OK this is getting hard now', but we wouldn't need to do this outside of the fiction, because we had roles that were developed because of the night; yes, they aligned with roles in *Medea*, but actually at the trickiest time of night who do you have? You have a nanny;

you have someone there genuinely caring for you. And that was intentional and supporting people not to feel abandoned.

JB: Sometimes things are dangerous or challenging or difficult and that's fine but it's the way that invitation is made and then the way that that exchange is grown and facilitated between you and participants, and I think that's something – and I never got to experience *Hotel Medea* (2006–12) – but it's definitely something I feel when you talk about it. Having experienced your work since then, I can feel that carrying through; that ethos and that spirit is always at the heart of the work.

PJM: Because isn't it also interesting in terms of what we're seeing in the world today post-pandemic? What you do affects the behaviour of other people and so when you have any kind of power – and let's face it – if you go to a show who is in power at that moment are the artists because they're in the know – and so today's immersive events, they're designed to encourage, often white, very privileged audiences, to tap into their worst sort of colonial impulses. We've seen it ourselves: sometimes we've been to things and people have come to our work and we're just looking at them because like, 'What are you doing mate!' Because they're just striding through spaces they've never been in before, completely entitled, this is a total colonialist aspect of white culture which is like, 'I'm here now, what is this, what is here for me, I shall be here, and I shall take as much as I want to because I'm entitled'. Thoroughly colonialist behaviour. Going through an abundance of spaces, rummaging, pillaging, trying to open locked doors and completely tripping out on their own neocolonial adventure. This is something that people have been encouraged to do through the work of big spaces and 'big monies' productions like Punchdrunk. What we do is completely different! Completely different. I've been in that situation with our pieces, where people have just completely ignored what's happening and just gone, opening drawers. The thing is we don't make anything like that, so if you open a door, you literally will see a broom cupboard! There is no secret; there's no fucking 'Alice in Wonderland'. The only reason why I mention that is because I think that version of immersive does touch on colonial behaviours and we're always talking about things in a post-colonial way. It's interesting for me to see a reversing, reverting back to that kind of Brexit type 'woah, I'm here and I'm important, we're British', that kind of mentality.

JB: After *Hotel Medea* (2006–12), your work has shifted; there's a lot more adoption of technologies. Could you talk a little bit about your relationship with TAG[5] in Montreal and how that relationship has kind of shifted the way in which you've been making work more recently?

JLR: In 2011 a project we were invited to do something, which was our first ever, to my memory, invited commission by someone who had come to us. And that was *Trade Secrets* (2012); it was an exhibition in Liverpool. It was *Humble Market* (2012), which was a more performative version that happened in Preston, Preston Guild, during the Cultural Olympiad. It happened in connection with things that were going on in Londonderry and also in Brazil.

We still had strong relationships with the company members from *Hotel Medea* (2006–12), so many of them were invited, as well, but it was a technology-led project. It was our first technology-led project, so some things did not need any performance, so it was like, 'Oh how do we square this?' That helped us to realize that there were things that we wanted to move forward with, but we had retained things from the past that not just were no longer relevant, they were actually barriers, for instance a theatre company model. One thing that stayed with me at that moment after *Hotel Medea* (2006–12) was if genuinely following a new enquiry and finding out what form it will take, how can we start that already with actors, how can we? Because we can never ask around the room at a certain moment, 'Hi guys, what do you think, do we need actors for this?'. You can't ask that because that's already a given; you already are a theatre company, so you've got to use everyone. There was a realization that in order to start a project that genuinely could go anywhere, we had to start from zero.

We had to start us in a room, maybe one more person, maybe two, and always being really honest and upfront saying, 'We don't know what this is going to be, and we don't know what people we will need and what skills we will need, we just don't know, all we're doing is working for three months on this idea, at the end we have a conversation again'. I think that was a big difference in the format, not seeing ourselves as a theatre company, not assuming that we were starting with anyone or any form, we would just follow an enquiry that we were really excited about and then see where it led.

JB: A lot of the work that you've made since 2014/2015 has been on that intersection with gaming/

PJM: Well, it's funny we talk about games, but actually everyone comes from a culture of games. Games was something that travelled with us from my Para Active days. When I started to work in exchange for space, what I did was I used to teach drama to kids and of course, it's just pure games. All you do is set them up for game after game and then maybe do a bit of thinking about the plight of the bees or whatever but it's basically games led! I worked a little bit as well with Clive Barker and of course Jorge came from Brazil and was super influenced by Augusto Boal. Jorge and I had different experiences of forum theatre, but I was mainly interested in the games. I used to use games as ways of devising, so meeting with TAG was really incredible, thinking about this kind of gaming up of our work. We already started in *Humble Market* (2012) to create things that were bordering on looking like quite classic games.

My difficulty with all the TAG stuff was still about how to hold on to what was real? So even though our experience with gaming goes all the way back, when we were really influenced by people like Keith Johnstone, Boal and Barker and also mixing that with the games and dynamics from the cultures that I come from, which is Yemen and India. Then for Jorge the rituals and games from Northeast of Brazil – the movement, vocabularies. I was personally very excited to touch base again to games, because there's something that I believe about games, which is that they are transformative, like I see them transform people in very, very amazing ways.

Games done well transform people in really amazing ways. What I personally love about that is that they then surprise themselves and they do things that they would never have expected themselves to do in that situation. They wouldn't predict their own behaviour. They couldn't predict their own behaviour, but in the moment of the game people turn out all kinds of hidden aspects of themselves; they become revealed. Games are a way in to create something that needs to be accessible, especially for audiences who aren't gamers.

One of the big differences between us and TAG is that they are a game community and everyone around them is very sophisticated in gaming. That was one of the barriers really between me and them. I was constantly looking at what does the game experience bring up on the level of intimacy and humanness? They were not, it was like there was a really weird thing where I would say, 'Here's the game we're going to do' and they would just try to break the game constantly. Slowly through this long collaboration we've started to influence one another.

JB: How have you still maintained this really integral intimacy and relationship between human beings through the use of the technology that you've been using in your recent work?

JLR: Short answer is the quality of Jadé's writing, and not putting technology first. Does it serve its purpose? If it doesn't – dump it. If it does – go with it. It's important to just talk about the quality of the writing because that is such a huge journey. Jadé suddenly becomes the writer and, in the beginning, with very little support, because we didn't quite understand that that was the thing, there wasn't a name to it. Recently when that became so clear we had to try and change the company's mentality and support Jadé to grow as a writer. None of our work, none of it, stands up without that care of the writing, the instruction-based writing and the way in which it's written and tone.

There are two things that I wanted to mention: one is how game design, as opposed to the actual games or video games, was very interesting to us as additional methodology to create our work. Because games have to imagine the journey of the player, there's no choice; with game design you have to think, OK player starts here; these are the options; what do they need to know here? I'm asking them to do this, but they'll never be able to do it unless I introduce it here. The whole focus is not on the thing. Yeah, sure, you might have a nice vision or story or fiction or whatever, but the journey of that player is absolutely core. Just that shift of mentality was already useful, whether or not we're making games, and in fact most of the things we make are not really games; they're either game-y or they have games in them. We don't really make games. We didn't set out to make games and certainly not video games, but what we did do is to interrogate the kind of approaches of game design and especially thinking of this player that isn't an audience member, that isn't a spectator, but is a *guest* that has been invited to activate something.

All that process in that way, which was a natural development from dramaturgy of participation, which is where, in our own way we try and reframe dramaturgy as something that is from the audience. It's about their experience as opposed to a stage dramaturgy.

So that's one level of game design. And the other level in terms of the relationship with TAG specifically is, although I don't think we were aware of it at the beginning, why we were so attracted to each other, is that TAG is a research centre for technoculture, arts and games. Most of the people do not come from games studies; they have been attracted to game; they're also outsiders. They already had interest in virtual and physical games – they weren't just a video game centre. They were already making movement-based games and multiplayer games and the journey we've been through is this: 'who is it for and who is it by, who is it with and does it need to become a game, even if it starts off as a game, can it be a walk, can it be an audio piece, can it be...?'. We're now entering a joint R&D, which is the next stage of developing of this game that we're making.

JB: I have come across VR in lots of different ways, and I found it very isolating and very inaccessible, but I think with the project that you did *Goodnight, Sleep Tight* (2017–), that connection between the world of VR, but haptics of real bodies, making connections in the space. It was kind of incredible actually, the way that you brought those things together and, again, I think that's because of that central drive that you have which is about creating moments, creating connections, creating temporary kind of communities or temporary moments between people that matter. There's always something very warm about the way that technology facilitates that through your work, that I haven't seen in other work. And I wonder if it's because of working within that gaming sector but with people like you say, Jorge, that are coming from outside of that and have a very different kind of perspective on it.

PJM: Yeah, I think so; games is a technology and when we talk about not letting the technology take over, in a way I put games in with that as well, because I've really struggled – and I'm struggling now actually with this one – this idea of 'oh how can we make it more game-y?'. I'm a bit like, 'Who says it needs to be more game-y; why do you keep saying that?' So now we're going into a process where I have to just allow the work that I've made to be made more game-y, which is something that I did with *Binaural Dinner Date (BDD)* (2016–). It was really hard because my question is, are there just some things that you can't make games about, is there anything you can't make a game about? We'd already been looking at that sort of thing across everything that we do, so whether it's about death, like, in *Good Night, Sleep Tight* (2017) and with the mother and child relationship, whether it's about suicidation, whether it's about dating. They tend to be quite hefty subjects and we're always trying to create games out of hefty subjects in a meaningful way and it never really quite works. I've thought a lot about why that is, because in the beginning of our meetings with TAG we were learning how to break games down, we were understanding them, how they function in terms of risks and rewards and all the vocabulary that comes with it in terms of levelling up or badges or point structures, etc. And in my heart, I think it was just about wanting to make a game that could behave like any other sort of art form, that might talk about any of these subjects, just like dance can, novels can, films can, music can, any other form of storytelling. It was interesting going on this journey to find out if games were as capable and as equipped to talk about any kind of subject, including heavy ones, even though you might think dating isn't a heavy subject, but actually I disagree: I think it's very heavy! Especially in the way that I was approaching it, which was making it about life or death, love lost and heartbreak and loss and grief and regrets and all kinds of other issues about having to understand yourself before you could offer yourself in a relationship to another person. This wasn't a light-hearted dating; this was going to be hardcore, hard-work dating!

It was very hard in the end and we just didn't succeed really in making *BDD* a game. What we did was, we had lots of games in it and it is a super playful experience but, importantly, in trying to make it a game loads and loads of other things come out, it doesn't matter in the end; it doesn't matter that *BDD* isn't a game; it doesn't matter that *Good Night, Sleep Tight* (2017), isn't technically a game. What matters in trying to make it a game is you discover loads of other really important shit. Why do we want it to be a game? And obviously the main reason is because we're looking at interaction and participation.

JB: And transformation. There is something in coming together under specific rules that are aside or other to the ones that we usually function within and, like you said, that becomes transformative, and it brings people together and quickly. That's one of the things I've discovered about games, is rules in games can very quickly offer an invitation that people can take up, jump in and run with very swiftly in that moment and sort of getting on-board with that helps to facilitate the intimacy and the temporary communities or connections that I think your work manages.

JLR: With a game or with role play, that is based on a function; it's really enabling invitation because as long as you know that it unlocks something for that person, they go like, 'Oh that's what you mean, yeah sure'. So, if I want you to take the spotlight and I want you to sing and I want everyone to just, kind of, take everyone with you, they go, 'What!' But if you say, 'Here's a karaoke, here's a microphone', it's a completely different thing. When we talk about hacking familiar contracts or familiar rituals, what we're talking about is these contracts that already exist, people already express themselves, they already play games, so it's about what already exists, rather than creating this 'thing here', spending a lot of money and time and effort getting people to believe.

PJM: In some ways, like games make things a bit more natural, what we're working with is the human being. We work with who they are and we work very much in the here and now, so like Jorge said, we're not doing things like *War of the Worlds* (2019), where the first thing that happens is a person comes out and says, "OK, I don't remember exactly what it is, but we're on the run from these monsters and we now have to go to learn about astrology" and then we're like, "Oh yeah OK we're all in it". We're just much more like, "Hi, thanks for coming"!

(Laughs) You know what I mean? This idea of makers, often I've heard them say that, 'Well, we work with audience members, and we expect them to meet us halfway'. I'm like, 'Dude, they've already met you halfway, they've organized a babysitter, they've got on some fucking shitty transport and they've turned up on time to your deal, that's already meeting you halfway'! This idea

that the audience has to somehow work is a bit problematic. Because if you're in a real collaboration why is someone paying the ticket price? It's just very messy.

JB: I wanted to ask one of the sorts of 'hush-hush' questions which is always about money, and I know you've talked a little bit about that obviously with *Hotel Medea* (2006–12), and how that was sort of extraordinary and completely unsustainable. Since then, how have you been able to fund and facilitate your work?

JLR: In every possible way within what we have judged to be ethical. We've looked into academic and research funding; we've looked into arts funding and, more often than before, social impact. Funding that is about culture and art but is directed at very specific metrics of a specific community or group or demographic. This is very recent for us, but some of our work fits into that category in what is expected of those funders and some of our work certainly doesn't. It is already hard as an independent art organization to get core funding or regular funding but when you are an organization that tends not to repeat a form or a pattern or way of working, you just make it three times as hard for yourself because what you're doing is you're reinventing the way in which you communicate and present yourself to partners and the world. It's very hard to have one coherent way of presenting the work, which is what you want; you want a strong case for a funder. So that's a difficulty, but what we've managed to do is always through the quality of the work, always building on a funder's understanding of 'if we say we're going to deliver, we'll deliver'. The values are there, the ethics are there, the commitment is there, we can do it really well, so that's the difference between us now and ten years ago is we have a track record, and we have a track record that is a range of very well-managed projects in very different settings. That's the benefit of being where we are today, we can prove that we can do it, where before we had to convince funders/commissioners that we could do it.

JLR: The way in which we tend to fundraise our work has mirrored the model of making that we started to do after *Hotel Medea* (2006–12), which was prototyping and playtesting. We already had this sense of R&D in the work and having to have stages anyway, it would be impossible to get a single funder to pay for everything; no one will fund the whole thing straightaway. Little pockets of development, of prototype, R&D, playtesting, always means that by the time you've closed that fund you'll deliver what you said you would. But now you can change your mind and pick something else or a new stage. That's what we do now, we break everything down into fundable amounts or structures and then we keep our eyes open for what's out there, whether it's a 5K thing or 50K thing or a 30K thing. We just apply for as many things as we can because law of averages, we'll get a few!

We spent two or three years when we didn't get anything. It was the two or three years we applied for the most things, I don't know, sixteen applications in a row, not one single positive. That was a lesson in two things: one is having people write funding applications for you or help you write them doesn't really work; you should write about your own work, really. You can communicate that vision and the passion yourself; you're the one that can go, 'It's my responsibility. I will do it'. If I claim that I will do something on the form, I'm not doing this on behalf of somebody else or another group. It's knowing *how* to talk about your work and also being responsible for what you write. We've been a lot more selective since and only write a 'thing' that we think we have high chances of getting.

JB: I can see some things that come from *Hotel Medea* (2006–12), in terms of that kind of incremental developing and this back and forth and back and forth of developing a project. Is that how the audience slide into this work and into the way that you make work now, is it a case of get to a certain point and test that, get it inhabited with participants and then move and move along and keep bringing people in like that? I guess what I'm asking is, what moments do you test? How do you put that to an audience if it's not necessarily about getting a show out, how do you get inhabitants into that process?

PJM: We have moved to a playtesting model, which was a very difficult move for me because I found it very hard to show work that wasn't ready. That was a massive mental shift that had to happen in my head, coming from such a precise discipline where everything was exactly how we wanted it to be, but the shift comes because we're putting the audience at the centre, not only of the experience but actually of the making of it, you know, building off of – to a certain extent – and these are all things that aren't sorted out. We have arguments in the company; there'll be weird tensions because there's a line where we playtest and then we're taking on people's feedback – they're being asked questions about how they felt and blah blah blah. Then the group are like, 'Oh one person said so and so, so and so' and I'm like, 'Yeah so what are we going to do, like, change the whole thing?' I'm not so concerned with what people say afterwards. I like to watch people, so I'll watch people do the thing and I'll watch how they behave, and I'll watch what happens and where they look like they're a bit confused or where they get lost, so I'm quite practical. I like to see how people behave in response. I'm not so interested as an artist in what people say afterwards, because I think that's a very clouded area of judgement anyway. What seems to me more truthful is actually how do people participate in the piece? But on the other hand, it's not entirely true; sometimes someone's just said something that's been like 'wow', you get twenty feedbacks but in this one feedback there's something that's so clean, it articulates something that was bothering me, and they've just articulated it really well. It is really part of that model of cross-disciplinary collaboration; it's a bit of an extension of that; it's about letting go of this 'one author' of every piece. There isn't; there's multiple authors. There's this devising process that is a lot more collective.

I'll tolerate them, and they tolerate me; we sort of bump along together. I'm not like Jorge. That goes back to the horizontal and vertical, I go really inwards, and I go really deep and I'm very closed and Jorge gets his influences sideways and very lateral. That's wonderful and I'm just not like that; I'm not built like that; I'm not like that at all. But I guess, yeah, both of those things serve each other but/

JB: /Those things rub together. Maybe those tensions are something that keeps it lively and alive and moving?

PJM: Yeah, it can get a bit tiring though.

I think this is really important in terms of some of the things that we've been speaking about, separating commercial immersive from arts-based products. Part of the problem is that art projects tend to want to be successful in the same way that businesses are successful and so all their projections are in market value terms. Now that we're coming out of the pandemic, I feel this should be a moment of looking at things a bit closer and going, 'Yo, hold on!' and bigger institutions are doing that. There's been The

Tate and the British Museum that have just come up in the news about you need to stop taking money from BP. In Brazil the arts are sponsored by big companies and is that going to continue – are we still going to think that's OK?

JB: Immersive is becoming increasingly commercialized. You can even buy levels of experience; you can buy levels of comfort and that's the same as buying cheap standing tickets at the last minute, isn't it? It's the same/

PJM: / it's the same as having private healthcare and private education; it's the same.

JB: Yes, yeah.

PJM: It's the same structures of wealth and elitism.

JB: Yeah. And we see that played out and like you were talking about the way that it encourages behaviour, it does encourage productivity and consumerism and all of those neoliberal values, but they're packaged as something, as being 'a good audience' and 'getting your money's worth' and 'getting value'. It's that kind of entitlement and take-take. I would never have dreamt of selling anything at one of my experiences. I'm very keen – and I always have been – that my participants leave with something. With me it's usually cake or tea or something that we've made together that they can take away but because I would never dream of saying, 'OK well if you want tea it's going to be five quid and if you want a piece of cake it's going to be this much', because it's part of the exchange, it's part of that coming together, this gift of me, of time, of them, of their time and taking that away with them, I would never have dreamed of selling t-shirts for example! *(Laughs)*

JLR: I think it's impossible to find the perfect model where an organization, you know, wants to, or has to pay everyone they work with properly and they're large scale and they have big names attached to them so, you know, we're talking about the big players; there's a lot of pressure for them to pay people properly and there should be. So, they're going, 'OK, where do we get income from?' Now I think what is problematic and, in some instances, lazy, is to just go for how to maximize income from this event; if you get that angle, you're going to do that – you're going to create a shopping centre as part of your Secret Cinema experience. Where it's a thematic shopping centre, it matches the theme of what you're doing but ultimately, it's stall after stall after stall selling your stuff. Like VIP experiences, you pay more, and you get more but you're already starting at, I don't know, 70 quid, you've already excluded shitloads of people anyway already.

JB: This leads me into the big white elephant which is 'immersive'. I think one of the issues that we have is that we are all nestled underneath this giant umbrella called 'immersive'. I know you have written very explicitly about this in the 'Post-immersive Manifesto' (2020) and so I kind of wanted to start to draw things to a close by bringing you to talk about that.

PJM: I like that you said we're going to bring things to a close by/

JB: /*(Laughs*), dropping a hand grenade at the end! *(Laughs)*

PJM: *(Laughs)* First of all it's really important to say that we absolutely distance ourselves from the term 'immersive' now, because it doesn't represent what we started out with when we were in the first wave of creating immersive. The belief was so simple; it was just this belief that we have a lot to offer each other just by being present with each other, just by turning up. However, immersive now has been turned into the direct opposite of shared presence; it's been turned into this thing that is a plaything of privilege, something that is exotic and yet you can have it because here in the West we can have whatever we want! It has to be attainable, something that can be held and sold and reproduced and the irony is that this obsession with material things that can be owned prevents this deeper, lasting effect; it's totally against the spirit with which we built those early encounters, which were always very evanescent; they kind of fade into the past as soon as they're over. But they leave this memorable legacy of personal impact – but that impact, as we've already spoken about today, requires so much work, so much training and an extraordinary amount of genuine personalized care to get right. Not fake personalization, which we've always also spoken about. And I think it's a bit like the fact that we get – we started *Hotel Medea* (2006–12), in 2006, we finished it in like 2012 or 2013/

JLR: /Yeah, 2012/

PJM: /and we still get emails about it; we still get people saying, 'Hey, didn't contact you before but I just want you to know what an effect *Hotel Medea* (2006–12) had on me, it changed my life, dah dah dah, now I do this, I just wanted to let you guys know' or whatever it is, we'll still get an email a month at least! We're talking a decade later. I think that is the true testimony to that work. Now, immersive is controlled by the same people that control everything else and so it's not on the outside anymore and we started, didn't we, today talking about outsiders and being on the outside and I think that's what's really important, that this is what needs to change because art for commercial gain loses that power to disrupt. By not taking corporate money we still have the power to disrupt and to engage with the specific communities from where this work comes from. So that key issue of being able to still have the power to disrupt things is really important because those big immersive shows require scalability. At that level of scale, art is rarely going to be able to address the kinds of things that we're addressing because the ability to be intimate and spontaneous has been sacrificed on the altar of engaging the widest possible audience, well, the widest possible paying consumer.

JLR: Immersive inherits so many problematic old school models of the arts industry when it had the potential to re-invent them. The more branded, professionalized, commercialized it becomes, the more it's following mentalities around the big players in theatre, art galleries, museums, festivals and inevitably will replicate the same thinking around income generation. Immersive has inherited that, inevitably. Or mainstream immersive has. But what's also even more problematic is that immersive is a lot harder to get right than most other art forms and it takes a lot longer and is a lot more expensive.

The advice for new emerging makers of immersive is don't do it!

JB: *(Laughs)*

JLR: Unless you try and really commit to the long term, if you're in it for the long term and you understand just how hard it's going to be, harder than any other more established art form because there are spaces and understanding for those and there's ways to create in different disciplines that are more straightforward. In immersive, to do it well you need so many different art forms and approaches and disciplines and thinking and support.

JB: Jadé, is there anything you would tell emergent or young makers who want to engage audiences?

PJM: Always considering who it's by, so always know what your privilege is and what you're bringing to the table and how you might be responsible for continuing and propagating the same privileges. Always consider who it's with and always consider who it's for. Who are you actually making the work for? In terms of who it's by, I think everyone needs to be more transparent about what our privileges are and define our position in relation to class or gender or ethnicity. I think that kind of intersectional thinking as a way of establishing awareness around power and privilege also means that you are obliging us to explicitly take up, to name, to address our positionings. In the *Post-immersive Manifesto* (2020), we're always talking about trying to be transparent about who we work with, who we're consulting with, who we have as our allies, who playtests our work, who we'll do books with. Recognizing our methodologies, sources and crediting the people that came before us. Anyone who's interested in creating post-immersive performances can't ignore all the barriers for participation that the mainstream tends to impose. It's worth remembering that it's not about proving that your work is good to a small group of people that are 'in the know'; it's about creating work that is allowed to grow and develop at its own pace, whether or not it's art is kind of irrelevant, because it can be genuinely innovative, not because it's seeking to be the next new thing but because it's really unique to its context, to its creators and to what we're looking for. And then finally, who it's for. The audience is not this kind of everyman, but this image of the audience or the player is so ingrained, isn't it, that it influences other makers to inherit the mainstream understanding of who the audience is, what they look like and how they behave. And, sure, that might be the audience that exists at the moment, you know, a very sophisticated, white mainstream audience member. But you should keep in mind who the audience *could be*.

Notes

1 Para Active Theatre was founded by Jonathan Grieve and Bill Aitchison in 1993. In 1997 Persis Jadé Maravala joined as lead performer, later becoming co-director.
2 ZECORA URA Theatre was founded in 2001 by Jorge Lopes Ramos; it has been based in London and Rio de Janeiro since 2001.

3 Founded in 1974, Salisbury International Arts Festival is an annual multi-arts festival that delivers over 150 arts events each year in and around the city of Salisbury, England.
4 Gahambars / gahanbars are six seasonal festivals when Zoroastrians assemble to eat and share food communally.
5 Technoculture, Art and Games (TAG). TAG is an interdisciplinary centre for research/creation in game studies and design, digital culture and interactive art based in Montreal, Canada.

FIGURE 8 *Image details Dr Joanna Bucknall in the process of podcasting a TAIT episode. Photographed by Nigel Tuttle on 21 March 2022.*

CHAPTER 7

Possible futures round-table discussion with Joanna Bucknall, Oliver Lansley, Persis Jadé Maravala, Jorge Lopes Ramos, Joseph Thorpe, Ruth Cross, Bertie Watkins, Owen Kingston and James Seager

Speaker key:
JB: *Joanna Bucknall*
OL: *Oliver Lansley (Les Enfants Terribles)*
PJM: *Persis Jadé Maravala (ZU-UK)*
JT: *Joseph Thorpe (The Lab Collective)*
RC: *Ruth Cross (Cross Collaborations)*
JLR: *Jorge Lopes Ramos (ZU-UK)*
BW: *Bertie Watkins (COLAB Theatre Productions)*

OK: *Owen Kingston (Parabolic Theatre)*
JS: *James Seager (Les Enfants Terribles)*

[The round-table discussion was recorded over Zoom on 13 May 2021.]

JB: In what ways have you been able to continue your practice under restrictions and lockdown conditions? And what have been the challenges of working in that way? Have there been discoveries of working in the digital realm?

OL: I would say nothing is maintained; I think early on we realized that just trying to keep going as 'normal' wasn't going to work. I think there was a period at the start where everyone was; if we just batten down the hatches, we can ride this out, and I think we got to the point where we realized we didn't really have a long-enough leeway to do that. So, I think as a result we did start at looking into the kind of ways of doing work digitally. I think there are a lot of positives and negatives. But one of the main positives that's come out of the pandemic for me is the huge potential for working more digitally; obviously, it's exciting. It gives other people access to the work but particularly what it does for access in terms of physical access for people that can't necessarily physically access our work in the same way. Whether that's due to having a disability or being in a different country or whatever reason it might be that they can't come and access us direct, to be able to make work for those people and also the financial restraints of accessibility as well. Like coming into London and seeing a theatre show is not a cheap business. So, being able to create work that people can access, to me, that's been one of the massive take homes of this type of work and something that I don't want to lose.

I think something that we should now be thinking, when the world does open up, when we start opening up our big physical shows again that actually, this feels like an important companion to that, as opposed to just the stuff that we did while everyone was locked in their homes. We did a few different digital things. And you could sort of see the progression of them as we did them, but we ended up doing basically a full digital immersive show with our *Sherlock Holmes* (2021) show. It was challenging, but I think on the whole, I'm really pleased that we were forced to explore those things further. I think there's a lot of stuff that will come out of it that I want to make sure that we don't just go, 'Oh, that was then and now we go back to where we were'. But there's a lot of this stuff which should be a very important part of our work moving forward for those reasons of access.

JB: It really heartens me to hear you talking about access because I think it's one of the big conversations that was starting to emerge before lockdown and before the pandemic. The scene is very London-centric still. In terms of financial access, I think lots of things are starting to emerge that we can utilize to have those audiences alongside our traditional audiences. So, it's really great to hear that those are some of the things that you'd like to hold on to. Now/

OL: /I think they can be complimentary of each as well. The idea with immersive stuff is you always have different tiers of audience interaction. And whatever that may be in some experiences, it's about how much you pay for. Or in some experiences, it's about how brave your audience member is. But for us doing immersive theatre, you're always catering with the audience member who wants to come in and start talking to actors and wants to engage 100 per cent, but you also have to cater for people that don't necessarily want to engage in that same way. It's just another tier potentially that we could have people interacting with live audiences, digital audiences, interacting the same way, in the same experience with live audiences. It's important to see this is a really exciting thread to add to our toolkit.

JB: I know that many of you have probably been working in some way within the digital realm during all the restrictions that we're under. Jadé, you've been doing a great digital work in terms of 'shows' like *Project Perfect Stranger* (2021) and connecting with audiences globally through this medium. And I know access is something that you feel quite strongly about.

JM: Yeah, I suppose in some ways, what I think is, what things can truly be changed? I think that we've seen, I definitely have, the chance this year [2021] to take stock of our industry and be a bit more articulate about the problems that I think the pandemic has exposed; what it has cracked open in terms of privilege should be clearer to a lot of the people. I hope that is something that is kept on, that discussion continues to be spoken about in terms of class and privilege, who gets to access this kind of work. Lockdown was, we felt, going to be super temporary, and it was kind of a fun way to have a well-earned rest and take stock. Things got very, very middle class for a while, didn't they? There was lots of baking of sour dough bread and learning of foreign languages, and you know feeling quite pleased with ourselves doing paper mâché projects with our children, and blah, blah, blah. In some ways, you could really see how the discussion around lockdown was defined by 'middle classness'. It was quite sickening.

We [ZU-UK] started to meet online because the whole world migrated online. What were you going to do? We had to just carry on making work with whatever we had at our disposal. And we started to meet people and see that the situation was so new, that this feeling was so new which was that we were all bonded by the pandemic. We felt newfound connections to other people across the world who we didn't know yet, but at the same time, we were super atomized and separated and alone and isolated. And so, we're all kind of, it's just very new. At the same time, we're meeting separately and unable to really be together. And for us touch is like, touching the body is a big aspect of our work so that was hard. And yeah, we're getting these first-row seats into each other's bedrooms and into each other's houses which meant seeing into each other's lives in a way that we hadn't been privy to before. So, it was simultaneously very separating and very intimate.

I thought that was one of the things we really wanted to move forward with. And we did create projects that were absolutely responding to very serious and very grown-up matters but acknowledging and incorporating all these limitations and all the idiosyncrasies of this context and how playful approaches could be used to unlock potential for creativity.

But my main thing, aside from using things like creating a game show, my main thing, really, was about hoping that it's going to be a way of seeing how we are going to live post-pandemic: not just looking at our trajectory as how we have progressed and where we have got to through 200,000 years of existing, but rather what we have learned. What systems are we going to continue with? And that way of being able to see the way that we live is just one system out of a myriad that we could be choosing from is important. So, I think that was the main thing that I've been wanting to use in terms of game designing and revealing what's underneath the paint work sort of thing.

JT: We [The Lab Collective] had a real problem when looking at the digital. We discovered that yes, we could expand our audiences and get international visibility for people to see our work and interact with us over remote space. However, the concerns that started to come into my brain was 'who is able to actually have access to that digital in the first place?' I got very, very worried. And also concerned that actually we were thinking along the lines that we are being accessible. We were cutting out a large proportion of the population from being able to experience our work. I've been trying to play with digital and other means; I've been moving over to look at RPG and more role-playing games. Looking at streaming and finding ways that audiences are able to interact with and change stories, narratives and character choices through this kind of game play. But something that we saw, the same as what Jadé was just saying, is how the systems which are built around us and the services available to us continue to promote feelings of remoteness, of individual experience and aloneness. Everything from Amazon to Deliveroo, these services that are placed to make sure that we don't have contact with people, and I think we've begun – especially Joe Iredale [Core member of Lab Collective] – looking into what is brand and what is 'brandalism'[1] to explore how services are delivered to us, questioning if art is something that could end up going that way, which I find quite interesting. I have participated in a few digital experiences recently and I found myself not being able to access it mentally, becoming tired, becoming unable to kind of throw myself into something. Even having nine pictures on the screen now is difficult to focus on! And so, I think I have become really interested in remoteness and how to tangibly connect non-digitally while not being in a physical space together. And I agree with Ollie that bringing in digital elements into live play is probably really important. We've been working with a couple of app developers to create a standalone app that can go alongside one of our experiences, but that was also a way, originally, we were looking at it – as a standalone. We found that we needed the live element to be able to create a discussion, to create the actual 'meat' of the show, and the app was then just a way of being able to control the structure. I agree that we've been very much looking at a middle-class concept and maybe that's what we've always been doing with immersive work. Maybe we've always been looking at the middle class.

JB: I agree and I think, I think there is a fatigue, and I think it's becoming sort of peaked now. We spend so much of our time looking at digital screens whether that be through Zoom, on our phones, and it's obviously been exacerbated by the context that we're in. And there has been a rise in work that is happening 'postally'. Ruth, obviously your work has operated in that kind of remote but tangible and material way for a very long time, and I wondered if you wanted to add something about that idea of remoteness and deliverable art in some way.

RC: Yeah, sure. I'm in Spain right now, and I'm in Spain because my wife is Spanish, so I was living between the UK and Spain, then lockdown happened, so, I've been in Spain for the last year [2021]. And my practice has moved very much to working with migrants and refugees. I've been making performance, immersive performance work with local people and migrants and refugees over the last two years, particularly here in the rural areas where I'm living in the South of Spain. And as I'm listening, I'm thinking in terms of these questions: how does that work translate to digital access when often the people that I'm working with don't have access either financially? They don't have the skills. They don't have access to iPads and laptops. Most people that I work with have smartphones and are very good at communicating on smartphones but don't have access to other resources. And so, there's something around the way in which I've been trying to focus myself during this last year. It has been to bring the qualities of what I'm creating as an immersive practitioner and the culture of care that I want to create with audience members and also the performance that I'm working with migrants and refugees is to look at how do I extend that out beyond a formative theatre experience out into how do we create this kind of sense of a culture solidarity during this time where there's so much divide?

And speaking of this kind of 'middle-class sour dough making' which is true of my personal experience to a certain extent. And also, being able to create these kinds of connections between people. It hasn't been performance making for a public audience. It's been sending WhatsApp's to groups of people so that we've been creating these social exchanges, gatherings, but online in ways that are really able to be accessible. I guess it's enabled me to breakout of thinking theatre happens for a paying public to thinking about what *actually* is theatre. What happens traditionally in cultures? Theatre is a place where people came together to exchange and to celebrate, to create, I guess to be seen, to be witnessed, to be in this kind of place of exchange. And so, that's what I've been trying to focus on in my current context. But I can also speak of the letter project *Post, Present, Future* (2010). I'm still doing it. And people have been receiving this kind of one-on-one experiential gifts, let's say in the form of a letter that they've written to themselves. People receiving their letters from five years ago are often surprised. So many people have said to me, 'I've been wanting time and space to reflect' or 'I've been craving time and space to reflect because my life is so busy'. And then they receive their letter, and they open it. And they're like, now, I have time and space to reflect. It's interesting how, to me through the pandemic, there's been lots of opportunities that have been created performatively and also there's something about having space in our lives to be able to deepen into. I think someone else had mentioned the sense of taking stock of the industry, but not only of the industry but also where are we as humans right now living together. What is it that that we're moving towards? In this sense of going back to the 'new normal', what does that mean? We have a responsibility as theatre makers and shapers to look at, what sort of invitations or provocations do we want? What kind of imaginary futures are we enabling people to step into that help us to kind of take those steps towards, well, for me anyway, very important and more integrated in terms of cultural diversity?

JB: I really love what you said about the idea of an exchange and the idea of a gift. And going back to the sort of the fundamental site of theatre as a place to be witnessed and to witness and to share. Because it's moving off the laptop-based approach to performance and into something that I think most people have in their lives which is some kind of smartphone or device.

JLR: I very much empathize with Ruth's reflections around when you engage with specific groups of people who you listen to and who you make work with and who are telling you, 'Those things that you do sound great, but I've got WhatsApp.' Over the years, there have been the things that have moved us away from the kind of large-scale massive mammoth kind of events where everyone just kills themselves to create something beautiful, maybe transformational, often for middle-class audiences, to something that is like, okay, hold on, maybe there's a lot of people we're putting off here. And we might be putting them off for a number of reasons. It might be access, that is physical access or access needs. It might be the price of things. But actually, a lot of the access issues around the work Jadé and I have been developing over the years have been around the sense that a number of people feel they don't belong. It's not their thing. It's not for them. And either the image that represents it or the way it's spoken about, the way it's covered, where it's cited just feels like to a large number of people, they're like, 'No, no, yeah, looks cool but nah, thank you. Like even if you give me a free ticket, I wouldn't go. Even if you give me a coach in front of my house and took me to it, because I will just feel uncomfortable, it's not for me. It's for other people that don't look like me or don't talk like me', and so on. Which is not easy to address and especially the comments that I've been seeing in the chat around the history of theatre versus history of immersive is that something that Jadé said as well, is that a kid can just jump up in a costume and start making theatre, right? How do you start making immersive?

The usual kind of mainstream version of what's become the infrastructure required relies on so much stuff that some theatre does, but some theatre doesn't. And it feels that there's a lot less options for kids just interested in getting into immersive: but how do I start if I don't have the contacts, if I don't have networks, if I don't feel confident about what I'm doing, if I see no role models that look like me and so on?

So, when we started engaging, and these are often not just communities in Newham where we're based, but also in Brazil and Colombia where we work often. We're like, 'Yeah. WhatsApp. Sounds great. I've got it. I've got 3G. What can we do?' And that was the beginning of *Project Perfect Stranger* (2021). We've been working with WhatsApp and SMS for a while because even, I guess, before *Hotel Medea* (2006–12), which was one of our large projects, we were fascinated by the technology, not the technology that is high end but the technology that people have understood as part of their bodies. We've been working with SMS in the past and it just felt like a 'no-brainer' to return to that.

We often kind of hack our own work as well, about ten years later, twenty years later. We just kind of triangle back to that stuff that we put so much time into. And the other thought that came up was the *Pick Me Up (& Hold Me Tight)* (2020 & 2021) project because again, it's looking at infrastructure; it's accessible to a wide number of people. Pay phones, they are, most people would agree, considered obsolete, yet to a large number of the population, they have that intrinsic relationship with our understanding of connection over distance, our connection with other humans, bringing people closer, even if now, some people don't really understand why they exist at all . . . So kind of ringing all the phones and inviting people to just come and pick up the phone circumvents the kinds of questions that often lead to people feeling excluded from the grammars of immersive conventions: 'Will I feel dumb, or will I feel, like, exposed? Will people laugh at me because I don't get it?' A ringing phone that you pick up, a letter that you write, a WhatsApp that you send, I feel are excellent ways into a world, so we've been fascinated with obsolete technology/

JB: /I have a real thing about audio tapes. I've still got lots of blank tapes because I bought loads before it looked like they were about to go out of circulation. I've got lots of tape and recording devices. There's something still very beautiful about the slide clunk and click of that and the hiss of when you press play. So, I very much share that fascination with obsolete tech. And a telephone, like the kind you pick up and put your hand around in the middle with two heavy bits at either end. There's something really tangible, intimate. And I don't know if that's because of my generation? I have memories of standing in phone boxes, talking to boyfriends, making collect calls to my mum to pick me up at 2:00 a.m. So, for me, it is a very embodied experience. Bertie, can you wade in here? You have been working to provide spaces in your venues that are accessible for young and emerging makers.

BW: Yeah. Well, we kind of, it came down to what the government allowed us to do. And obviously because that's our main priority. We found that what was lovely about the online things, like what we were saying about the accessibility, is that we didn't need to provide spaces for people physically anymore, which was wonderful because they had the whole internet to go roam around in and make their own shows. My personal excitement that came from all the online stuff was not necessarily how it's changed immersive theatre but kind of how it's changed the mechanics within immersive theatre and what the sphere can bring to the future of theatre and how those sorts of hybrids can become a thing.

I was also desperately sad, and the more online shows I saw because again, like we were saying, there's just something so lacking at looking at the screen rather than being in a room full of people. And it's just something that the more I saw, the more I kind of got more and more sad and by not being able to see other people's faces smiling and seeing their body language and seeing people, sort of, make friends within a room. And it sucked the joy out of it. And it also lost the conversations that come with theatre, what happened when you do put people in a room is that something happened, whatever that is, and it sort of goes back to Thespis,[2] the whole point of why it was created.

My big thing was what can we do without screens and how can we support people to find doing things without screens as you know that's one of the biggest challenges for putting anything online is immediately, it's a screen-based thing. So, we offered our spaces for some theatre companies to come and use our space as sort of like a 'geotag' location and ways to access the space being Covid-friendly. And then also, being able to create a sort of online buzz for people to be able to explore different experiences, to be able to try and maintain some sort of hub of being able to share the immersive work.

Because what's also been fantastic is the amount of immersive work that has come out of the last year [2020/2021]. Considering there's no venues open and we were really desperate to open them up again. Annoyingly when we did, we had to shut down pretty soon after again. So, that was quite a frustrating experience, but it's been really lovely to just see the immersive work blossom into something that it wasn't before. Now it will become a hybrid jungle of immersive ideas which is really exciting thing for us. I think everyone is now going to be thinking of shows that are socially distanced. And of all the shows that I know opening this year [2021] have very much taken social distancing into account.

There are hundreds of shows opening that are hopefully changing the face of theatre and not just immersive theatre which I find exciting.

JM: I just wanted to offer a counterpoint to what Bertie is saying. It's just that you know everyone is going, 'Oh god. I'm on Zoom and it's so terrible'. First of all, it's sort of saved us. And let's be honest about that, it has! Because what would we have done without it? And secondly, I think that it's really important that it is recognized as a tool that actually favours certain kinds of people because in person, meetings and negotiating physical space with other people is sometimes fraught with all kinds of rules and codes about: who's allowed in the space, who belongs, who's a fluent speaker, who's got a really nice vocabulary, who's dominating the talking? All these kinds of ways we recognize privilege, rights, in terms of gender, in terms of race and in terms of class, all come out a lot more when you're in this 'zoom' space. This year has been such a great leveller in terms of Zoom. I certainly know it has been for me with all my 'whatnots' going on that make me a complex person just like everyone is. It has actually been a real relief and a real way of grounding and being able to be in a space where everyone's got exactly the same size square as everyone else is incredibly democratizing and incredibly releasing of some of those pressures that I think we go through, especially people who are like me. I'm not a White person. I'm not middle class. I'm not a man. I don't have a posh name. I haven't been to a good school. All of those things that might make me... I am very much speaking from, you might say in academic terms, as an embodied – embedded subject. So, I can only really talk about what I've experienced. I think that's just a good counterpoint. And we try to, with *PlagueRound Game-Show* (2021), even though it was like a bit of silliness, the main priority of the playground was just being silly and playing games because silly is very serious. It was also recognizing that this was a space that people can interact with on a bit more of an even playing ground or playing field, yeah, you know what I mean. That's all I wanted to say just as a counterpoint.

OK: It was very interesting for me to hear people talk about class and screens because I had completely the opposite viewpoint on that. When you think about when people go out to consume dramatic arts in whatever format it is – like if you're upper class, you get the opera. If you're working class, you get the cinema. And then you've got everything in between. But the presence of the screen for me has often denoted more of a sort of working-class perspective. These days, everybody's on a screen. My children come home; they're not going to school anymore; they're doing all their work on screens. Pre-pandemic, they've watched some telly, but they wouldn't really engage with a computer hardly at all. And then suddenly, they were on the computers all day long, every day. I live on a council state in South London; all the families around me have got screens. My kids are unusual in, they don't have smartphones. But most of the families around us, their kids, similar age, have got smartphones. So, for me, the screens thing seemed like actually quite a good way for most people to be able to access stuff in a less intimidating way than going out of your house, going to a place that's not familiar, maybe having to dress up, you know. But there are a lot of people who live around me who would probably love the shows that we do, but they feel put off by that barrier of culture capital, not feeling like they belong in the world that they're going to go and visit physically. So, for us, because as I say we do a lot of gameplay-based theatre, but it is still theatre, going online for us really did seem like a natural thing to do. It made our work more accessible to people who would have really struggled to come along to it in person; we've seen that not just through international audiences but also through the sorts of people who've become fans of our work brought virtually to shows whereas they would have really struggled to get them to show up in person. So, to give you an example, one of the first things we did online was a World War II-themed show [*England Expects* (2020)]. We love our history in Parabolic, and it was all about naval vessels in the Mediterranean in an alternate history of World War II. And we had a lot of older people come who were mostly parents or grandparents of people who would normally come and see our shows in person. They, for whatever reason, either because they don't live near London or they're house-bound or they just wouldn't have thought it was their kind of thing, they would never show up to one of our shows in person, but they did come along and engage with what we were doing online which meant we had to work really hard to keep it as simple as possible and accessible which for us is always a challenge because we always tend to veer towards complexity.

And in the first couple of months of doing it, we were having to teach people how to use Zoom for twenty minutes before we could start the show. I mean we probably wouldn't have that problem now [2021], a year on, but this time last year [2020], there were still a lot of people who weren't using it and I know for a fact we taught some elderly relatives to use Zoom to do our show, and then they were able to talk to their kids afterwards, which was quite a nice win really.

But in terms of translating what we would normally do in person and online, I think the main thing for us was bringing people into the world of the show. We call it immersive theatre. For me, the immersive part of it is making your audience part of the world of the show, not just physically present within the show, not just standing in the same set as the actors and sharing the same space but also sharing the same world. And that's where the interactive thing comes in for us and for the audience to be able to *affect* that world makes them feel that they share that world with us. And then we tell a collaborative story within a shared world and that was the hardest thing for us to really crack. Because you can make a game available and make that work online and we did that several times. But drawing people into that world, a huge part of that for us would be the environment that you bring them into, so trying to do that over a little screen was harder, but it is possible, and films do it all the time. So, for us, looking at the techniques that filmmakers use to help immerse you in their story was a key thing.

I don't know that we cracked it completely 100 per cent, but there's a lot of good stuff that we've learned about not relying on the physical environment as much. And I think from the point of view of access and getting some new faces into our shows, we're definitely persevering with it.

We're about to announce a show which is going to be an online and in-person hybrid. So, the idea being, that we can preserve some of the game play elements for people who are online, who will then interact with people who are physically present. And the people who are physically present will be sharing the things that they discover and find with the people who are online and create a meaningful connection that feels realistic. So, that for us has been a useful takeaway to try to see how we can preserve that stuff.

JB: What do you hope for it in terms of all the things that have emerged out of being under restrictions so all the things that we've talked about, what do you hope to carry forward from that and what do you hope the 'post normal' landscape will be not just for your practice but also in a broader term?

JS: It's a big question, isn't it? I think it points a little bit to Bertie's point, what we're all talking about is connectivity. And that's what immersive theatre does and *is*. It's connecting people. You look at the music industry, and you see why and how that shifted and how they make money. It's all in the live shows. And in the live economy, the experience economy that people keep talking about, so I've missed that like Bertie. But at the same time, I'm desperate to get back into theatre, I'm desperate to have that connectivity, I'm desperate to do live immersive shows, but as I said earlier, we have a learned a lot doing online shows, and we want to see how we can use that now, in this kind of hybrid that Owen is talking about.

How that can benefit, how you mix it, how you can have a live show but with people playing at home, and we're working on something next year actually. It's forced us to do is to think of them on equal terms, the live experience and the online experience.

I think it's an exciting time and a challenging time. But what I discovered over the last four years of the people working in the immersive industry is that they're some of the most talented and exciting people working in the industry who think outside the box. And sometimes the people who work in that box, traditional theatre people, they're sometimes not scared but sometimes they're surprised at the ingenuity but there is ingenuity in that industry of course. The ingenuity and imagination and all of it and the traditional theatre industry has been forced to think about how they can react. You only have to look at the National Theatre.[3] Initially, they started putting out just the film shows online and then they started doing crazy things with *A Midsummer Night's Dream* (2020). They've been forced into thinking that way. We all have but I think what excites me is that the immersive industry is growing so much and so popular because the people that work within that sector are always thinking what next, what can we do next, how can we push ourselves. I think it's exciting to see how the two worlds can co-exist.

The other crucial point is how they can co-exist and not compete because what I always keep thinking is that I don't want to do a live immersive experience and then have a digital one and then suddenly everyone does digital and not come to the live or vice versa. If you can solve that then both can co-exist, then you don't have to see them as competition.

OK: That's spot on. I think they need to be complementary if you're going to try and involve both those things at the same time and make them co-exist, alongside each other. What I'm most excited about for the coming year is I'm really hopeful; there's going to be some new show structures and concepts. You tend to see the same basic structure rolled out time and time again and really you were just changing the sort of the internal creative elements of that, but it was essentially the same structure 'under the hood'. And I think what online work has forced us to do is to completely reimagine how we structure our work and that excites me because that's my favourite bit of it! At Parabolic, we're always looking for new ways, new structures that we can hang a story on. So, if we can find some new ways of perhaps online working, incorporating that, it busts open some of the structures and makes us rethink stuff.

I think that's exciting for audiences as well because, ultimately, if you go to a show where you go into one room then you go into the next room and some people coming behind you in the room that you've just been in and you know they're there and then you all move around together in a big carousel, that's alright and it's fun and it's lucrative, but you know that's happening as an audience. And if that's all, immersive theatre ever is, then we've got a problem. Obviously, it isn't that. There are other structures out there but I'm just using that as an example because that's one of the ones that's been beaten to death; if we can change up the underlying structure of how these sorts of shows work, the more exciting they will become.

JLR: I couldn't agree more with James and Owen's input around the structures and the thinking and where usually the thinking comes from. Often, it means that it's just a very limited amount of risk taking and a very limited frame of what's available to us. I guess we are talking here today to new makers, emerging makers, researchers, so as a maker who came to the UK twenty years ago, couldn't speak a word of English, my immediate response as an immigrant, as working class, as a person with no contacts, I just absorb the culture and just go. Everything that comes to me must be the right way, must be good, must be proper and so that comes from the way I learned English and the person who I had as my reference, this imposing White man with a posh accent, to know the models that were out there. Our first big push to make it in the theatre was to go, go, go, go, go, make it work economically, make it work in the models that were out there and *Hotel Medea* (2006–12) was the outcome of that blind drive to just be the best and be the hit of Edinburgh and go to the South Bank. Yes, we made it! And when we got there, we were there. There was a big poster in the Hayward Gallery[4] with our face on it and we looked around the audiences and were like, 'This is so not what we want to be doing'. These people they have access to culture. They are great people, I'm sure, but what about other people who we came from? What other models were we not aware of because, especially I can speak for myself, I'm blindly following these things that I think are just the right way to do it? So, it will never come from the *National Theatre*, the solution to our problems. It will never come from the established ways of thinking. It will come, if the space is given, and the voices are heard, from quite straightforward-thinking solutions, structures and mechanics. Some of them have been in place for seventy years, just in a different discipline. When that 'penny dropped' just after the big mammoth production . . . Well, we just killed ourselves to do it.

It was just unsustainable on every level. We then went, okay, hold on. Are we just following blindly various models that we think there's no way out of? So, we stopped really referring to what we did as theatre.

We're very questioning of the term 'immersive'. And we started looking at game design, cooking, experience design, archaeology, why not and I guess that if I was talking to people who are trying to get in and not quite making it, I'd just say, 'You're probably the one that's going to come up with the best possible solutions and ideas for your context and the people who you make work with and for so try not to get distracted by this idea of what we need to do and what's available to us would be'. The current thing we're testing is for shopping centres. It's a three-player game. It's available: I'm talking as if it's ready, it's definitely not ready! But we're testing it – and that's another thing we've learned from other disciplines is just keep testing it; test again and test again with the people who you intend for it to be with and for and by. Just bring them in and go like, 'How is this?'

JM: Returning to Joanna's question though about moving on. We've got loads of new terms since the pandemic to describe everything that we've all been experiencing. And this thing about the 'new normal' is a bit of a farce, isn't it? It's like, what is normal anyway? We just generally think that it's the state of connecting yesterday with tomorrow. It's just continuity, isn't it? The way we've actually been living this last 100 years and last 20 years is that change is so accelerated that this feeling of a 'reliable normality' is just an illusion. So, this idea of a 'new normal' makes it sound like there was an old normal but the old normal was constantly mutating and so maybe the new normal will be just as illusory because it's all about transition.

We're in a time of upheaval, we're in a time of not knowing. And there are all these paradigms and values from the 'old normal' that have got no place. In the world post-Covid, all these old orthodoxies and established ways of thinking are dying. We just need to grow up and forget about returning to normal because that was the problem in the first place. It wasn't just the pandemic that happened, was it? It was also Black Lives Matter movement happened. It was also a way that we could see how people were being radically house-bound, now knew what it was like to actually be house-bound and have connections with that and realizing that working from home is a total privilege because there were all these people, people that live in East London and grew up on a council estate and the people that I'm in connection with – our frontline workers (my neighbours are nurses and teachers), and these people had to keep going out; my whole street got Covid at one point. It really shows those cracks. I think it is important to carry on with because we live in this hyper-interconnected, interdependent, complex world. In order to go forward, it's in all of our interest no matter who we are to adjust to the new reality in which the solutions are going to come from change, right? And change might mean moving over sometimes and making room for other people or change might mean not just how are you going to get back to your own aspirations but actually how about questioning what we are as a society, what does it mean to even be a society and what are other roles of artists in that. Instead of this really comfortable chummy, chummy – because we know that inequality is a backdrop for commercial immersivity. Sorry, but that is just a fact and that scales across the social, the cultural and the aspiration.

Our industry is suffering for that. It suffers without diversity of thought. We have to consider who the work is really for. What is this work for? Who's it really going to benefit? It's just all self-serving – it seems to me – I'm not from this but I don't say I make immersive theatre because quite frankly, I hate it. I really do. I don't like it at all. I don't like what it represents. I don't belong to it. I don't like it when people call my work immersive. I've written a 'post-immersive manifesto' (2020) which details everything that I'm saying much more clearly, with some other people.

But we are WEIRDOs,[5] right? WEIRDOs is the psychology acronym for Western, educated, industrial, rich and from a democratic society. We make work for WEIRDOs by WEIRDOs. And what this means is that everything is framed as universal and generalized to all human beings when it actually only pertains to WEIRDOs. And WEIRDOs are a small amount of the global, in terms of the global population. WEIRDOs, we, as WEIRDOs, are a minority. So, all the time just translating something into another language is a cosmetic repair. It doesn't really mean anything.

And so, it's about who belongs and I think as we go forward, the three things that I always think are really important are: always consider who it's by – Jess Marcotte is this intersectional feminist games designer, and they always talk about, before any meeting – we could have with this one as well – before any meeting, all the cards are out on the table and all interests are declared. Really advocating that kind of intersectional thinking as a way of establishing awareness around power and privilege. Always consider who it's with. That would be the second thing. I think it's really important, who plays. I mean I struggle with this as well. We struggle with this. Who's playtesting our work; who do we consult with; who do we take advice from; what are the models we're trying to emulate? That's important because anyone interested in creating post-immersive performance needs to be able to make it genuinely relevant to all kinds of people.

Hannah Nicklin is this games designer. She's in Copenhagen now but I really like the way she describes how 'the player' is used as if it's a neutral term, some sort of societally neutral term. And you know just as God created Adam in his own image, White middle-class men shape audiences in theirs. And so, when we have this as a lens for our world, we forget that the masses are made up of people and white cis gender, het, middle-class men are a minority in that. And I also have been guilty of thinking of this audience as this so-called kind of 'everyman' and it doesn't exist. I think this neutral audience member doesn't exist and I think those are the three things that I would take forward.

RC: For me, it's crucial, crucial, crucial that we think about whose reality counts. We have this way of, I mean even within the context that I'm working in, I was making social theatre work with local people, with migrants and refugees around belonging so around exploring these themes of belonging. We would come together, and we'd had a developing process of several weeks. And then we would create a performance, a theatre piece, experiential theatre piece but we'd always start with sharing food from different cultures. We'd go exploring this kind of process of migration as people moved through physical sites, so we'd have this sense of travel and exploration. And obviously creating work like that with hundreds of people coming together hasn't been possible, I haven't been able to do that for the last year. One of the things that I've become fascinated by and the reason that I'm in Spain is because I'm working on a project called *La Bolina*,[6] which works to create sustainable livelihoods for migrants and refugees.

We're looking at migration of young people out of rural areas and the increase of migrants coming into the south of Spain. We have got this phenomenon of depopulating rural areas, older population who are becoming increasingly isolated, particularly during the pandemic, and an increase of migrant and refugee workers. The project that I've been setting up and working on here with my colleagues from the Gambia, from Morocco and we're working on an alternative food system here that we're interested in. We've been going to the *Plastic Sea*,[7] which is in Almeria. Which some of you might have heard of the *Garden of Europe* it's called but it's basically this gigantic, massive, massive greenhouse, four kilometres. You can see it from the moon. It's this huge matrix of greenhouses. And I've been going there with the migrant workers who are working often in slavery conditions in these spaces. For me, it's been an amazing opportunity to be able to step into the shoes of the 'other', to be doing theatre work with each other as a small group as researchers but researchers, you know, they would never class themselves as researchers. They wouldn't class themselves as theatre makers. And I've been using a GoPro camera to try to create the closest way of stepping into these environments, considering, how can we, how can I take you there?

And I'm interested in terms of what you're saying James about these blended performances; it feels like this last year has been a real research period. And going forwards as well as creating this video work with GoPro, that is allowing audiences to kind of experience through what it is to be, getting up at that time, working all day, not knowing if you're going to get paid or not. How do then we take audiences to go and experience that life? I'm interested in how we create that as an 'interactive thing' that's happening online and also live.

We're very, very much led by the migrants who are there working in these spaces. I think, I could carry on. *(Laughter)* I guess maybe just one thing to say is on a personal level this last year, being here in Spain for the whole time, has enabled me to slow down and to put focus on research. And I'm not sure if that's the same for others amongst us but there's been, I've not had the pressure that I felt to be creating so I've had time to really just be with the themes and the topics that are of deep interest to me and to try to create spaces to visualize the invisible. This is what I think I've always been interested in. All my performance work, really coming back to this reality counts and how do I use my resource and my skills, my capacity to be able to give, to be able to kind of co-create and co-empower the people to be able to visualize their experiences that they wouldn't necessarily be able to gain access to?

And the food systems across Europe, Sainsbury's, every Aldi, every supermarket, has food that is grown by the people that I'm working with. For me, it feels like these are crucial topics particularly during the pandemic. It's just thrown up, the vulnerability of our food systems, the vulnerability of the people who are growing, they're still there. We're all in our houses with our face masks on but they're on the fields, they're working. They don't have face masks. They don't have time off. They're ill but they still have to keep working. For me, I'm interested in how to give access to that, to visualize that? It was Jorge who was saying how do we, encourage the young makers to not get stuck in the labels, to deconstruct and just to be true to what the things are that are really calling you because then we're not replicating the current systems that are not working. Our work and our theatre making to be able to be representative to the things that are truly interesting rather than replicating a system of power that we don't want to see.

JB: We're still saying the same things that this term immersive is so problematic because it's sort of come from the outside. And I know that in the post-immersive manifesto, you very much raised this and it's something imposed upon us and something that draws audiences, certain audiences in, but also, really alienates others. It feels that all of this is coming to a head now. I suspect as we move out of this [Covid-19], that terminology will become more and more troubled offering us a broader dialect. Once with which different voices can be heard. I hope that we can start to have the room to articulate our own work in ways that isn't driven by this externally imposed publicity monster that immersive has kind of become. Joe, I wanted to just turn to you. Joe, your work previously has very much been about bringing people together to make sort of transient and momentary communities and I wondered what your concerns were for sort of continuing and developing that work as we move out of this because your work is very much about bringing people together.

JT: As I said before, I'm not able to work on Zoom for long periods of time, so work has been stretched out and conversations take three months rather than a week of intensive work or intensive rehearsal. But that's allowed me to consider audiences. We've been saying 'people'. And something that becomes really, really important, especially with post-immersive manifesto, is the emergence of the individual and ways they become part of a temporary community. Being able to not just understand yourself but understand others is something that I've become incredibly interested in as a participatory practitioner.

The other thing that is important to me is creating the invitations to generate action – to move forward – for two people or more to move forward together. So, whether that will be performer and participant, or whether that be participant and participant, or performer and performer – how do you enable those people to create something *together*. I am thinking more about how do we give focus and time to allow people to have that engagement with each other? I'm becoming less and less interested in maths. I've become more interested in commitment to each other. And before, I said about how inspired I was by Ruth, your work looking at letters, physical objects and memory – watching the moment that my co-artistic director, Natalie Scott's letter arrived and watching her sit and read it. And that joy that she felt. She put it down, and was like, 'God, I was stupid'. *(Laughter)* But that moment of holding something and allowing herself to talk to herself, and to guard herself. I think the idea of temporary community is important. I was lucky enough to go to a camping event recently. And what was wonderful was this huge mix of different communities, all coming together for these two days, being a temporary community and being able to share things. So, I think there was a conversation I had with a gentleman called Matt Gunter and he was talking about how we've all been able to kind of create our own morals and ethics away from each other during this time and yet as a society, we've been unable to share this. We haven't had the space yet to really talk about those things. I think that's where my hope comes from. If we can function again not only as individuals but also consider each other, being able to sort through those thoughts and have time to meditate, talk, and communicate, can create something very, very beautiful that's not only just about this space but also the external and the possible, the larger space. Talking of space, I've also become very interested in, where does space lie for this kind of work? Do we need buildings? Do we need the mind? Do we need the digital? These are all valid spaces to play within. And the more deeply that we can engage with these spaces, the more exciting – not only for us as artists but in the ability to turn others into artists too – and we can move forward! This is where I think my hopes are, and my fears. There is also something very different about the immersive world. Because I also work in the immersive world, looking at system-based things or management-based things and that's where I make, funnily enough, that's where I make a substantial part of my living and my artwork is something very different.

JS: What are your fears?

JT: I'm just scared of – I think as we said before – about the hope that we can create new systems and that we don't go back to relying on old systems. I know that there's a lot of conversations about television rights and film rights and that type of experience. And they're still kind of being placed in the same bubble of immersive and I'm really hoping that as you say we're able to define these things and see and explore these different areas. Because all of us here do different types of work that could be branded as immersive. And I just really hope that we can continue to take risks and try something new and different and take all that learning and move forward, instead of trying to kind of go back to what was, as Jadé said, 'normal' again.

OL: I think for me like what the pandemic, what the shutdown did was made you realize how much of a reset we needed in many, many different places. Just to briefly talk about theatre specifically. If we talk about the theatre and the fact that for a family of four to go and see *Harry Potter and the Cursed Child* (2016) in the West End is going to cost them 1,000 pounds that's an industry that needs to start again. That is an industry that is problematic and is not doing what it should be doing. What happened, the first thing that happened is those big, big theatre institutions, those were the ones that couldn't adapt. Those were the ones that had to shut down and they're still shut down. They're the ones that dug their feet in and went, 'Well, this is theatre, and this is how it works'. And I think you've got to understand when we talk about the normal, people talk about going back to, it's normal that worked, extremely well for a lot of people hence the desire for a lot of people and particularly a lot of commercial institutions to return to that. What was sort of extraordinary about the pandemic is that it, those behemoths of commercial theatre, just couldn't work around it. You could not, you know, a show like *Harry Potter* runs on something like 80 per cent occupancy to/

JS: /Breakeven.

OL: /To breakeven. And those models, there was no way of changing that and so they were forced to stop and that period of downtime, I really hope in a lot of ways has made people realize that actually, wow, we really, really needed a reset on a lot of things! And then I hope that space, in time, will provoke in people that fire to not allow, if there's going to be a 'new normal, then it needs to be different. I think we can't let it go back to that and we've all got a responsibility in that to not go, 'Oh, that was okay, now, let's get back to that as quickly as we can'. We've got to dig our feet in the ground and be like, no, that's we want to go forwards. We don't want to go backwards. And I think again, rounding it up and going back to theatre, a lot of these changes can be expressed or driven through the arts which is why it's such a catastrophe that our government have bled the arts dry for so many years now. Governments over the last two decades have decimated funding for the arts but that's where – for us, lucky enough to be in it, it's about raising up those voices, giving people the confidence and the skills to be able to have those voices and stand and try and keep and things moving forwards and not allow us to just get dragged down that path again.

OK: I think we should be really careful about being snobbish about licensed content and there's a good reason for that. I think it massively improves accessibility. If I go to 'Tony' who lives next door to me, who's a builder and I say to him, 'Tony, do you want to come to see one of my shows? It's about the Second World War and it's about politics', he'll find a good reason not to come. If I said to him, 'Do you want to go and see a show up in London. It's immersive Doctor Who [*Doctor Who: Time Fracture* (2021)]', he'll go, 'Oh yeah, the kids love *Doctor Who*. We'll all come'. Now, the two experiences are very different.

What's in Dr Who may not be what's in *my* show. But if he goes to *Dr Who* (2021) and he enjoys it and they have a great time talking to a dalek or whatever and then they come home again, next time, I go to him and say, 'I've got one of my shows on. Do you want to come to see it? It's a bit like that *Doctor Who* (2021), thing you saw and it's also a bit different', he's much more likely to say, 'Oh yeah, I'll give that a whirl', because the ice has been broken. That idea of going up London to go and see an immersive show, that is something Tony and his family now do. Whereas before, they wouldn't have done it because that was for the middle classes. So, I think we've got to be really careful. There are big licences that are out there to be got, my company is probably too small to get any of them. Some other companies are much bigger and would be able to do that and all power to them, if they want to go and do that. In terms of breaking the ice with new audiences, in terms of opening up an industry that uses the buzz word 'immersive' to cover a whole spectrum of work, it can make our own work much more accessible to people who wouldn't come and see it otherwise.

JB: I agree. That's another side of accessibility that I think mustn't be forgotten, is the power of IP. We know how powerful IP is. Les Enfants have worked with IP and Bertie I know you've worked with existing IP as well. It is a very particular way to access and speak to audiences who have exactly what Jadé was talking about which is that 'it's not for me'. But some of those IP's can make that connection/

OL: / We shouldn't be snobbish about content. And there should be something for everyone. What we do need to try and do is to make it possible for people to be able to access it and for people to be able to experience it. We sort of got into like this arms race of ticket pricing /and it's mad!

OK: /We also need to be careful that we don't link class with economics as well. I'm the poorest person in my street and I'm surrounded by people who consider themselves to be working class. They're all tradespeople. All the doors down that way, and all of them that way, they're all tradespeople but they all earn more than me. Some of them earn more than double what I earn because I'm a poor struggling artist. We talk about the working class not coming to the theatre. I don't think economics is necessarily the barrier. There's a family two doors down from me; they love *Hamilton* (2015). They've seen it six times; they were over the moon when it came on *Disney+* because they're like, 'Oh, we love that show'. So, money was not a barrier to them going to the theatre. It was more *what* the theatre was offering. I think we can talk about very socially engaged, very aware, very 'woke' content for our shows but a lot of people who are working class, who we might even think could be the target of those shows, might not want to come and see it because of how it's marketed. There are, I think, distinctions to be made between how you market things, who your audience *is* in terms of culture and who your audience is in terms of economics. And our assumptions there are not necessarily correct.

JB: You tapped into something very interesting. As an industry we make massive assumptions about audiences, but we actually have no evidence to support them whatsoever. There is so little research done beyond 'what's your postcode and your age and your bank balance', that we actually couldn't possibly really know some of these things other than anecdotally from practitioners who might work in smaller ways that do get to know their audiences and capture some of that stuff in a much more sort of holistic way.

OK: The people in my street would prioritize entertainment over pretty much anything else. They have all got big tellies in their front room. There is a huge priority on entertainment over pretty much like over food, well not necessarily over food but over other things that other people from other cultural backgrounds might consider differently.

OL: That speaks to the greater problem of decades of cuts to the arts and to creating the sense that theatre is elitist which becomes a self-fulfilling prophecy. But if in primary schools you've got kids being able to go and see plays and if you've got art on the curriculum in a meaningful way, then/

OK: /That feeds cultural capital/

OL: /Exactly, exactly. Then suddenly, it doesn't seem like something that is alien to them when they're growing up. But that's the thing: it's about making sure that people have access to art. And not just art, art that they see themselves represented in, art that they see people that look like them represented in because not every kid is going to want to jump up on the stage in front of the rest of the school and perform a monologue, but I think that's the key/

OK: /It also works further up the cultural food chain as well. I would consider myself to be middle-class culturally, probably not economically if you're going to tie those two things together but definitely culturally. I would not go and see opera. I have no interest in opera. I've been to the ballet exactly once. People who consider themselves upper class culturally that's their cultural preference. We have to believe so, given how much money the Arts Council England[8] (ACE) spends on it. *(Laughter)* Those artificial cultural barriers and divides are something; post-pandemic, we've got a real shot at taking a sledgehammer to it all, but not if we tie ourselves to the cultural assumptions that are also tied to economic assumptions that mean that we wouldn't put on a big licensed production because we think the poor people will never come and see it. Well, who are the poor people? Actually, the poor people is *me* at the moment. And I probably would go and see it. *(Laughter)*

JT: Thinking about licensing, it's that idea of what *is* that license, what *is* the content you create within it and how do you subvert the thoughts within the world of that license? So, for instance, I also make licensed work. I worked with the Dank Parish's *Legitimate Peaky Blinders Festival* (2019).

I'm turning around to these suited and booted males that are inside the world of this play. They can create violence. And these audiences can create misogyny and be that gangster they've always wanted to be in this world we're replicating. How do I subvert this? How do we try and change this? Okay, we need to push a different story. Some of it was successful. Some of it was not. But it's that thing of what is the type of content that you're putting out and how does that change? There is some interesting, licensed work out there and yes, it is a great gateway. But I also hope that we can find a way to be defined from other forms of immersive work in some way. I also think culturally again, Joanna, what you say about where our assumptions lie is a really interesting question, which is why we are looking at temporary communities. I have friends of ours who use *Dungeons and Dragons*[9] as a role-playing interactive way of working with children with mental health conditions, to help them understand social interactions. That creative, interactive, theatrical experience is being made on a table in a school in the middle of Lewisham. We need to be able to move to them, not them to us, I think.

OK: We had the experience of trying to work out how we could tour For *King and Country* (2018), which is not a huge show and is in theory 'tour-able' in the back of a van. But we worked out we couldn't do it, simply because we couldn't charge the ticket price; we needed to charge to sustain the show outside of London. We can't take it to another city in the UK and charge that same money and actually get it without funding support. It just wasn't viable. And rather than not make any work at all, we're like, 'We'll just keep doing what we're doing then'. The Arts Council is the body that has the power in theory to step in and enable that kind of stuff, but they don't really seem to care about the weird kids of British theatre; they prefer conventional theatre. They understand that and they know how it works and they've got a model for it so they'll stick to funding that, and we can fend for ourselves. It's what it feels like from my perspective.

JB: I think one of the things that really is striking me through these conversations is we need spaces to do *this* more and we don't have those. It feels to me like there needs to be a space where we can start to put our voices to work so that we can build cultural capital and cultural value and start impacting on the way in which we might be received, understood, perceived.

Notes

1 'Brandalism' is a revolt against the corporate control of culture and space. They are a collective that stage art interventions in public spaces and have published a manifesto to outline the goals of the movement. You can access the manifesto at http://brandalism.ch/. Accessed 01 January 2022.
2 Thespis was an ancient Greek poet who has been credited, largely because of Aristotle's accounts, for being the first to present a character on stage.
3 The National Theatre was founded in 1963 and has been operating since the opening night of *Hamlet*, starring Peter O'Toole on 22 October 1963. The National Theatre is located on London's Southbank.
4 The Hayward Gallery is an art gallery situated within the Southbank Centre, London.
5 WEIRD is an acronym, standing for 'Western, Educated, Industrialized, Rich, and Democratic', introduced by Henrich et al. (2010) in their article 'The weirdest people in the world?'
6 *La Bolina* is an eco-project that was launched in 2017; you can access more details about the project on their website: https://labolina.org/en/home/the-bolina/. Accessed 01 February 2022
7 Poniente Almeriense is a comarca in Almería, Spain, also known as the 'sea of plastic' (*Mar de plástico*). The comarca contains ten municipalities and covers an area of 971 km^2.
8 ACE is the national development agency for creativity and culture. It holds and distributes public arts funds.
9 *Dungeons & Dragons* is a fantasy tabletop role-playing game originally designed by Gary Gygax and Dave Arneson in 1974.

Conclusion

Joanna Jayne Bucknall

Introduction

It has been a genuine delight to cultivate the necessary relationships, over the last five years, to bring to fruition the knowledge exchange opportunity that this volume represents. Curating and crafting the conversations that have blossomed out of those relationships, and to be able to share them with the associated knowledge communities, is a privilege. Generating a space where makers can share their praxical 'know how', expertise and perspectives is an important step towards decentring and diversifying the currently narrow canon of immersive theatre scholarship and practice. At times, the discussion in this book has been startlingly frank and generously candid, particularly around previously undisclosed topics such as financing, funding, privilege and accessibility. The conversations in this volume directly address some of the key concerns, anxieties, challenges and tensions the immersive sector faces in the current (2022), rather hostile, sociopolitical climate. In the Conclusion, I will draw out some of those challenges and tensions in more detail; however, it is important to recognize the novelty in providing the space for this discussion to be had, let alone disseminated beyond the context of the venue bar. These conversations represent a bold step towards demystifying certain aspects of the ways in which immersive theatre gets made, warts and all. Broadening the canon, in this very praxical way, is important for increasing both the reach and impact of a more diverse range of practices along the immersive theatre spectrum. Increasing the reach of a broader multiplicity of work is essential for ensuring a more inclusive and diverse representation of the immersive theatre sector in terms of its cultural visibility and, ultimately, its legacy. It is vital to the future vitality of the form that a more varied cross section of the immersive theatre spectrum is captured and disseminated. Documenting and highlighting a broader range of immersive and interactive dramaturgies, in a primary resource that has been generated first-hand by the makers, provides new praxical insights that have the potential to feed into the future of audience-centric practice. The conversations here not only contribute fresh insights, approaches and 'know how' that will both feed and enrich existing practitioners' toolkits but also, perhaps more significantly, offer aspiring and emerging immersive theatre makers access to and insight into more varied practical routes into engaging audiences.

Excavating value

Les Enfants Terribles have received recognition and critical acclaim for their immersive theatre making; however, despite their success, they have been almost entirely overlooked in scholarship. Beyond reviews, press releases and a brief case study in an article by Alston (2019) regarding financing, their work has been marginalized and unrepresented, critically and conceptually. As pioneers of the 'carousel' dramaturgical model that has become a prevalent form in the immersive sector, they have not received any significant critical attention. In Chapter 1, with Lansley and Seager, the conversation offers insight into those performance innovations. Although those innovations are not conceptualized in this volume, the primary resource that the chapter presents provides fresh access that will facilitate the possibility of further critical analysis. Watkins and Kingston have been hugely successful in building the grass-roots community of makers and audiences, not only through their own performance work but also in their endeavours to nurture and support new talent. Their fundamental commitment to grass-roots community building and knowledge sharing has been enacted through their involvement at Matthews Yard, the COLAB Factory and COLAB Tavern. Their film- and game-influenced dramaturgies have succeeded in building relationships with non-traditional theatre audiences. Despite their success in community building and innovations in hybrid dramaturgies, their work has also been neglected, failing, until now, to gain visibility within the canon or the broader performance landscape. Watkins and Kingston's work sits at the heart of the non-commercial London fringe; they have been a touchstone influential within the pop-up, DIY immersive community in terms of their approach but also their facilitation of networking and knowledge exchange at a localized level. Their inclusion in this volume seeks to acknowledge their position within the immersive landscape and extend the reach of their hybrid dramaturgies beyond the community that they have nurtured and sustained; offering key insights into the ways in which they have achieved that individually but also documenting the ways in which their endeavours have intersected to establish their success.

Like COLAB and Parabolic, The Lab Collective have been a core driving force of the London immersive scene; their work has often intersected with some of the dominant more visible companies in the sector, such as Punchdrunk, but their contribution until now has remained mostly unacknowledged. The Lab Collective have pioneered socially engaged approaches to immersion and interaction, with the impact of that work quietly unfolding across the pop-up and DIY sector. Behind the scenes they have also developed some of the first high-quality professional training opportunities with their innovative series of master classes. In addition to this they have broadened the impact of their expertise to the wider sector through consultation work and by holding key posts with large-scale immersive projects and performances. The Lab Collective have developed dramaturgies of interactivity that have the potential for generating radical transformation for the audiences who encounter them. However, these innovations and knowledge exchange activities have been shared tacitly until now; this volume highlights their contribution to the field and extends, in a more concrete way, the impact of their novel interactive dramaturgies. Our discussion here not only captures the praxical expertise that informs their work but also documents the role that they have played in community building through initiatives such as *Lighthouse*.

Ruth Cross established her intimate and care-based dramaturgical approach during the first wave of the immersive cultural phenomenon. Her work has impacted upon and influenced numerous first-, second- and third-wave immersive performance makers, including myself and Joe Thorpe from The Lab Collective:

I said about how inspired I was by Ruth, your work and looking at letters and looking at physical objects and looking at memory but watching the moment that my artistic director, Natalie Scott's letter arrived and watching her sit and read it. And that joy that she felt. She put it down, it was like, 'God, I was stupid'. [*Laughter*] But that moment of holding something and allowing herself to talk to herself and to guard herself. (See p.198)

Her work is widely respected and celebrated by makers, producers, venues and performance festivals across Europe. However, despite her undeniable impact on both practice and audiences, her work seems to have entirely evaded meaningful capture by critics or the academy. The inclusion of Cross Collaborations in this collection of conversations is vital in ensuring Cross' work receives the visibility that it deserves. She has tirelessly worked to develop socially engaged, audience-centric dramaturgies that draw upon concepts of care, ethical responsibility, radial amazement and ecological activism. Her current practice of working with migrants and refugees in Spain has shifted into a far more holistic, cross-disciplinary space than can possibly be described by the moniker of theatre; however, her contribution to the emergence of immersive theatre needs to be acknowledged along, as does her current practice in relation to the boundaries of the immersive theatre spectrum. My dialogue with Cross provides fresh insight into the ways in which one can utilize immersion and interactivity as a tool for social change and activism. It is vital to share Cross' work as an exemplar of socially engaged practice because it illustrates how immersion and interactivity can be utilized to meet not only some of the emergent and urgent challenges facing the sector, such as accessibility, diversity and inclusion, but also the most pressing societal challenge of our age, climate change.

Like Cross, ZU-UK were part of the first wave of immersive theatre; their groundbreaking work *Hotel Medea* (2006–12) has been widely documented, theorized and conceptualized; it holds a firm place within the immersive canon. *Hotel Medea* (2006–12) has legendary status within the annuls of immersive theatre practice; its innovation and success have been widely celebrated by makers, critics and scholars alike. ZU-UK themselves have disseminated through various critical writing, which explores the dramaturgy of *Hotel Medea* (2006–12). Despite the widespread acclaim of their work, their practices since *Hotel Medea* (2006–12) have not generated the same cultural currency nor been given the same consideration within the canon. It is vital to include their conversation in this volume for two main reasons. First, in our discussion, they scratch the veneer of the legacy of *Hotel Medea* (2006–12) to reveal some key concerns with the approaches that they employed in making that work. In their chapter, they add and extend the discourse around the show, and with the privilege of hindsight, they expose some of the challenges in making the work and offer insight into why they abandoned that way of theatre making. They also unpick aspects of the challenges they faced in making the work that have become obscured by its legacy. ZU-UK and I were keen to extend their 'voice' beyond the cultural romanticization of *Hotel Medea* (2006–12). As Maravala explains in Chapter 6:

> [E]very artist who works against the mainstream ends up, you know, you can get into some really dark places when you don't have the kind of support that other groups who are accepted. I was seeing at that time companies around Battersea Arts Centre for example, other known places for theatre and they're just very clique-y. I cannot stress how left out we were, how that felt miserable. I'm sick of it being a romantic idea, because I think a lot of people talk to me and they're like 'oh yeah it's so cool'; it wasn't cool, it was fucking painful, it was horrible! You just were getting knocked back all the time and with *Hotel Medea* (2006–12), we were getting knocked back all the time. And it's not cool. It was really hard, and we didn't get any support. (See p.157)

Second, they candidly discuss the ways in which they have been making work since *Hotel Medea* (2006–12) and how it has led them to the publication of 'The Post-immersive Manifesto' (Ramos et al. 2020). ZU-UK speak frankly about some of what they see as the central challenges, concerns and anxieties facing the sector but also the ways in which they have been responding to them and navigating through them. By including ZU-UK in this volume, they represent the elasticity of the spectrum and the challenge being made to the form through digital technologies and cross-disciplinary practice.

There is value in the volume beyond the curatorial ones that I have outlined here, and I am going to briefly explicate the ways in which various contributions to knowledge and praxical 'know how' might be extracted from the conversations that this book holds. There are eight central 'pillars' upon which each conversation in each chapter is scaffolded by:

- Dramaturgical designs, the 'nuts and bolts' of the performance-making approaches
- Rehearsal process and strategies
- Finance and funding models
- Methods of audience activation, inclusion and participation
- Privilege, accessibility, diversity and inclusion
- Holistic influences, histories, genealogies and legacies
- The immersive theatre spectrum; positionality, distinctions and definitions
- Futures, substantiality and advice

Each 'pillar' has been used as a launching pad to ignite discussion and conversation around clusters of common themes across the volume and to draw out dialogue around related themes and topics in areas that have been previously masked, hidden or undisclosed. Together, these conversational 'pillars' generated new primary source material that presents novel access and insight. The conversational 'pillars' work to elicit dialogue that forges an understanding of the ways that leading performance makers and companies, from across the spectrum of immersive theatre, make their work. This compendium of praxical 'know how' has the potential to influence and impact upon the next wave of experience making in the UK and beyond.

Immersive dramaturgies and the spectrum of immersive theatre

The 'nuts and bolts' of each dramaturgy that is unfolded within each chapter vary significantly between the companies that have been curated to represent the various points of the immersive theatre spectrum. However, what is striking are the ways in which the three discrete areas articulated by the spectrum I have modelled here echo the positionalities that the makers themselves perceive for their own practices within the broader immersive theatre landscape. The positionality of each contributor's work is explicitly considered in the discussions that respond to the seventh conversation 'pillar': the immersive spectrum, positionality, distinctions and definitions. It is also echoed more implicitly in the conversation surrounding design, production and dramaturgical methodologies that each chapter unfolds. Les Enfants Terribles articulate a dramaturgical approach to experience design that is most closely aligned with more traditional theatre making practices, as Seager explains, 'people have started to call us an immersive theatre company, which is not true. We're a theatre company' (see p.33). They suggest that they begin their work with a consideration of the two central elements of site and story. They suggest that they secure a performance site and then develop a script. These two aspects are then subjected to the core question of 'what do we want the audience to feel', which informs the development of the overall dramaturgy. The practicalities and strategies developed to achieve that spring-board from these three fundamental starting points; story, site, sensation are the key drivers for the development of the overall performance design. In the introduction of this volume, as well as previously, I have asserted that space and the invitations couched to audiences are the fundamental aspects of all immersive theatre regardless of where it rests within the immersive theatre spectrum. In Chapter 1, Lansley and Seager confirm this assertion to be true of their work, and then they discuss the central roles that site and audience engagement play within the development of their distinctive immersive theatre style. The intricate complexities of the carousel dramaturgy that they innovated and applied in the design of *Alice's Adventures Underground* (2015) are explicated. They also explain the ways in which their dramaturgical devices have been devised to respond to other factors like existing IP material, such as *The Twits* (1981), and configured to account for working in site-responsive ways within unusual or heritage spaces. They firmly locate their own work as theatre because of its relation to recognizable theatrical storytelling features and practices.

Watkins unfolds his process in Chapter 3, articulating a much more relaxed, organic and less rigid script-based process than that described by Les Enfants Terribles. Watkins outlines the impact that film, cultural genre, game and pop-culture influence his own creative process. However, the fundamentals of space and audience invitation are crucial to the core of his particular dramaturgical methodology. Watkins explicates the way in which space and concept are the launch pad of his creative process. His dramaturgy hinges on using recognizable pop-culture genres as a skeleton structure to build upon, and the audience invitation is often devised to present the opportunity to become immersed within a genre-based, filmic construct. Watkins explains the way in which the genre experience on offer to audiences in his work is then constructed through gamifying that recognizable world. He says:

> What really helps immersive shows a lot is those sorts of tropes that people already know, it's already downloaded, you know what they are. If you put it in front of audiences, if you're a gangster you know what you do, if you're a policeman there's all these codes across the board that everyone already has in their back pocket they can get out because they've been watching it, since they were a young person. They know exactly how to act and that, on top of the narrative, allows them to be 'in world'. Existing within is so much easier, basically it gives them that license, it allows them to explore the world without having to expose themselves too much. They can be themselves as such within this sort of genre, it just gives them enough ammo to be able to experience the show. (See p.86)

His work has utilized a variety of repurposed spaces but has also unfolded across the streets of Southeast London. The adoption of the central facet of liminal space in COLAB's work is sometimes a site that the audience enter into but also has been an 'everyday' space transformed into liminal space through game play. COLAB's dramaturgies rely on a series of gamified opportunities to bring the space to life for audiences and thus locate them more towards the centre of the immersive theatre spectrum. Although COLAB's work leans towards the more theatre end of the middle, like Les Enfants Terribles, but in a more informal way, script and traditional theatre rehearsal practices rest at the heart of COLAB's approach.

Parabolic Theatre's work resides most firmly in the central gamified space of the immersive theatre spectrum. Kingston's work with Parabolic Theatre confidently represents a distinctly gamified approach to theatrical audience's experience making outside of the commercial, immersive entertainments puzzle game sector. Parabolic Theatre is an exemplar of gamified theatre; their dramaturgical risk-taking has quickly led the way in innovating the hybridization of gaming and theatre. In Chapter 2, Kingston generously and candidly offers detailed insight into the role that game mechanics play in their particular style of experience design. He articulates the granular detail of the ways in which mechanics structure 'world building' and audience activation in his dramaturgical methodologies. He explains how game mechanics function in conjunction with space and characters to manifest as a series of mini invitations for instigating audience activation and theatrical play. Kingston's unfolding of the 'nuts and bolts' of his dramaturgical approach again confirms the centrality of liminal space, invitation and play to his creative process. As Kingston explains:

> For Parabolic we've really tried to inject into the broader immersive conversation is to embrace the audiences potentially in collaborating with you in the telling of a story. To place them right in the heart of it, they are the central characters. They're the protagonist. In order to give them that agency and in order to make it meaningful, not just tell them that they're hero, actually make them the hero. Because their decisions are meaningful. Because a hero is only a hero if they could fail. (See p.75)

Space and audience inclusion are highlighted as core devices in Chapter 4 by The Lab Collective. Their work is interesting because it is more mobile than some of the contributors that sit towards the theatre end of the immersive spectrum, and therefore 'space' is conceived and generated in a different way. The Lab Collective explain that they rarely build or utilize a constant or concrete space to house their work because they toured it. Instead, they discuss the ways in which space is generated through the structural mechanics of the invitations made to audiences rather than being an aspect that is entered into; it is instead conjured between the performers and audience collaboratively through game play. This is one of the features of their work that I want to suggest locates them at the 'reframing' end of the immersive theatre spectrum. Liminal space is not necessarily a concrete construct but is more conceptually generative as a contingent state for the duration of the performance. The Lab Collective provide a keen explanation of how this is achieved practically; they describe the way they build the relationship between audience and facilitator through various task-based mechanics. Joe Iredale explains:

> Our kind of performance, a lot of the time were saying that 'you're not the show, you're a facilitator in the show, you're just the subtext' and I think that's maybe what we were trying to get to a bit earlier. This is your scene but you're serving a higher function, you've got your own little text but it's not about you, it's about their experience and you're facilitating that. You are the shop assistant to the show. (See p.107)

The Lab Collective outline the ways the collaborative and collegiate ontology of their dramaturgical methods is employed to explore the ethics of responsibility. The Lab Collective's work utilizes the radical potential of liminal invitations, and liminoid acts as a tool for instigating the possibility of social change. I suggest that this represents a mode of interactivity that resides quite firmly towards the opposite end of the spectrum to the theatricality of Les Enfants Terribles.

Like The Lab Collective, Cross' work also takes up co-creation and creative collaboration as generative dramaturgical strategy. Cross articulates the ways in which she reframes and refunctions 'the everyday' through performative acts and provocations to conjure a fragile and contingent liminal space and activate audiences. In Chapter 5, Cross reflects in detail on the strategies and devices that she adopted to develop the projects *Post Present Future* (2009) and *Meridian* (2014/2015). She shares the strong ethos of care and socially engaged action that inform the methods she employs to empower audiences commit small but transgressive or transformative acts. Works such as *Post Present Future* (2009) slip across time and extend the audience engagement, thus extending its transformative potential far beyond the originating audience encounter. Cross explains:

> I love that you can put a stamp on an envelope, you post it. Then it gets touched by so many people on this chain, it goes on its own experiential performance. And then it's always struck me as such a magic process when that actually arrives in the post box of the person who's receiving it. I love writing letters anyway, the

art of writing letters in my day-to-day life, so there is something about really focusing on gifting that. It felt like a gift. (See p.131)

Cross Collaborations' work does not reside comfortably within the spectrum of immersive theatre; her work conceptually and formally significantly stretches the elasticity of the moniker. Despite this, the same two fundamental tenants of immersive theatre can be detected in her work: liminal space and play, albeit in the form of acts rather than games, underpin the approaches that she unfolds in the chapter. She unpacks her more recent shift into the unchartered, hybrid, cross-disciplinary space of arts activism when she discusses *Asociación La Bolina,* accounting for the approaches that drive her strategy for engaging non-actors and marginalized communities in collective, transformative experiences.

In Chapter 6, ZU-UK go into considerable detail to unfold the challenges and issues surrounding the creative process of developing *Hotel Medea* (2006–12) and describe the methodologies that drive the work they have made since that landmark production. They open up the rationale behind their decision to abandon the model of making work as a collaborative theatre company, explaining the ways in which, over the last six years, they have shifted into a much more horizontal approach to developing audience experience. ZU-UK frame their shift to a more cross-disciplinary approach to engaging audiences against the backdrop of broader financial and sociopolitical concerns, which also indicates a shift in the ethos that underlies their new direction. The conversation in Chapter 7 draws out the ways in which gaming, antiquated and domestic technologies have transformed their dramaturgical strategies, pushing it from a more theatrical approach into a far more nebulous field of creative practice. Both Maravala and Ramos precisely articulate an approach to experience building that is informed and influenced by gaming and pedestrian or pop-culture practices. They unpack the role that digital technology and social media platforms and strategic cross-disciplinary collaborations with creatives from other fields have played in helping them to innovate forms of instruction and task-based dramaturgies aimed at reaching new audiences. They offer insight into their pioneering strategies for using social media and task-based devices to build intimate and transformative opportunities for audiences to engage with each other, across the globe. Like The Lab Collective and Cross Collaborations, highly distinctive approach to experience making uses tasks, rules and instructions as a generative tool to establish the liminal space in which audiences have the potential for a transgressive or transformative encounter. *Project Perfect Stranger* (2021) is an astonishing exemplar of this strategy. Maravala explains:

> Games done well, transform people in really amazing ways, what I personally love about that is that they then surprise themselves and they do things that they would never have expected themselves to do in that situation. They wouldn't predict their own behaviour. They couldn't predict their own behaviour, but in the moment of the game people turn out all kinds of hidden aspects of themselves, they become revealed. (See p.163)

In Chapter 6, ZU-UK reiterate and expand upon the positionality they laid out in 'The Post-immersive Manifesto' (2020), suggesting they operate beyond the spectrum of immersive theatre. I would suggest that although their work does test the ecstaticity of the spectrum to its very limits, they are still not fully able to unhitch their work. They assert that their work might be considered as 'post-immersive'; however, the 'post' suffix acknowledges the thread that still binds them to immersive theatre, even if that is as a beyond. It must also be acknowledged that their practice still relies upon the two foundational tropes, but which one can identify as immersive theatre: the use of liminal space and a reliance upon play. It is for these reasons that their work can comfortably be considered beside the other contributors' work.

Rehearsal strategies

Each of the contributing companies and artists articulates a very different approach to engaging in 'rehearsal'. As one might now have come to expect, Les Enfants Terribles' rehearsal strategies most closely resemble traditional theatre approaches to working with actors. They explicate a process that involves working with scripts, blocking, entrances and exits that are the familiar territory of mounting a theatrical production. Despite this familiarity, they also draw out the challenges of doing this on such a grand scale and with the additional character of the audience, which is inevitably absent for the entire rehearsal process. On the other end of the spectrum, Cross Collaborations and ZU-UK work in an organic way that is more centred around R&D processes, than as something that could be recognized as rehearsal. Cross, Maravala and Ramos present insight into a process that replaces rehearsal with research and development (R&D); each in their respective chapters outlines instead the steps that they take on their unique modes of R&D journeys for brining work to audiences. Cross explains a process of refinement and reflection that might be understood as a responsive mode of engaging with the ways that the work evolves with and through the audiences that encounter it. I would suggest that her process is reflexive, responsive and accumulative. Whereas for ZU-UK, beta-testing and refinement is something that they identify as a mode which replaces the notion of rehearsal. There is something scientific about the process of 'test–refine–test–refine–test' that they explain in their chapter, which again seems an inevitability of their positionality on the spectrum and their distance from more recognizable theatre practices. However, in taking an overview of the work discussed in the chapter, it is evident that it is work that sits towards the middle of the spectrum that has developed albeit recognizable but complex systems of rehearsal.

It is interesting to observe that the most complex modes of rehearsal have come out of the context of explicitly gamified audience experience. In Chapter 2, Parabolic offer insight into the unique and localized way that they manage rehearsals for actors and the other creatives involved in the process. Kingston draws attention to the constant battle that he faces to resist the fixing down of material for actors and for those running the show during the live events. He suggests that there is a desire from actors to fix down text and how it is a challenge to push back at that desire to generate script. In Parabolic's gamified dramaturgies the carefully constructed mechanics that marshal the activity demand performers and show runners to trust in their efficacy to engage audiences and keep the event moving forward to its conclusion. The Lab Collective provide a detailed account of the new roles that they have developed to facilitate their more elastic, mechanic-driven approach to making audience experience. They have developed lots of different roles and tools for training immersive performers and makers. One of the most significant roles they have defined is that of the 'pit boss'. In their chapter, The Lab Collective account for its emergence through their own process and offer insight into the 'pit boss' roles function within their broader task-based dramaturgies. All of the chapters offer practical knowledge that accounts for the devices and strategies that each artist employs to realize practically their very particular mode of experience making. The rehearsal conversation 'pillar' is a thread of the conversations that offers aspiring and emergent practitioners a very 'hands on' orientated resource that they could apply in realizing their own practice.

Finance and funding models

The discussion thread surrounding finance and funding that runs across each of the chapters highlights the disparity in the approaches that each company takes to both support and sustain their work financially. What becomes evident from an overarching perspective of the different strategies is the distinct lack of infrastructure and financial support for the sector. The approaches range from raising capital in more traditional theatre ways through to public funding, operating as a not-for-profit organization and accessing funds by locating the work within the parameters of research funding; despite these disparate funding models, there is a clear culture of precarity and personal financial risk that sits beneath the practices presented across the spectrum of immersive theatre. Although Alston has previously acknowledged this dark undercurrent beneath the belly of British immersive theatre, he suggests that there is 'a dark underside to a rapidly expanded market for immersive theatre in London that can leave theatre makers open to profound vulnerabilities' (Alston 2019: 238). The conversations here starkly testify to support Alston's concerns and expose the ways in which those risks currently impact each of the companies in this volume. Public funding along with the theatre establishment has been incredibly slow and resistant in supporting this sector as it has emerged. Even now as immersive theatre finds itself in a third wave of creative endeavour, that support is only beginning to emerge. The strategies shared in the conversations here for financing this mode of work suggest a 'wild west' culture within the immersive theatre sector. There is a feeling of operating within a context of precarity, expressed by all of the makers, which I want to suggest needs to be addressed for the sector to achieve more stability and sustainability, a topic that dominated the round-table discussion in Chapter 7.

Future work

The generosity and quality of the knowledge exchange captured in each of the chapters of this volume indicate an appetite within the immersive community to engage in the work of building more substantial cultural, visibility, credibility and a more robust legacy for the immersive theatre creative community. If the community aspires to meaningfully increase the cultural currency of the form, then the knowledge exchange activity represented in this volume must be systematically built upon. To continue consolidating, expanding and diversifying the canon, this type of dissemination needs to be more regularly facilitated. I suggest that, in many ways, it is scholarship's responsibility to function as cultural custodians, but to do so in ways that recognize and capture the diversity of the creative cultural landscape. There are, I am sure, many more practices that have thus far evaded capture both within the immersive theatre spectrum and within the even more elastic category of 'immersive entertainments'. The TAIT podcast series was the 'ground zero' that ignited the impetus which has led to the knowledge exchange opportunity that this volume presents. TAIT emerged as a DIY, accessible resource in 2016 and is a platform that continues to engage makers in the important activity of sharing their tacit 'know how' and expertise. The series goes some way in filling the praxical-shaped hole in the canon, and this book extends the credibility of that knowledge exchange work.

The more inclusive the documentation can be in capturing the practice-based knowledge of a broader range of voices and approaches working under the immersive umbrella, the richer the potential impact might be for the sector and scholarship. The need for diversity and inclusion is not an issue that is just endemic to immersive theatre but indeed the theatre industry more broadly.

> British theatre needs to be 'completely rebuilt' in the wake of Covid-19 to make it more accessible to people from diverse

backgrounds, according to the director of a web series about the challenges facing people of colour in the industry.

(BAKARE 2021)

Ultimately, developing a body of work that captures and disseminates a broad range of approaches, perspectives and outlooks can only increase the cultural currency of the role that immersive theatre plays within the broader experience economy and begin to map out a cultural legacy for this mode of performance making. The legacy needs to reflect the variety and breadth of current practices, not just certain dominant dramaturgies. Building a rich, diverse and inclusive knowledge community is one of the desires that has driven the creation of this publication. I have been concerned for over ten years about the cultural visibility, currency and legacy of the form of immersion and interactivity.

REFERENCES

Alston, Adam (2013), 'Audience Participation and Neoliberal Value: Risk, Agency and Responsibility in Immersive Theatre', *Performance Research*, 18 (2), 128–38.

Alston, Adam (2016), 'Tell No-one': Secret Cinema and the Paradox of Secrecy', in Anna Harpin and Helen Nicholson (eds), *Performance and Participation: Practices, Audiences, Politics*, 243–64, London: Red Globe Press, Macmillan International.

Alston, Adam (2016), 'The Promise of Experience: Immersive Theatre in the Experience Economy', in J. Frieze (ed.), *Reframing Immersive Theatre*, 243–64, London: Palgrave Macmillan.

Alston, Adam (2016), *Beyond Immersive Theatre: Aesthetics, Politics and Productive Participation*, London: Palgrave Macmillan.

Alston, Adam (2019), 'Immersive Theatre in Austerity Britain: Les Enfants Terribles' Riot in the Saatchi Gallery and the Liquidation of differencEngine', *Contemporary Theatre Review*, 29 (3), 238–55.

Bakare, Lanre (2021), 'British Theatre Urged to "completely rebuild" to Improve Diversity', https://www.theguardian.com/stage/2021/mar/11/british-theatre-urged-completely-rebuild-improve-diversity-blackstageuk-gabrielle-brooks, Retrieved on 8 April 2021.

Biggin, Rose (2017), *Immerisve Theatre & Audience Experience: Space, Game & Story in the Work of Punchdrunk*, London: Palgrave Macmillan.

Boal, Augusto (1985), *Theatre of the Oppressed*, New York: Theatre Communications Group.

Brecht, Bertolt (1964), 'A Short Organum for the Theatre', in B. Brecht and J. Willet (eds), *Brecht on Theatre: The Development of an Aesthetic*, 1st ed., 233–46, New York: Hill and Wang.

Bucknall, Joanna (2016), 'Liminoid Invitations & Liminoid Acts: The Role of Ludic Strategies & Tropes in Immersive and Micro-Performance Dramaturgies', *Performance Research*, 21 (4), 53–9. Routledge Journals, Taylor & Francis Ltd for ARC.

Bucknall, Joanna (2017), 'The Daisy Chain Model' an Enunciative Modality: Epistemic Mapping as a Mode of Performative

Documentation and Dissemination of PaR', in Annette. Arlander, B. Barton, Melanie Dreyer-Lude and Ben Spatz (eds), *Performance as Research: Knowledge, Methods, Impact*, 50–74, London: Routledge.

Bucknall, Joanna (2023), 'Selling Secrets: The Role of "elusivity" in the Liminoid Invitations of Immersive Theatre', in Finola. Kerrigan and Chloe. Preece (eds), *Marketing the Arts: Breaking Boundaries*, 2nd ed, Routledge.

Bucknall, Joanna and Kirsty Sedgman (2017), 'Documenting Audience Experience: Social Media as Lively Stratification', in Toni Sant (ed.), *Documenting Performance: The Context and Process of Digital Curation and Archiving*, 113–30, London: Bloomsbury.

Bucknall, Joanna J. (2017), 'The "Reflective Participant", "(Remember)ing" and "(Remember)ance": A (Syn)aesthetic Approach to the Documentation of Audience Experience', *PARtake: The Journal of Performance as Research*, 1 (2), Article 6.

Dahl, Roald and Quentin Blake (1981), *The Twits*, New York: Knopf.

Dahl, Roald and Joseph Schindelman (1964), *Charlie and the Chocolate Factory*, New York: Knopf.

Dinesh, Nandita (2018), *Memos from a Theatre Lab: Spaces, Relationships, and Immersive Theatre*, Wilmington: Vernon Press.

Dinesh, Nandita (2019), *Immersive Theater and Activism: Scripts and Strategies for Directors and Playwrights*, Jefferson: McFarland & Company, Inc., Publishers.

Eng, Dave (2020), 'What are Megagames'?, https://www.universityxp.com/blog/2020/10/22/what-are-megagames, Retrieved on 19 January 2022.

Farrier, Stephen (2005), 'Approaching Performance though Praxis', *Studies in Theatre and Performance*, 25 (2), 129–44.

Frieze, James (eds) (2016), *Reframing Immersive Theatre*, London: Palgrave Macmillan.

Gardner, Lyn (2021), 'Punchdrunk's The Burnt City', https://stagedoorapp.com/lyn-gardner/punchdrunks-the-burnt-city?ia=1011, Retrieved on 16 December 2021.

Gill, Jonathan (2021), 'Accessibility and The Future of Podcasting', https://www.forbes.com/sites/forbestechcouncil/2021/03/05/accessibility-and-the-future-of-podcasting/?sh=764f2c2d22d9, Retrieved on 17 December 2021.

Henrich, Joseph, Steven J. Heine and Ara Norenzayan (2010). 'The Weirdest People in the World?', *Behavioral and Brain Sciences*, 33 (2–3), 61–83.

Jarvis, Liam (2019), 'Narrative as Virtual Reality 2: Revisiting Immersion and Interactivity in Literature and Electronic Media', *International Journal of Performance Arts and Digital Media*, 15 (2), 239–41.

Knight, Steven, et al. (2015), *The Peaky Blinders*, Warner Bros. Entertainment.

Lanthimos, Yorgos, Olivia Colman, Emma Stone, Rachel Weisz and Mark Gatiss (2019), *The Favourite*, Twentieth Century Fox Home Entertainment, Inc.

Machon, Josephine (2009), *(Syn)aesthetics: Redefining Visceral Performance*, Basingstoke: Palgrave Macmillan.

Machon, Josephine (2011), *(Syn)aesthetics Redefining Visceral Performance*. Reprinted, with a new preface, Basingstoke and New York: Palgrave Macmillan.

Machon, Josephine (2013), *Immersive Theatres: Intimacy and Immediacy in Contemporary Performance*, Basingstoke and New York: Palgrave Macmillan.

Machon, Josephine (2016), 'Watching, Attending, *Sense*-Making: Spectatorship in Immersive Theatres', *Journal of Contemporary Drama in English*, 4 (1), 34–48.

Michaels, Anne (2009), *Fugitive Pieces*, Toronto: Emblem Editions.

Norros, Miila (2015), 'Immersive Theatres: Intimacy and Immediacy in Contemporary Performance', *PAJ: A Journal of Performance and Art*, 37 (3 (111)), 131–2.

Ramos, Jorge Lopes, Joseph Dunne-Howrie, Persis Jadé Maravala and Bart Simon (2020), 'The Post-Immersive Manifesto', *International Journal of Performance Arts and Digital Media*, 16 (2), 196–212.

Shakespeare, William, 1564–1616 (2000), *Romeo and Juliet, 1597*, Oxford: published for the Malone Society by Oxford University Press.

Slade, David (2018), *Black Mirror: Bandersnatch* [Netflix streaming], United States: Netflix.

Warren, Jason (2017), *Creating Worlds: How to Make Immersive Theatre*, London: Nick Hern Books.

Warren, Jason (2017), '"There is so much left to discover": Jason Warren on Creating Immersive Theatre', Nick Hern Books, https://nickhernbooksblog.com/2017/06/23/there-is-so-much-left-to-discover-jason-warren-on-creating-immersive-theatre/, Retrieved on 17 November 2021.

White, Gareth (2012), 'On Immersive Theatre', *Theatre Research International*, 37 (3), 221.

White, Gareth (2013), *Audience Participation in Theatre: Aesthetics of the Invitation*. London: Palgrave Macmillan.

INDEX

accessibility 7–8, 52, 97, 163, 181–8, 201, 219. *See also* privilege; WEIRDO; working class
ACE (Arts Council England) 11, 28, 49, 202
acting 38, 91. *See also* actors; performer
action 20–1, 106, 109, 142–3, 158, 197, 214
active 106, 112, 116, 151, 159, 163
actors 35–7, 39–40, 42, 46–8, 59, 66, 68–71, 74–6, 79, 86, 88, 90–2, 106, 160, 162, 179, 189, 219. *See also* performer
adaptive narrative 28, 72
advice for new and emerging practitioners 53–4, 80–1, 97, 122–3, 148, 173–4
aesthetic space 19
affect 12, 20–1, 28, 116, 161, 189
agency 20, 58, 72–5, 83–4, 92–6, 104, 116, 213
Alice 40–9, 161
architect 72. *See also* pit boss; world building
audience 1, 12–15, 18–23, 25, 39, 43, 47–8, 51, 53, 58, 60–4, 80, 83, 86, 89, 92, 95–6, 100, 103, 109, 111, 114–15, 120–3, 146, 152, 155–61, 163, 173, 179, 181, 184, 188, 191–2, 195–7, 201–3, 206, 211–17

audience-centric 1–4, 7–10, 23–5, 28–9, 157, 206–8. *See also* inclusion; participation
audience engaged dramaturgy 100. *See also* inclusion; participation; tropes
audience experience 2, 5, 18–19, 21–2, 25, 29, 62, 160, 211–15, 217
authenticity 71
author 170
authority 7

bad behaviour 108–9
bar 25, 79, 94–5, 152, 205
bar income 94
behaviour 10, 23, 105–10, 139, 161–3, 171, 216
beta-testing 217. *See also* dry run
Binaural Dinner Date 18, 22, 166
Black Lives Matter 193
Boal, Augustus 57, 61, 144, 163
Brecht, Bertolt 57, 64

care 24, 30, 31, 86, 116, 123–4, 136–40, 158, 164, 172, 182, 207–8, 214. *See also* culture of care
cast 37, 46, 52, 68, 91. *See also* casting
casting 46, 91. *See also* dry run; performers; workshop

INDEX

character 20, 42–7, 64–9, 71–5, 86–91, 109, 112–16, 135–7, 147, 181, 213, 216. *See also* improv; narrative structures; performers
childish 84, 88. *See also* children's play
children's play 84–8
co-creation 22, 214. *See also* inclusion; participation
COLAB Factory 13, 18, 25, 29, 92, 206. *See also* COLAB Tavern
COLAB Tavern 206. *See also* COLAB Factory
COLAB Theatre 20–1, 26, 29, 83
collaboration 21–3, 117, 148, 153–70, 214–15
collaborative 8, 91, 189, 214, 215. *See also* collaboration
community 24, 51–2, 118, 143–5, 147, 159–60, 168, 197–8, 206–7, 219–20
consumerism 171. *See also* productivity
core desires 103–4, 214. *See also* psychology
COVID-19 8, 15, 193, 197, 219. *See also* pandemic
creative community 5, 14, 219
creatives 2–3, 7–8, 14, 25, 30, 72, 215, 217
Crisis? What Crisis? 28, 63, 74
CROOKS 21, 29, 80, 87–9, 92, 96
cross collaborations 4, 18, 22–4, 26, 30, 127, 135, 208, 215, 217
Crypt 28
cultural 1, 4, 9, 11, 13–17, 24–5, 52, 121, 131, 146, 183, 194, 202, 204, 206–11, 219–20
cultural currency 15, 146, 209, 219–20
cultural legacy 15, 220
cultures 30, 153, 157, 159, 163, 183, 195

cultures of care 30, 86, 116, 123–4, 136–40, 158, 164, 172–82, 207–8. *See also* socially engaged

D&D (Dungeons & Dragons) 64–5
depopulation 144
design 2, 8, 24–5, 35, 40, 43, 45, 65–6, 96, 102, 109, 111, 114, 120–1, 192, 211, 213. *See also* designed; design mechanics
designed 45, 67, 73, 84, 161
design mechanics 65–7, 72–3, 84, 96, 109–14, 120–2, 161, 164–5, 181, 192, 194–5, 211–13. *See also* game mechanics; mechanics
devised 211, 212
dialogical 6–7, 129–30, 135
dialogue 27, 100, 104, 118, 146, 208, 210
digital 50–1, 178–82, 191, 198, 209. *See also* Zoom
digital immersion 78
digital practice 16
dining experience 45–6
director 44, 57, 72, 76, 113, 220
diversity 143, 183, 194. *See also* WEIRDO; working class
DIY (Do it yourself) 14, 22, 207, 219
document. *See also* documentation; documented
documentation 2, 5, 14, 16, 208, 219
documented. *See also* document; documentation
dramaturgical 9–11, 18–19, 206–7, 211–15. *See also* dramaturgies; dramaturgy; tropes
dramaturgies 2–3, 5–6, 9, 11, 17–23, 26, 34, 100, 165, 206–8, 210, 212, 215, 217–18,

220. *See also* dramaturgical; dramaturgy; tropes
dry run 68. *See also* rehearsal process

eco-feminist 136–7
ecology 136, 139, 141, 144
elusive 3. *See also* elusivity; secrecy
elusivity 11–15, 50. *See also* elusive; secrecy
embodied 3–7, 11, 139, 145, 185, 187. *See also* lived experience
embodiment. *See also* embodied; lived experience
entertainment 93–4, 123, 202
entertainment industry 17, 213, 219. *See also* entertainment
environmental activism 136–7, 143–5
estate 44–5, 50, 62, 193
ethical 102, 104, 110–11, 136, 142, 168, 208
ethically charged participation 9, 22, 30, 118, 142, 148, 155, 168, 198, 214. *See also* inclusion; invitation; socially responsible
ethics 64, 118, 142, 148, 168, 198, 214. *See also* ethical; ethically charged participation
ethnographic 6–7
ethos 2, 8, 25, 118, 161, 214–15
excluded 142, 172, 185
experience 2–6, 31, 35–6, 41, 46, 50, 84–5, 100, 103, 109, 113, 139, 141, 143–7, 157, 160, 171–2, 179, 181, 186, 196, 200. *See also* experiential
experience building 26, 215. *See also* world building
experience design 24, 192, 211, 213

experience economy 1–4, 17, 50, 190, 220
experiential 3–6, 10, 14–17, 21–2, 131, 138–9, 146, 183, 195
experiential turn 4, 16
expertise 4–6, 14–15, 25, 205, 207, 219

facilitate/facilitated 22–3, 68, 91, 105–7, 117, 119, 134, 145, 167–8, 206, 217. *See also* facilitation/facilitator
facilitation/facilitator 68, 76, 91, 105–10, 146, 214. *See also* performer
factory 13, 18, 25, 92, 93, 95–6, 206. *See also* COLAB Factory
feedback 69, 109–15, 119, 138, 170
fictive 17, 19–21, 23
fictive world building 17, 19–23
finances/financial strategies 48–9, 107, 135, 218–19
finances 117. *See also* finances; finances/financial strategies
financial 11–12, 14–15, 25, 48, 78, 95, 137–8, 178–9, 215, 218. *See also* finances/financial strategies
For King and Country 20, 21, 28, 63–6, 69, 71, 73–4
forum theatre 58, 61–2, 64, 163
foundational 18, 102, 216
found spaces 14, 52. *See also* London-centric; pop up
function 64–6, 71–4, 79, 107, 166–7, 213, 218

game 64–8, 87–97, 188. *See also* game mechanic; mechanics
game mechanic 20, 63, 73, 94, 111, 213
game play 100–1, 121, 181, 189, 212–13. *See also* game; gaming
gamification 18, 83, 90, 96

INDEX

gamified dramaturgies 20–1, 26, 68, 87, 96, 212–13, 217. *See also* game mechanic; mechanics
gamifying 86–8, 212. *See also* gamification; gamified
gaming 21, 31, 75, 86, 109, 163–5, 213, 215. *See also* game
gift 108, 131, 138–9, 148, 171, 183, 215
goal 97, 110
Good Night, Sleep Tight 165
graft 153–4
Grotowski, Jerzy 58, 97, 152
guest 165

help 27, 49, 59, 61, 77, 95, 104, 134–5, 169, 183, 203
herd mentality 107. *See also* psychology
hero 75, 106, 213
hidden 25, 163, 210. *See also* elusivity; secrecy
holistic 5–6, 140, 202, 208
host 3, 4, 7, 149
Hostage 18, 21, 29, 89, 94
Hotel Medea 9, 24, 31, 151–6, 161–2, 168–9, 172, 184, 192, 208, 209, 215

immersed 43, 79, 120, 138, 144, 212. *See also* immersion; immersivity
immersion 2, 9, 12, 19, 24, 26, 120, 146, 207, 208, 210. *See also* immersed; immersivity
immersive community 219
immersive theatre 2–4, 9–14, 16–19, 33, 36–7, 52–3, 63–4, 79, 83, 96, 121–2, 146–7, 186, 189, 194, 205–6, 208–18. *See also* umbrella term
immersivity 194
immigrant 31, 156, 192. *See also* migrant

improv 42, 46–7, 71, 88, 108. *See also* actors; performers
inclusion 213, 219. *See also* invitation; participation
incoming/exodus 18, 22, 30, 111, 114, 115
infrastructure 1, 25, 184–5, 218
interactivity 24, 70, 73, 85, 101, 103, 109, 119–20, 121–3, 181, 203
intervention 17, 142
intimacy 35, 136, 164, 167
invest 49, 86. *See also* invested
invested 49, 57, 87. *See also* finances; invest
invitation 21–3, 85, 101, 106, 129, 158–9, 161, 167, 197, 211–14
invite 62, 70, 85, 122, 133, 147. *See also* invitation
IP (intellectual and licensed property) 9, 11, 17, 20, 45, 49, 88–9, 93–4, 117, 201, 211

keen 13, 92, 171, 209, 213
kinaesthetic 6–7. *See also* lived experience

Lab Collective 22–4, 26, 29–30, 181, 207
Land of Nod 28
Les Enfants Terrible 9, 13, 19–21, 26–8, 95, 201, 206, 211–12, 214, 216
liminal 12, 18, 20–2, 114, 148, 212–13, 215, 216. *See also* liminality; liminal space; pop-up
liminality 18, 23. *See also* liminal; liminality; liminal space
liminal space 18, 21–2, 212–18
liminoid invitation 21–3, 214
lived experience 22, 160

INDEX

live-directed 74
lockdown 90, 178–82. *See also* pandemic; Zoom
London-centric 1–2, 6, 179. *See also* pop up
lost 59, 68–70, 101, 108, 153, 166, 170, 186

mechanics 20, 37, 64–75, 89–90, 105, 109–15, 186, 192, 213–14, 217. *See also* game; play
Medea 9, 24, 151, 154, 156–7, 159–72, 184, 192, 208–9, 215. *See also* Hotel Medea
megagames 66
Meridian 135–44, 214
migrants 143–5, 182, 195–6, 208. *See also* immigrant
Montagues & Capulets 29, 87

narrative 19–21, 28, 31, 42–3, 45–6, 63, 72–81, 83, 85–93, 101, 106, 181, 212
narrative genres 85–6
narrative structures 19–20, 42–6, 72–4, 86–93, 101, 181

one to one/one on one/one-on-one/one-to-one 23, 58–9, 77, 102, 123, 128–30, 139, 183

parabolic 13, 18, 20–1, 26, 28–9, 57, 59–60, 70, 72, 75, 77–8, 188, 191, 207, 212–13, 217
participation 2, 12, 21, 30, 62, 141, 147, 165–7. *See also* inclusion
payoff 87. *See also* win
performers 22, 42, 66, 100, 103, 107–17, 138, 213, 217
pervasive 17, 20–1
Pick Me Up & Hold Me Tight 185
Pinstripe Trilogy 30

pit boss 112–13, 217–18
plastic sea 31, 144, 195
play 2–3, 60, 70, 74, 84–5, 89–91, 100–10, 121, 167, 181, 189, 203, 212–13, 215–16. *See also* game; game mechanic; mechanics; player; playtest
player 108, 164, 174, 195. *See also* game; game mechanic; mechanics; play; player; playtest
playtest 168–9, 194. *See also* game; game mechanic; mechanics; player
political 61–2, 102, 139, 143. *See also* privilege; WIERDO; working class
politics 61, 102, 139, 143, 200. *See also* privilege; WIERDO; working class
pop culture 85
pop-up space 13–14, 25, 133, 207. *See also* liminal space; site responsive
post, present, future 183
post-immersive 24–6, 172–4, 194, 197, 209, 216
post-pandemic 161, 180, 202
praxis 5, 7, 11, 205–6, 210, 219
precarity 14, 218
previews 36–7, 47–8, 92
privilege 78, 172–4, 179–80, 187, 194. *See also* socially engaged; working class
productivity 12, 60, 171
psychology 103–7. *See also* inclusion; invitation
Punchdrunk 19, 57–60, 83–4, 120–2, 196

rabbits 36. *See also* Alice
radical 12, 30, 123, 130, 139, 141, 143, 207, 214. *See also* liminal; liminoid invitation; politics

radical amazement 141–2
R&D (research & development) 90–2, 165, 168–9, 217
reflective participant 7, 16
reframings 22, 213. *See also* ritual
rehearsal process 47–8, 66, 69, 90–1, 115–16, 216–18
rituals 18, 21–2, 147, 163–7. *See also* reframings
RPG's (role play games) 65, 67, 181
rules 22, 65, 92, 110–11, 123, 167, 187, 216. *See also* tasks
runs 68, 70, 135, 199, 218

safeguarding 25–6, 112
salon 119
Schumacher Institute 140–3. *See also* holistic; radical amazement
scripts 53–4, 89–94. *See also* narrative structures
secrecy 2, 12–14, 50, 60. *See also* elusivity
seed money 78
Sherlock 41, 49–51, 178
sites 18–21, 40–1, 183, 195
site responsive 40–1, 211
social distancing 186
social exchanges 182. *See also* socially engaged
socially engaged 22–3, 26, 130, 148, 201, 207–8, 214
socially responsible 9. *See also* socially engaged
Souk 100, 117
storyboarding 90. *See also* narrative structures
sustainability 118–19, 137

TAIT (talking about immersive theatre podcast) 1–2, 4, 6–8, 15–16, 18, 25

tasks 22, 65, 110. *See also* rules
theatrical 19, 53, 73, 86, 211, 213, 215
training 29, 75, 91, 94, 103, 106–7, 110–11, 114, 118, 121, 151–5, 172, 207, 217
transformative 130, 139–43, 163, 167, 214–16. *See also* socially engaged
tropes 10, 86, 212, 216. *See also* mechanics
trust 5, 7, 59, 70, 102–3, 112, 116, 120, 217

umbrella term 16–17, 24, 96, 152, 172, 219. *See also* immersive theatre
uncanny 22
under-represented 3, 16. *See also* diversity

Vaults, the 18, 39
venue 13–14, 29, 138, 146, 154, 185–8
visit 69, 188

WEIRDO 194–5. *See also* political; privilege; working cl
West End 49–50, 52, 199. *See also* theatrical
win 23, 43, 110–11, 189. *See also* game; game mechanic
working class 62, 154, 157, 188, 192, 201. *See also* political; privilege
workshops 46, 88, 91, 94, 159. *See also* rehearsal processes
world building 72. *See also* mechanics

Zoom 8, 51, 182, 187–9, 197
ZU-UK 4, 9, 13, 18, 22–4, 31, 209

www.ingramcontent.com/pod-product-compliance
Lightning Source LLC
Chambersburg PA
CBHW062147300426
44115CB00012BA/2037